Pro ASP.NET SharePoint 2010 Solutions

Techniques for Building SharePoint Functionality into ASP.NET Applications

Dave Milner

Apress®

Pro ASP.NET SharePoint 2010 Solutions: Techniques for Building SharePoint Functionality into ASP.NET Applications

President and Publisher: Paul Manning
Lead Editor: Mark Beckner
Development Editor: Matthew Moodie
Technical Reviewer: Shannon Bray
Editorial Board: Steve Anglin, Mark Beckner, Ewan Buckingham, Gary Cornell, Jonathan Gennick, Jonathan Hassell, Michelle Lowman, Matthew Moodie, Duncan Parkes, Jeffrey Pepper, Frank Pohlmann, Douglas Pundick, Ben Renow-Clarke, Dominic Shakeshaft, Matt Wade, Tom Welsh
Coordinating Editor: Jennifer L. Blackwell
Copy Editors: Ralph Moore and Mary Behr
Compositor: MacPS, LLC
Indexer: Julie Grady
Cover Designer: Anna Ishchenko

Distributed to the book trade worldwide by Springer Science+Business Media, LLC., 233 Spring Street, 6th Floor, New York, NY 10013. Phone 1-800-SPRINGER, fax (201) 348-4505, e-mail orders-ny@springer-sbm.com, or visit www.springeronline.com.

For information on translations, please e-mail rights@apress.com, or visit www.apress.com.

Apress and friends of ED books may be purchased in bulk for academic, corporate, or promotional use. eBook versions and licenses are also available for most titles. For more information, reference our Special Bulk Sales–eBook Licensing web page at www.apress.com/info/bulksales.

The source code for this book is available to readers at www.apress.com.

For my wife Rita,
whose understanding of people teaches me far more
about collaboration
than any software ever will.

Contents at a Glance

Contents

About the Author

 **Dave Milner** is a Senior SharePoint Architect and the Products Lead at ShareSquared where he builds SharePoint products and helps companies implement their SharePoint solutions. Dave is a technology professional with deep understanding of Microsoft technologies, including 19 years of IT experience and experience with Microsoft technologies spanning over a decade.

Dave has an MBA with a technology management focus, and is a Microsoft Certified Trainer as well as having obtained other advanced Microsoft certifications in the .NET and SharePoint areas. He also is a Certified Scrum Master, having successfully implementing Scrum methodologies with several application development and solution teams. In the technology community, Dave is a frequent speaker and trainer at local and national SharePoint and .NET related events. He serves on the leadership team of COSPUG (the Colorado SharePoint User Groups) and helps run the local branch in Colorado Springs; he's also involved in other local technology groups. When he's not working on technology, Dave enjoys the outdoors of Colorado Springs where he lives with his wife and two children.

About the Technical Reviewer

 **Shannon Bray** is a SharePoint evangelist and Microsoft Certified Trainer. He is currently employed with Planet Technologies as a Technical Architect and works exclusively with Microsoft SharePoint. Shannon specializes in architecture design and solution development using Microsoft technologies. He is the President of the Colorado SharePoint User's Group and has presented SharePoint topics at Microsoft's TechReady and TechED.

Follow Shannon on Twitter: @noidentity29.

Acknowledgments

As you are undoubtedly aware, the work involved in writing a book of this magnitude is not the effort of one individual, but rather a great effort by a team collaborating on all aspects from the initial ideas and viability of the topics to the outline of the chapters to the content itself.

Therefore, I would like to thank of all my editorial team at Apress, headed up by Mark Beckner, my Acquisitions Editor. Without all of you, this project would not have been possible. The team maintained the schedule, modified content, suggested approaches, and edited chapters. In other words, they were the behind-the-scenes glue that made this project work. They also helped me keep my sanity through all of the process. Specifically, thanks to Matthew Moodie, my content editor; Jennifer Blackwell and Anne Collett, my schedule editors; and Ewan Buckingham and Dominic Shakeshaft for administrative support. Apress is a fantastic company to work with; I highly recommend it to fellow authors.

Special thanks to Shannon Bray, my SharePoint colleague in community endeavors with the Colorado SharePoint User's Group and other things. 00Shannon, as my main technical editor, helped ensure that statements were accurate and code examples were precise and best practices.

Also, special thanks to Reza Chitsaz with the Visual Studio Team at Microsoft. Reza provided great ideas and specific feedback on Chapter 2, which highlights all of the SharePoint 2010 features in Visual Studio 2010. Great work on the developer story for SharePoint 2010, Reza and team!

Thanks as well to others specifically involved with content editing: to David Yack for reviewing the initial content ideas and outline and to Ted Iverson for helping out with content reviews and suggestions.

I also want to thank fellow session members, speakers, MVPs, and MCMs in the SharePoint community that contributed indirectly through discussions of the concepts involved in this book. Your comments around sessions at SharePoint Saturdays or SPTechCon sessions provided valuable insight into the content of this book, and I look forward to collaborating with you in the future.

Thanks also to David Kruglov and my fellow colleagues at ShareSquared for supporting me by providing content, inspiring conversation, and great camaraderie.

Thanks as well to William Ramey, Jr., Chuck Roberts, Matt Lindgren, and the SGIBU SharePoint/.NET team at SAIC. Many of the projects I worked on there provided the questions that this book was developed to answer.

And last but not least, thanks to my wife Rita, my son Luke, and my daughter Dori for supporting me through the writing process—all of the time involved, the late nights, the excess work. I love you!!!

Introduction

Code re-use is the Holy Grail of software development. Countless hours of refactoring, countless books, countless software development tools, components, IDEs, and platforms have been dedicated to pursue this elusive quality.

Why is this? As software consumers, we are used to seeing very rapid advancements in technology. Every year, we see more amazing things accomplished in hardware and software. We see new gadgets, new technologies, and new concepts all conspiring in new and wonderful ways to make our world smaller and more manageable. The pace is almost beyond comprehension. When you think about where we have come from and some of the history of computing, it's mind-boggling. We now carry in our pocket in a mobile device the computing power that used to take up an entire building. We can reach around the world at the speed of light to connect to information and people. We can store more information than our mind can comprehend on a device the size of our thumb. And we have built for ourselves somewhat of an expectation of magic and miracles.

The people that we build software and solutions for have similar expectations. They expect us to do more with less. They want the power, the reach, the magic, and the miracles. And they want it all on a meager budget.

As software developers, as architects, as solution providers, we do not have the luxury of re-discovering fire on each project, for each client, and at each juncture. We need to amass the ability and the tools to pull together large infrastructures of information, people, and feature sets in a short period of time. We need to start our journey as far down the road toward our destination as possible.

That means learning how to utilize the tremendous platforms we have available to us to deliver compelling solutions to our customers. There are so many development platforms from which to choose. Each selection has tradeoffs in performance, footprint, and feature sets. One of the greatest challenges for the solution provider, architect, or developer is to decide which platform in which to invest time, energy and resources, and which to recommend to clients. SharePoint is one of these great development platforms—one that I will examine in detail in this book.

The topic of SharePoint as a development platform is one that has recently been gaining a tremendous amount of traction in the .NET and SharePoint developer communities. Microsoft events are focused around this topic, books are being written with this concept in mind, and Microsoft has dedicated a large portion of the SharePoint 2010 and Visual Studio 2010 product features to improving the developer experience for SharePoint.

SharePoint as a product offers many outstanding built-in platform features. Extensibility of web sites and collections, user authentication and authorization, document management, calendars and tasks, blogs, and wikis are a few of the popular features encapsulated within the SharePoint platform that can help companies move to a more collaborative working environment. All of these features within SharePoint are engineered in a way to make them extensible with the tools available in Visual Studio 2010.

■ ■ ■

CHAPTER 1

SharePoint as a Development Platform

Water, water everywhere, Nor any drop to drink...

Rime of the Ancient Mariner by Samuel Taylor Coleridge (1798)

Some of the first questions that face a developer when initially looking at a platform like SharePoint are such questions as "Why should I use SharePoint for a platform as opposed to some other solution?" and "What features does SharePoint have that are compelling enough to make me select it as the center of a development platform in order to deliver the best solutions to my employer or customers?" These questions are all the more overwhelming with the number of solutions that exist. There are large numbers of frameworks to choose from with which to build upon, everything from code generators to web site extenders, development tool extensions to fully functional portal frameworks. Evaluating the pros and cons of each possible environment is a huge task that is impossible to accomplish on a budget.

One common approach is to read the community reviews of these tools and put together a short list of tools or technologies to build upon and do feature comparisons or prototypes. While the complete methodology to flesh out this approach is beyond the scope of this book, we will endeavor to examine in detail the features of SharePoint 2010 that allow for including it in this type of analysis and to then build a compelling case to use SharePoint in our ASP.NET development solutions.

Let's examine some of these features and formulate a few ideas about how they may be to our advantage in solution development. Also, let's note that while some of these features may be explained fully in other literature, from different perspectives, what we are interested in examining is specifically how they can help us as a development platform. This may involve adjusting our viewpoint a little bit and examining these features from a different perspective. Also, while the extended range of features in SharePoint 2010 Server includes many more offerings that are compelling to an ASP.NET developer, we will primarily focus on features available in SharePoint 2010 Foundation. These features offer a significant advantage, in that they represent to the ASP.NET developer a platform from which to work in an environment that is distributed free or without charge by Microsoft.

■ **Note** Licensing changes for the SharePoint 2010 product differ from the 2007 offerings. Windows SharePoint Server 3.0 (WSS) was available as part of an operating system license with Windows Server 2003. With the 2010 release, Microsoft has separated out the SharePoint product from the operating systems. Now, SharePoint 2010 Foundation will be scheduled and developed along with the SharePoint product release cycle as opposed to the Windows Server release cycle. Also, Microsoft has committed to making SharePoint 2010 Foundation available as a free download. A free, feature-rich platform offers a compelling argument for ASP.NET development, especially in some of the specific areas these features represent.

SharePoint Features

SharePoint has enjoyed a rapid rise in scope and use in the marketplace. Since its inception around 1998, SharePoint's mission has been simple, according to Corporate Vice President of Office Business Systems Jeff Teper:

> *To have one place to go to organize, share, and access information wherever it lived.*
> *(Hoover, 2010)*

With such an aggressive mission, SharePoint's features have evolved rapidly toward the organization and sharing of information. To facilitate the rapid sharing of information, one of the forefront features in SharePoint is its extensibility.

Extensibility

In some ways, the word *extensibility* is vague. Its basic meaning is simply the capability of being easily extended. This is a fairly common claim among software architecture and development platforms, as well as coding techniques. To pinpoint qualities of features such as extensibility, generic descriptions are not very helpful. For example, in the Microsoft .NET class libraries, System.Object is about as extensible as you can get. You can build almost anything with it. Yet taking advantage of that type of extensibility is meaningless, as it provides no real code reuse or time savings in the approach.

The problem with the word *extensible* is that the value of extensibility generally does not exist in the broad strokes of the concepts behind the extensibility, but in specific attributes. Architectures can be tremendously flexible in one direction, and yet extremely brittle in another direction. There are trade-offs made in any design. Furthermore, in my experience, the full impact of these trade-offs typically is only found out two weeks before your project is due to be deployed to production. The devil is in the details, as they say.

So with that preface, this leads us to ask "In what ways is SharePoint specifically extensible?" To understand this, let's first examine the hierarchy of the SharePoint object model found in the Microsoft.SharePoint DLL.

DISASSEMBLING SHAREPOINT DLLS

If you would like to disassemble the `Microsoft.SharePoint.dll` or other SharePoint-related DLLs with the .NET Reflector tool to examine their code construction, most of them are stored locally in the Global Assembly Cache (GAC) on a machine that has SharePoint 2010 Foundation installed. You can load them by selecting File ➤ Open Cache. This loads a window in which you can select the SharePoint-specific DLL. If your version of Reflector doesn't show these, usually you can edit the Reflector.cfg file to add in a section such as the following, which will allow you to disassemble GAC and related DLLs:

```
[AssemblyCache]
"%SystemRoot%\Microsoft.net"
"%SystemRoot%\Assembly"
"%SystemRoot%\Assembly\GAC"
"%SystemRoot%\Assembly\GAC_MSIL"
"%ProgramFiles%\Microsoft.net"
"%ProgramFiles%\Reference Assemblies"
```

Web Site Extensibility

The SharePoint object model hierarchy is broken down into the following components, shown in Figure 1–1: Farm, Web Application, Site Collection, Site, List, and Document Libraries.

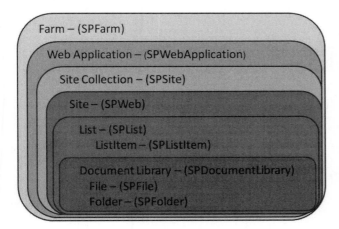

Figure 1–1. SharePoint object model hierarchy

SPFarm

One of the first things to notice with respect to extensibility is the top-level object: Farm, or SPFarm. SharePoint 2010 Foundation is designed out-of-the-box to enable you to deploy it onto a multi-server web farm and handle the level of traffic that a web farm produces. Farm deployment, under normal conditions, can scale up to multiple web front-end servers (WFE Servers), with most deployments for scale utilizing between two and five WFE Servers. Built-in tools allow you to manage multiple WFE servers using NLB load balancing or individually managed server deployments. These types of configurations can be centrally managed by a built-in administration tool and scaled out very easily using PowerShell scripts that have built-in SharePoint extensions to manage setup and deployment of SharePoint environments.

This, in and of itself, is a very compelling feature for consideration in web development. The scaling of a web application for load balancing and heavy traffic can be a resource-intensive portion of a web solution, and the built-in tools that SharePoint 2010 provides can help defray the cost of such a solution. SharePoint 2010 Foundation and Server both include a Central Administration web site to help administer farm servers. Central Administration also has the ability to configure service accounts, track usage, and run reports.

SPWebApplication and SPSite

The next level of extensibility to examine involve the second and third tiers of the SharePoint object model – Web Application (SPWebApplication) and Site Collection (SPSite). Within a SharePoint farm solution, SharePoint runs on top of Internet Information Services (IIS) and ASP.NET. A SharePoint farm can host many web applications, each of which is a stand-alone ASP.NET application running in its own Application Pool. Within a web application exists one or more site collections, which are collections of web sites. The power of SharePoint in these tiers is far-reaching. With SharePoint's Central Administration web site tool (see Figure 1–2), as well as with SharePoint PowerShell extensions, this power is available with a one- or two-paged administration page or a few lines of a PowerShell script with which to deploy a whole new web application, as well as set up a new site collection. The advantage in this tier can be compared to the resources that it would take to roll out a whole new web application, along with a tool that allows your customers to customize specific subsets of the application and extend it down many tiers. The cost in a solution, considering these components, shows SharePoint to be a clear winner in the web-site extensibility area.

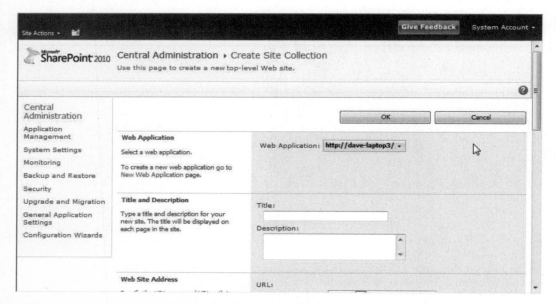

Figure 1–2. Central Administration site collection definition

Other features at the site collection and site levels that are compelling include galleries and libraries such as the master page gallery and site collection image library, which can provide a way for designers to provide a branded user experience across all the sites in the collection.

From the administrator's perspective, there are several features that are compelling at the site collection level. site collections have a unified scope and means of administration. For example, you can manage security, group policies, and features for a site collection. You can track web analytics reports, audit log reports, and other data for security and performance monitoring. Also at the farm level, each site collection can use a different content database, allowing you to monitor growth at that level. If a site collection gets too large, an administrator can move it to a different database resource.

SPSite and SPWeb

Another tier of extensibility exists at the site collection (SPSite) to site (SPWeb) level. Usually, in a SharePoint deployment, the SharePoint administrators are the resources involved in configuring web applications and site collections, at least at the top levels. But the extreme ease of extending SharePoint site collections into different sites has changed the components of web-site administration and brought into existence a whole new culture of administrators that, in SharePoint terminology, are called *site owners*. Site Owners are, many times within organizations, trained power users that are entrusted with the ability to make new SharePoint sites within their area of responsibility. Some of the areas of extensibility that exist at the site level include:

- *Site Templates:* Each site created can have a unique template upon which it is based. There are ten basic themes included in SharePoint Foundation 2010 (out-of-the-box), and many more will become available through open source projects and Microsoft code releases in the future. For SharePoint 2007, a set of 40 templates was released after the product came out, to address specific business needs.

- *Language:* You can install language packs with SharePoint Foundation 2010 to select a language-specific site template for a new site. This will enable multi-language site configurations and content.

- *Site Layouts:* You can make specific layouts and master pages available to a site.

- *Themes:* You can manage colors, fonts, and CSS layouts on each site via an installed theme.

- *Content Types:* You can make specific groupings of site columns arranged in content types available to a site.

- *Security:* Each site can have specific user groups and permissions.

- *Regional Settings:* Sites can have different time zones, locales, format for time, and calendar types.

- *Workflows:* Sites can have unique workflows defined.

- *Search:* You can configure the inclusion or exclusion of sites in search results, as well as specific search settings per site.

- *Web Pages:* You can define sites with a unique home page as well as other page definitions.

- *Navigation:* Sites can have unique navigation links included in various places on the site.

With all of these built-in features, the extensibility of SharePoint in the rapid deployment of web sites has taken off in a couple of areas:

- Internally facing intranets
- Externally facing publishing web sites

Organizations have taken advantage of SharePoint's web-site deployment extensibility to rapidly build out internal organizational web sites. Many of these internal web sites evolve in a few different directions.

First, SharePoint intranet web sites tend to be deployed centered on organizational structure. It is rare in an organization, with SharePoint deployed, to not see individual organizational hierarchies with their own team sites, document libraries, calendars, and collaboration.

The next area where SharePoint intranet web sites tend to expand are strategic sites. Many times, it is common in organizations to see cross-functional and cross-organizational teams being put together to address a particular strategy or objective. For example, if a particular team is working on a specific project for R & D, they might make their own SharePoint team site. As another example, a particular team working on a specific contract could have a collaborative SharePoint site dedicated to that contract. Also, depending on the size of the objective or strategy, a whole site collection could be deployed to address it.

Publishing sites are a second area where SharePoint has rapidly expanded. A publishing site is one that has an external-facing component, such as a large corporate web site. Content being published to the web site is developed by individual workers, while SharePoint's workflow feature is set up to route content to web-site area approvers prior to publishing it out to externally facing sites. This area is also large, and many features for publishing sites are in the category of SharePoint 2010 Server and do not fall under the free SharePoint 2010 Foundation features that we are examining.

All in all, the web-site extensibility of SharePoint 2010 is a powerful and compelling feature set. The ease of extending SharePoint and creating new site collections and SharePoint sites has moved the power of web-site administration from the specialized IT worker to the organizational worker.

Development Extensibility

Another category of extensibility to be considered, with respect to SharePoint as a development platform, ties into the architecture that provides the web-site extensibility, but is separate.

Development extensibility is examining how extensive the capability for code reuse is in a project or solution. With SharePoint, part of this is determining a strategy for using code in conjunction with the built-in web-site extensibility. If a developer uses the built-in capabilities to flow downstream with SharePoint's built-in features, then there is a tremendous potential for development extensibility. However, the internal parts of SharePoint are complex enough that if one does not "go with the flow" of SharePoint, then it can be very difficult to get a tremendous amount of code reuse.

A few of the ways you can achieve development extensibility within the flow of SharePoint will be examined in a later part of this book. However, some of the approaches can include:

- Using SharePoint Master Pages in ASP.NET development
- Packaging solutions within SharePoint features
- Using Business Connectivity Services (BCS)
- Using the Client Object Model (Ajax / REST / Silverlight)
- Taking advantage of the SharePoint Root

SharePoint custom development often takes place within a few types of common constructs:

- Web parts
- Application pages
- Site pages

Web parts are common constructs that you can place on any SharePoint site page. In SharePoint 2010, you can place them inline with text, images, or wiki links. Application pages are pages deployed to the SharePoint root with code-behind sections that run compiled code. Site pages are not compiled, but the end user can customize and store them. You can configure sites to allow a high level of user customization, with individual pages having configuration stored per user. These types of configuration differences are stored in a common content database stored in Microsoft SQL Server.

The features that are included in SharePoint that support extensibility make it a compelling solution as a development platform. To produce similar functionality from scratch in an ASP.NET solution would require thousands of staff-hours and a large price tag.

Document Management

Another main feature set of SharePoint Foundation 2010 is its handling of document management, including its integration with Microsoft Office. One of the main constructs of a SharePoint web site is a document library. Document libraries are special types of lists that contain additional functionality to store documents as opposed to simple list items. As a type of list, we can define additional functionality in content types and columns that are stored within the library, as well as interact with the document library through the SPDocumentLibrary built-in class that is part of the SharePoint object model.

One of the features available in document management is a versioning feature. It is an option to turn versioning on for a document library, and to specify whether to create major versions (ex: 1, 2, 3, 4), or major and minor versions (ex: 1.1, 1.2, 2.0, 2.1). You may also limit the number of versions retained for space conservation.

Another feature in document management is the ability to attach a workflow to a document library. One of the out-of-the-box features in SharePoint 2010 is an approval workflow, which routes a document to an approver before allowing it to be checked in to the library. Figure 1–3 illustrates both the versioning and approval features.

Other settings that are available to configure SharePoint Foundation 2010's document library include:

- *Multiple Content Types:* Each content type can have different document templates, columns, and workflows associated with them in the same document library. For example, one might have Microsoft Word documents and Microsoft Excel documents in the same library.

- *Document Template:* You can configure new documents to use an existing template with all of the characteristics available through the particular Office document template.

- *Default Behavior:* This allows the designer to define whether to open documents in a web browser or in the client application.

- *Folders:* You can allow folders to be defined within a document library.

- *Search:* You can decide whether or not a particular document library will show up on Search functionality.

- *Offline Client Availability:* You can specify whether or not to allow documents to be available to offline clients.

- *Site Assets:* Certain types of document libraries may be defined as a default location to store images, slides from PowerPoint, or wiki pages.

- *Datasheet Settings:* SharePoint lists, of all types, can provide the ability to bulk-edit content in a datasheet.

- *Dialogs:* You may specify whether interacting with library items occurs in an Ajax modal dialog box or fully redirects to a web page to interact.

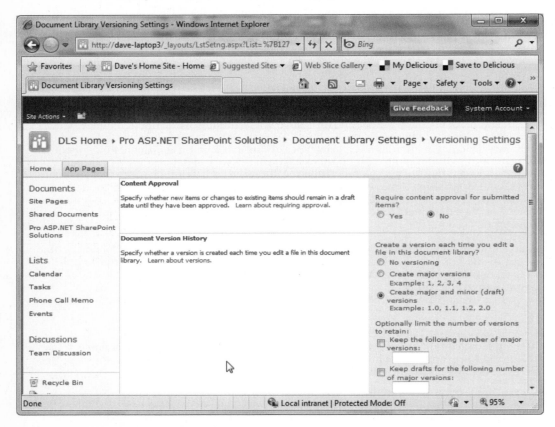

Figure 1–3. *Versioning and content approval in a document library*

Authentication and Authorization

Another feature to consider, in conjunction with SharePoint as a development platform, is user authentication and authorization. SharePoint 2010 has a rich authentication system that is flexible and extensible.

Authentication

Starting with SharePoint 2010, the authentication method has migrated from a classic mode authentication, which only supports one authentication per zone, to a claims-based authentication, which is based on the Windows Identity Foundation (WIF). Claims-based authentication supports the delegation of user identity between applications, and allows for solutions that implement multiple forms of authentication on a single zone. SharePoint 2010 provides for five different zones connected to authentication: the default zone, intranet zone, Internet zone, custom zone, and extranet zone.

All of the standard IIS Windows authentication methods are supported in SharePoint 2010, including anonymous, basic, digest, certificates, Kerberos (Integrated Windows), and NTLM (Integrated Windows). In addition, SharePoint Server 2010 adds support for identity management systems that are not based on Windows. Support is included for forms-based authentication.

The implementation of identity management in SharePoint is through the ASP.NET `MembershipProvider` interface, which is a provider pattern allowing for pluggable authentication designs. We will cover more of this topic in Chapter 3, but suffice it to say that this approach allows for implementing authentication solutions from almost any identity store, including Lightweight Directory Access Protocol (LDAP), SQL Server, or other databases, as well as other forms-based authentication providers.

Authorization

SharePoint offers a rich authorization model as well. Every artifact within the SharePoint site is secured through permissions from SharePoint's model. SharePoint Foundation 2010 includes five permission levels by default. Table 1–1 includes information about these levels.

Table 1–1. SharePoint Foundation 2010 Default Permission Levels

Permission Level	Description	Default Permissions Included
Limited access	Allows access to shared resources only. Meant to be combined with specific permissions to give user access to lists, document libraries, or other elements without giving access to the SharePoint site. Cannot be customized or deleted.	View Application Pages, Browse User Information
Read	Read-only access to entire SharePoint site.	Limited access plus: View Items, Open Items, View Versions, Create Alerts, Use Self-Service Site Creation, View Pages
Contribute	Create and edit items in lists and document libraries	Read Plus: Add/Edit/Delete Items, Delete Versions, Browse Directories
Design	Create lists, document libraries, edit pages	Contribute Plus: Manage Lists, Override Check Out, Approve Items, Add/Customize Pages, Apply Themes/Stylesheets
Full Control	Full control of the scoped area	All permissions

■ **Note** For a complete overview of user permissions and levels, as well as a more detailed version of Table 1–1, see the Microsoft Technet article entitled *User permissions and permission levels (SharePoint Foundation 2010)* at http://technet.microsoft.com/en-us/library/cc288074(office.14).aspx.

Microsoft Office Integration

Another of the advantages of SharePoint's document management is its tight integration with Microsoft Office. Microsoft Word contains built-in features to compare versions of Word documents with previous versions stored in the document library, as well as the ability to capture metadata for custom columns in SharePoint right within Word.

You can configure the Microsoft Outlook mail client to have a view into SharePoint lists and libraries, which includes unread new items in the list or library, as well as preview functionality. This makes it very convenient to interact with document libraries, as seen in Figure 1–4. Notice the folder entitled *SharePoint Lists* on the left side of the image, and underneath it, the folder for a particular SharePoint team site. Then underneath this you can see a particular document library entitled *Shared Documents*. Beneath this are specific folders, each containing documents. You can see in the second to the left pane a particular folder selected, along with a Microsoft Word document. In the to its right, you can see the document preview—all of this is very tightly integrated with Microsoft Outlook and provides the user a familiar interface with which to interact with SharePoint document libraries.

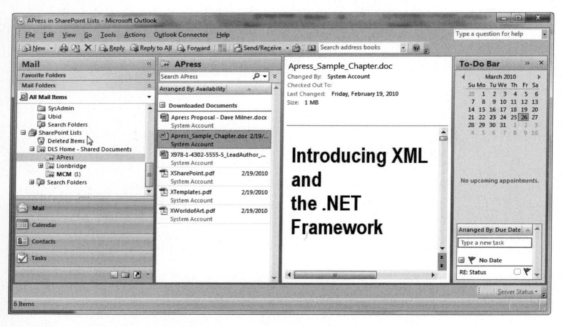

Figure 1–4. Microsoft Outlook integration with SharePoint document libraries

Another area of integration with Microsoft Office includes the ability to share and synchronize Microsoft OneNote notebooks in SharePoint document libraries. Another feature in Microsoft Word 2010 includes the ability to simultaneously edit Word documents stored in a document library alongside another user. Still other areas of Office integration are beyond the features released in SharePoint Foundation 2010, but include vast areas such as Business Intelligence and integration with Excel Services, KPIs and reporting, and handling large data items with PowerPivot. Microsoft Project services offer integration between SharePoint and Microsoft Project capabilities. While on the topic of integration with other Microsoft products, there are a few other areas to mention without distracting from the main focus of this book. One is continued integration with the Microsoft Dynamics product lines. CRM is building in more and more integration with SharePoint with every release, as well as the Great Plains and other tiers of Dynamics products.

SharePoint's integration with Microsoft Office is a feature that presents compelling arguments for building web-based solutions for customers. In an environment where most users will have Microsoft Office installed, the productivity gains involved with this tight integration will help to build compelling solutions.

SharePoint Designer 2010

Another perspective to consider when putting together ASP.NET solutions is how to provide the end users with the ability to modify their web sites and pages on their own. Many packages or solutions will include a page modifier with a built-in editor. SharePoint has quite a lot more to offer in this category. In the first place, all wiki-type pages within SharePoint are editable, and you can store modifications per user or for all users.

Next, SharePoint Foundation 2010 has a designer tool that is free to download and use for the express purpose of extending existing SharePoint web sites. With the 2010 product release, SharePoint Designer 2010 is even more integrated with the SharePoint environment than ever, offering rapid development paths to be able to modify SharePoint master pages, add CSS, build custom workflows with a designer tool, and quickly define external content types through Business Connectivity Services. It also comes with a quick InfoPath form editor (although InfoPath server does not come with SharePoint Foundation 2010).

SharePoint Designer 2010 (shown in Figure 1–5) is a rapid development tool for power users and developers. It provides the ability to interact with such components as lists, data sources, content types, views, forms, workflows, and external content types, all without having to write any code.

Consider the amount of development effort that it would take to provide an administrative tool of this type to a customer. A tool that communicates with and loads an active web site, provides interaction with lists, libraries, workflows, all site pages, and such assets as images, content types and columns, data sources, and master pages. SharePoint Designer 2010 also provides to a customer a WYSIWIG editor for master pages and site pages. To provide an administrative tool of this sort would mean thousands of hours of development time, and administrative tools are typically among the last features thought of and budgeted in web development.

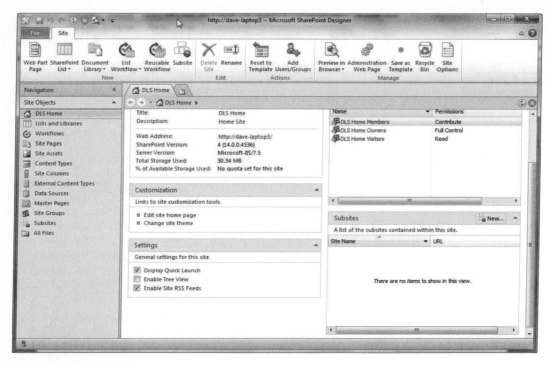

Figure 1–5. SharePoint Designer attached to team site

SharePoint Workspace

A common concern with developing Internet applications is how to offer customers the ability to interact with the application when they are not connected to the Internet. Several common approaches are taken to develop loosely connected applications that support an offline mode.

SharePoint 2010 has a whole feature set that has migrated from the Groove product in previous versions of Microsoft Office, which is called SharePoint Workspace. What this feature involves is a desktop application that comes free with SharePoint, which allows a user to interact with a SharePoint web site, go offline, and still work on the SharePoint items while not connected. This is done through SharePoint workspace. Subsequently, when the user is connected again to the Internet, changes made while offline are synchronized with the SharePoint site.

As a feature, developing a desktop offline client to an ASP.NET application represents, again, a significant development investment. To have a feature available free to customers is a significant advantage.

Visual Studio 2010 Integration

Another main feature that SharePoint 2010 offers is tight integration with Visual Studio 2010. With previous versions of SharePoint, the development story has not been as clearly defined and executed. SharePoint still offered a tremendous value as a development platform, but the developer's story certainly had not been focused on within the Visual Studio environment to the extent it has been with

Visual Studio 2010. Microsoft's SharePoint team offered up plug-ins to help bridge this gap with several of the VSeWSS tool releases, which offered a more automated way to develop web parts and features and several templates to help. Also, many common community-developed tools, such as STSDEV and WSPBuilder, offered Visual Studio plug-ins to help developers gain more productivity.

A good developer story is a more compelling feature than you might think when you start to evaluate development and maintenance costs for the solutions you are building. Good, intuitive development tools mean that it will be easier to train existing staff on SharePoint development, as well as make it easier to find existing resources for teams. In Chapter 2 of this book, we will more fully examine Visual Studio 2010 and new features included for SharePoint 2010 development. The Visual Studio product team has done a great deal of work in advancing the developer story for SharePoint 2010 through the feature set provided by Visual Studio 2010.

Common Approach to Application Development in SharePoint

With the rise in popularity of SharePoint as a solution in the enterprise, SharePoint has started to gain ground as a development platform and as something to customize. With that basis, one of the things to discuss is the typical progression of SharePoint in the enterprise, as well as a couple of likely paths to customization, and a popular approach to application development.

Intranet Scenario

In a common scenario at a company, SharePoint has started out with the free version deployed in a particular department to keep track of documentation, team schedules, and content related to the department. With authorization tightly integrated with Active Directory, team members are easily given permission to the free team site, where they start to use it, expanding it with new wiki pages, documents, calendar entries, announcements, and wiki page entries. There may have been some resistance to this from traditional web development groups perceiving a conflict of interest over intranet development.

After the initial rollout and popularity, perhaps the solution has expanded to a number of other departments for use. Custom development at these stages may consist of simple branding through SharePoint designer, the coding of simple web parts internally, as well as the use of common or free web parts from outside the corporation.

With a number of internal departments on board, at this stage, thought and resources are given to deploying a common SharePoint solution for an intranet option. Additionally, hosting is provided, an initial set of guidance is drafted up for internal users, and a common environment is provided for internal SharePoint use. At this stage, or a similar stage, an enterprise version of the SharePoint product is purchased with a view toward using features such as InfoPath forms for gathering information, or Excel services for reporting purposes.

In this type of scenario, one that is very common in corporations, the SharePoint environment has started small and content has grown and been migrated between a few environments, and the SharePoint content has grown consistently over a number of years.

This is the type of environment in which SharePoint is centric to any application development. The most important factors from a business perspective are the content already contained in the environment and the status and health of the SharePoint farm. Solution development in a scenario such as this is typically not the large insertion of an ASP.NET application, but rather feature development using web parts and other small constructs tied in to the intranet scenario. There may be concentrated development in a few areas where need is perceived, such as developing a more complex workflow structure to suit specific business needs.

This is perhaps one of the most common scenarios where SharePoint development is set. This is also what we like to term *traditional SharePoint development*. Much of the literature available will be helpful with this type of development, as will the first section of this book.

Publishing Site Scenario

Another very common scenario for SharePoint development is setting up an Internet-facing web site that has a lot of content that is necessary to update on a consistent basis. SharePoint is useful in this type of scenario, in that it provides a particular type of web site called a *publishing site*. These are often implemented as separate site collections for authoring and for a production site. They are commonly set up with workflow for approval levels between content authors and publication managers or editors.

The Publishing Portal in SharePoint 2010 starts with a hierarchy that includes a home page, a sample press releases page, a search center, and a logon page. This is the beginning template from which larger Internet-facing sites can be constructed and tied together with workflow approvals in the content publishing areas. The benefit to this kind of site is that anonymous users are supported while not giving them access to SharePoint application pages to allow site modification.

Underneath the Publishing Portal in SharePoint 2010, the publishing site with workflow can be extended. This site template allows for publishing web pages using approval workflows, and includes document and image libraries to store assets related to publishing web sites.

SharePoint Server 2010 also has two specific products geared toward these scenarios. SharePoint Server 2010 for Internet sites, both Standard and Enterprise editions, cover the scenarios of having a full-featured SharePoint solution with unlimited client access through an Internet site. There are also new features in SharePoint 2010 to help with managing larger Internet-facing sites and associated page libraries. Automated page organization, through the Content Organizer, is one of the features that helps with this.

This type of solution is also a scenario where SharePoint is centric to any application development. Common types of development associated with the publishing portals and sites can include customized workflows, content types and metadata, and integration with other data stores through Business Connectivity Services (BCS).

This is another common scenario that SharePoint development is set within. This is also traditional SharePoint development. Familiarizing yourself with some of the standard SharePoint development tools, terms, SDKs, and scenarios will be helpful in this type of environment. The first section of this book also will address these skill sets to build a foundation for all SharePoint development.

Sandboxed Solutions

Overall, the common approach to application development in SharePoint is one that involves the main feature set of the application, SharePoint itself. This is understandable in many cases. Just look at all of the features we have documented in this chapter. There are very compelling scenarios and deployments that work just in this fashion. With SharePoint as the main feature of a solution, application development is more peripheral. This means typically it is small feature sets that are being worked on and deployed at one time—a few application pages, a few site pages, web parts, a workflow solution.

In scenarios such as this, one of the most important approaches to solutions is to do nothing that might impact the health of the current SharePoint installation. One of the features in SharePoint 2010 that helps with this approach is sandboxed solutions (see Figure 1–6). Sandboxed solutions, rather than running in the main application pool thread, run in their own isolated thread. A higher level of control over SharePoint resources is maintained in these threads, and there are safeguards to ensure that a deployed solution cannot affect the health of the farm.

Sandboxed solutions allow for a much broader range of solution deployment in SharePoint. With the protections in place, permissions to deploy solutions can be opened up so that IT administrative personnel do not have to be involved in the solution deployment. They no longer need to run tools such as SPDisposeCheck to ensure that there are no memory leaks in sandboxed solution code, and they no longer have to monitor the farm subsequent to a solution deployment. Also, this allows for opening up solution deployment to online offerings of SharePoint.

Of course, with the common approach to SharePoint development, there are many scenarios that sandboxed solutions will not support. This leaves the more standard method of solution deployment, which does run in the main SharePoint application pool of the site. All of the standard factors of deploying DLLs to the GAC or Code Access Security (which we will cover in Chapter 3) apply to these solutions. For these types of deployments, IT administrative involvement is recommended.

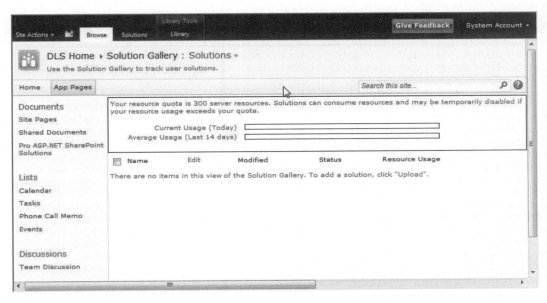

Figure 1–6. Sandboxed solutions in SharePoint Foundation 2010

Advanced Approaches to Application Development

Another scenario that we would like to investigate in this book is the concept of a few different advanced approaches to application development with SharePoint 2010. They are advanced only in the sense that they are not approached in this fashion in mainstream SharePoint development, not in the sense that they are necessarily extremely difficult to conceive or to execute.

One of the main goals that we have is to be able to integrate SharePoint's functionality within an ASP.NET solution. Some of the main reasons for doing that include solutions for which there is a complex requirement for database interaction. For example, we need to ensure transactional integrity across database actions. Or we need to utilize a many-to-many join structure in some of our database tables for a more complex business model.

With complex database needs, we can quickly approach the end of the scenario where the standard methods built into SharePoint to connect to external systems are most effective. Business Connectivity Services (BCS) has made tremendous advances with the SharePoint 2010 release, and offers compelling integration between SharePoint Designer 2010 and Visual Studio 2010 to build external content types. However, to perform anything such as transactional integrity or many-to-many joins is beyond the current capability of BCS. To try to force BCS into a solution scenario such as this would offer diminishing returns on effort. It would require a great deal of overhead in development effort to do advanced things in database interaction in BCS that are relatively simple with other approaches.

So, for this type of a solution that we will address in later chapters in this book, we will look to a blended method of more traditional ASP.NET development and SharePoint development for solutions here. Getting the touchpoints right with this approach is our goal. We view this blend as more art than science, and somewhat similar to cooking in the kitchen! With the right recipe and blend of ingredients, we may produce a tasty dish utilizing all our resources in an efficient fashion. However, with an incorrect blend, we may lose our popularity at the dinner table!

Another reason for a more advanced or different approach to SharePoint development might be that we are upgrading an ASP.NET application that involves a significant investment for a customer, and we do not have the budget or resources to build everything again from the ground up. However, as SharePoint proponents who recognize the tremendous value of SharePoint as a development platform, we would like to be able to leverage some key features in SharePoint for our customers, while retaining the business value of previous investments in a code base.

So, for this type of a solution, we also will look to different means to be able to blend traditional ASP.NET development with SharePoint development in 2010. A later chapter will highlight this approach and offer key recommendations and examples to help speed up the process to integrating solutions of this sort for customers.

In both of these cases, as well as a few others we haven't yet mentioned, a key business value proposition for utilizing SharePoint 2010 features could certainly be SharePoint Foundation 2010. With a rich feature set that is distributed free, it does make a compelling argument for solutions. One caveat to free, however: using SQL Server Express as your database host for SharePoint 2010 Foundation is free, but only supports up to 4GB of data in your deployment. Content sizes beyond that will require you to purchase an SQL Server Standard license or use one that you already have. Also not free is the license for the operating system on which you will install SharePoint. However, the techniques that we will show in this book will work equally well on SharePoint Server 2010 environments. We will say, for SharePoint server farm deployments of some of these more advanced approaches, that the involvement of IT administration will definitely be required and recommended, and this will include performance monitoring and testing of solutions to ensure adequate performance in a production environment.

Summary

All in all, SharePoint offers quite a feature set as a development platform, and makes a compelling argument to offer integrated solutions together with standard ASP.NET development. Extensibility, document management, Microsoft Office integration, built-in authentication and authorization, SharePoint Designer 2010, Visual Studio 2010 integration, and sandboxed solutions are a few of these features.

To be able to take full advantage of this platform, we will first delve into the development environment in Visual Studio 2010, then we'll dig deeply into the SharePoint API and core along with IIS and the .NET framework as it applies to SharePoint. We will also dig into SharePoint architecture and cover some of the common constructs to SharePoint development in master pages, application pages, site pages, and web parts. We will touch on the client object model and interaction with SharePoint from external applications. These endeavors are necessary to build a fundamental understanding of common SharePoint development.

After this, the next section of the book will be dedicated to examining advanced approaches to SharePoint application development, including the scenarios mentioned in this chapter.

CHAPTER 2

■ ■ ■

Visual Studio 2010–Advancing the SharePoint Development Environment

There is incredible enthusiasm among the developer community for SharePoint. We know that hundreds of thousands of developers have used the SharePoint platform in the past year, and we believe that will increase to more than 1 million developers over the next couple of years with the introduction of SharePoint 2010

Steve Ballmer, PressPass Interview 10/16/2009

To be able to use SharePoint as a development platform, we must first build an understanding of how SharePoint development works. We must learn some of the tools of the trade, and some of the standard approaches for performing SharePoint modifications and customizations.

The primary tool for building SharePoint development features and solutions is Visual Studio. Past versions of Visual Studio have not included the same extensive set of tools for interacting with SharePoint out-of-the-box that Visual Studio 2010 does. In the midst of the product cycle, additional tools and project templates for Visual Studio were released by the SharePoint team such as the Visual Studio Extensions for WSS (VSeWSS), with the most recent version released being version 1.3. Also, several SharePoint MVPs in the community have contributed with plug-ins for Visual Studio that have helped with SharePoint development. Some of the most popular plug-ins include STSDEV (http://stsdev.codeplex.com) and WSPBuilder (http://wspbuilder.codeplex.com).

This story has changed with the release of Visual Studio 2010. Visual Studio 2010 includes a comparatively large set of features for building SharePoint features and solutions. These features include 12 new templates for SharePoint projects as well as several new designer tools for the organization and deployment of SharePoint projects. Visual Studio 2010 also includes a highly customized build and deployment process for interacting with a local installation of SharePoint as well as tight integration with the SharePoint root, which is the physical location of a large portion of the SharePoint product.

The intent of this chapter is to present the basic tools of SharePoint 2010 development wrapped up in the features of Visual Studio 2010. While it is not necessary to learn all of the nuances of SharePoint 2010 development to be able to integrate SharePoint components into ASP.NET applications, it is necessary to build an understanding of the fundamentals of interacting with the SharePoint API, of the underlying constructs of some of the features of the SharePoint product, and to become familiar with the templates that Visual Studio 2010 offers for SharePoint development as well as the SharePoint Project Items (SPIs) that are available to utilize within the Visual Studio IDE.

Our goal in this chapter is not to present comprehensive coverage of SharePoint 2010 development through Visual Studio 2010, but to highlight the major tools and templates in Visual Studio 2010, to provide a couple of more common scenarios that represent standard SharePoint 2010 development, and to pique interest and curiosity in building further SharePoint development skills.

■ **Note** To further build upon skillsets in SharePoint 2010 development, several books are being published around the same time as this book that are dedicated solely to discussing standard SharePoint 2010 development skills. One book is *Beginning SharePoint 2010 Development* by Steve Fox (Wrox, 2010), a Microsoft evangelist with an advanced understanding of SharePoint, which will provide a pretty thorough foundation for getting started in SharePoint development. Another great resource is *Pro SharePoint 2010 Development* by Tom Rizzo, et al. (Wrox, 2010), written with other notable SharePoint MVPs. Tom Rizzo is a Microsoft manager with a long history of interaction with SharePoint. Also of note is *Professional SharePoint 2010 Development* by SharePoint MVP Sahil Malik (Apress, 2010). These books will cover a thorough foundation in SharePoint 2010 development that is recommended to build over time if you intend to build expertise and a career around SharePoint.

This book will help you to understand fundamentals necessary to get quickly up-to-speed in SharePoint 2010 development to the point of being able to understand what is necessary to integrate SharePoint features within ASP.NET application development.

It is also important to understand some of the basic tenets and principles behind good SharePoint development, as well as the reasons behind them. If you understand the purpose of some of the rules, then you can identify when you need to break some of the rules as well as some of the ways to mitigate risks and ensure performant applications under those circumstances.

Anatomy of a Visual Studio 2010 SharePoint Project

When you first fire up Visual Studio and select File ➤ New ➤ Project, and select the SharePoint 2010 Installed Templates, you will see a list of the 12 new templates that are available in Visual Studio 2010 (see Figure 2–1). Both C# and VB are supported by these templates.

Figure 2–1. SharePoint project templates

These templates are starting points for SharePoint development, and each consists of a unique common solution ready for SharePoint customization. These templates are for projects with the purposes outlined in the sections that follow.

Empty SharePoint Project

This template is a blank template that contains the absolute minimum for working with SharePoint. One effective way of working with this type of SharePoint 2010 project is to start with this template, and then add new SharePoint Project Items (SPIs) using the Add New Item selection on the right-click navigation menu. Figure 2–2 shows the project inclusions.

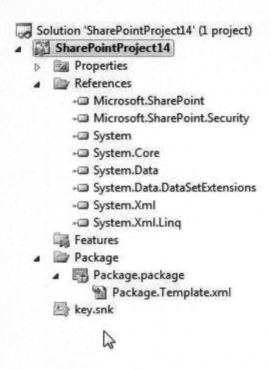

Figure 2–2. SharePoint blank project items

To go over the details of what is included in a blank baseline SharePoint development project, first we include the main references for Microsoft.SharePoint.dll and Microsoft.SharePoint.Security.dll. These two libraries contain the SharePoint object model and security APIs. Also included are core .NET libraries, as well as System.Data for interacting with DataSet elements. System.Xml.dll and System.Xml.Linq.dll are .NET 3.5 libraries that are used for data interaction and querying.

■ **Note** LINQ libraries are included because SharePoint has a new development feature called LINQ-to-SharePoint, which has replaced the old CAML XML interaction with a more language-integrated feature set. Visual Studio 2010 also includes a command-line tool called SPMetal to generate the necessary model classes for working with LINQ-to-SharePoint.

New folders are also included, called Feature and Package. These two folders correspond to two key aspects of SharePoint development as well as two new designers available in Visual Studio 2010, which we will cover in detail later on in the chapter. Both features and packages are important SharePoint development concepts.

Feature

A feature is a basic unit of work in SharePoint. Features are how the SharePoint product is constructed internally. Features consist of artifacts that can include assemblies, pages, controls, workflows, and are identified by specifically constructed XML files that identify the feature to the SharePoint product framework. This construct allows features to be scoped at a particular level of implementation, such as the web application level or the site level. A features scope allows it to be activated from within SharePoint administrative pages for use within a particular site collection in SharePoint or on a specific Site.

■ **Tip** I cover features in more detail in the "Using Features" section later in this chapter. You can also find more detailed information about features in the following MSDN article entitled *Building BlockFeatures*:

`http://msdn.microsoft.com/en-us/library/ee537350(office.14).aspx`

Package

The SharePoint 2010 Framework API provides a way to bundle extensions to the SharePoint 2010 environment. These extensions are packaged up in a solution package that consists of a single cabinet file with the extension .wsp. This packaged .wsp solution file can contain features, site definitions, application and site pages, web parts, workflow extensions, external content types, and many other constructs including assemblies and resource files. This SharePoint .wsp solution is moved to a SharePoint server environment and deployed as a solution.

■ **Tip** You can find more detailed information about Solutions and Packages later in this chapter as well as in the following MSDN article entitled *Creating SharePoint Solution Packages*:

`http://msdn.microsoft.com/en-us/library/ee231560(v=VS.100).aspx`

Both the Features and the Package directories are required to be in any SharePoint 2010 development solution, regardless of whether or not you use a feature in the solution you plan to deploy. We will cover features and packages in detail later on in this chapter.

These are the basic elements of any SharePoint solution. Within this window, you have the ability to add quite a lot of SPIs to your solution. Figure 2–3 shows some of these SPIs.

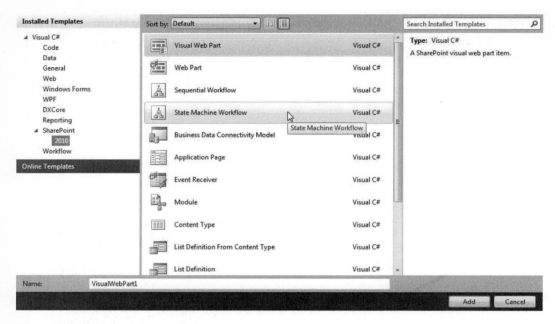

Figure 2–3. *SharePoint Project Items*

Many of these SPIs match up with specific SharePoint 2010 project templates, but many also are additional items. Let's go through some of the different project templates in Visual Studio 2010 that represent some of the key types of SharePoint 2010 solutions and elements of solutions.

Visual Web Part

The Visual Web Part template is one of the most common types of SharePoint solutions. The reason for this is that SharePoint itself is built upon web parts, and when you create a SharePoint visual web part, you can install it on an unlimited number of customizable pages in SharePoint. Thus the Visual Web Part is the number one most flexible type of SharePoint solution.

For ASP.NET developers, the environment and coding approach surrounding visual web parts is very similar to the User Control in .NET Web Forms development. You have a visual designer and access to a number of SharePoint controls similar to a subset of the ASP.NET Web Forms controls you would see in designing and coding a User Control. One of the SPIs in the Visual Studio template actually is suffixed with "UserControl" in the name.

There is an example Visual Studio 2010 solution to follow along with that is available in the code portion of this book. You can find it under Ch2, in the VisualWebPart folder. You will find the solution VisualWebPart.sln, which you can load into your Visual Studio 2010 environment to follow along with the text. All of the following examples in this chapter representing the different Visual Studio 2010 SharePoint templates will appear in the same fashion.

To design and code a visual web part solution for SharePoint 2010, open your Visual Studio IDE and select File ➤ New ➤ Project, and then the Visual Web Part template found under the SharePoint heading (Figure 2–4).

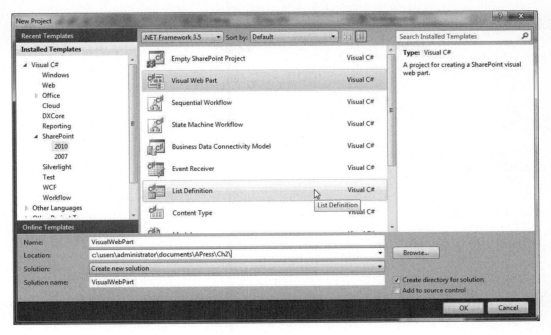

Figure 2–4. Visual Studio 2010 Visual Web Part selection

When you have selected the Visual Web Part template, the next screen that you see has a lot of functionality within it—and is actually a whole topic in itself.

SharePoint Customization Wizard

The wizard allows you to select the site and security level for the web part. SharePoint 2010 allows two separate deployment models for all SharePoint solutions. These models represent the security trust level under which you would like to deploy the solution. Figure 2–5 highlights the SharePoint Customization wizard.

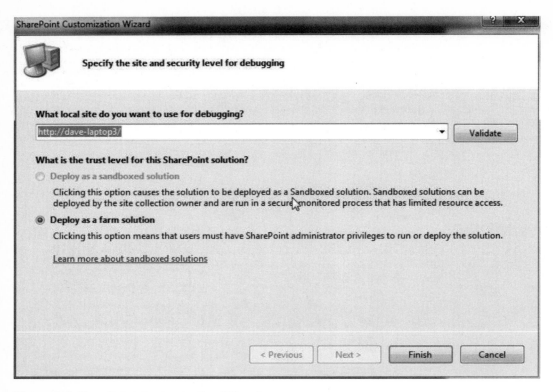

Figure 2–5. *SharePoint Customization Wizard*

First, you select your local development environment SharePoint URL, then you have the option to select two types of security levels, to either deploy your solution as a farm or sandboxed solution.

■ **Note** Visual Studio 2010 does not support sandboxed solutions for visual web parts. This is because the .ascx control in the solution will need to be deployed to the file system, and sandboxed solutions have limited permissions that do not include this capability. However, the SharePoint team has released a Visual Studio 2010 SharePoint Power Tools code release that offers the ability to do this. You can find this by searching on that phrase or at the URL http://visualstudiogallery.msdn.microsoft.com/en-us/8e602a8c-6714-4549-9e95-f3700344b0d9

You should also note that we are selecting our local environment as opposed to a remote environment. Visual Studio 2010 requires that to do SharePoint development, you must have the SharePoint product installed on the local environment that you are doing development on.

Deploy As a Farm Solution

Deploying as a farm solution is a higher level of trust than the sandboxed solution level. Typically, assemblies packaged in these types of solutions are deployed to the Global Assembly Cache (GAC). Code is run in an unrestricted fashion. All aspects of the solution will be run in the same application pool on your IIS server as the SharePoint site. This setting can represent greater control over the SharePoint environment, yet also represent a significant risk to the SharePoint farm if solutions deployed in this fashion are not handled in a judicious manner. However, with coding farm solutions in a best-practices manner this opens up a wide horizon of possibilities to take your collaboration solutions to the next level.

Deploy As a Sandboxed Solution

Sandboxed solutions operate in a whole different fashion. Instead of running in the same IIS application pool as the SharePoint site, there is a completely different service that is running that spawns off a completely separate process to run the sandboxed solution (see Figure 2–6).

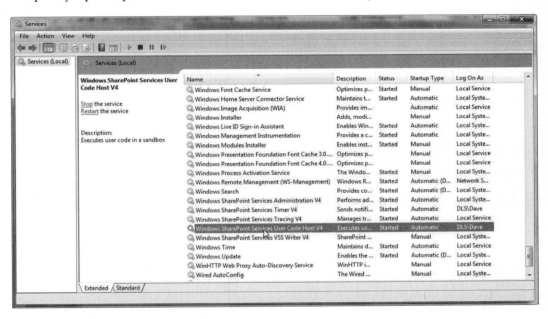

Figure 2–6. *Windows SharePoint Services User Code Host V4*

This service in SharePoint Foundation 2010 is the service that runs and provides sandboxed solution management. This service manages the threading, performance, and resource management of the sandboxed solutions deployed on that server.

Examining the Visual Web Part Solution

When you have selected the trust levels you want and the site that you are deploying your solution to, Visual Studio 2010 builds out the visual web part solution that you are aiming at. The solution appears as in Figure 2–7.

Figure 2–7. Visual web part solution

The visual web part solution, in addition to containing the same elements that the blank project shown earlier in the chapter has, also contains a new folder named VisualWebPart1. This folder contains all of the artifacts necessary to build a Visual Web Part. Let's go over the key files involved with a visual web part SharePoint solution.

Elements.xml

The elements file is an XML-formatted file that the SharePoint product knows how to interpret, which contains the module of the project, including the internal SharePoint URL path to the container folder, the list type that upon which the visual web part is based, and the name of the web part. The File element contains the internal path to the web part and the Property element as well as the Type, indicating its use in SharePoint 2010 libraries and lists.

```xml
<?xml version="1.0" encoding="utf-8"?>
<Elements xmlns="http://schemas.microsoft.com/sharepoint/" >
  <Module Name="VisualWebPart1" List="113" Url="_catalogs/wp">
    <File Path="VisualWebPart1\VisualWebPart1.webpart"
Url="VisualWebPart_VisualWebPart1.webpart" Type="GhostableInLibrary" >
      <Property Name="Group" Value="Custom" />
    </File>
  </Module>
</Elements>
```

VisualWebPart1.cs

This file is basically a container for the .ascx file—a SharePoint user control which is very similar to the ASP.NET user control. This container provides a path to the control as well as a Factory pattern for all of the controls in the .ascx control.

VisualWebPart1.webpart

The .webpart file is another XML formatted file that highlights necessary information about the web part, such as its type, error messages, and properties of the web part.

```xml
<?xml version="1.0" encoding="utf-8"?>
<webParts>
  <webPart xmlns="http://schemas.microsoft.com/WebPart/v3">
    <metaData>
      <type name="VisualWebPart.VisualWebPart1.VisualWebPart1,
$SharePoint.Project.AssemblyFullName$" />
      <importErrorMessage>$Resources:core,ImportErrorMessage;</importErrorMessage>
    </metaData>
    <data>
      <properties>
        <property name="Title" type="string">VisualWebPart1</property>
        <property name="Description" type="string">My Visual WebPart</property>
      </properties>
    </data>
  </webPart>
</webParts>
```

VisualWebPart1UserControl.ascx

This .ascx file is, as you can see by the file definition, a specific type of web part that was designed to interact with the SharePoint 2010 product. It has a code-behind file.

```
<%@ Assembly Name="$SharePoint.Project.AssemblyFullName$" %>
<%@ Assembly Name="Microsoft.Web.CommandUI, Version=14.0.0.0, Culture=neutral,
PublicKeyToken=71e9bce111e9429c" %>
<%@ Register Tagprefix="SharePoint" Namespace="Microsoft.SharePoint.WebControls"
Assembly="Microsoft.SharePoint, Version=14.0.0.0, Culture=neutral,
PublicKeyToken=71e9bce111e9429c" %>
<%@ Register Tagprefix="Utilities" Namespace="Microsoft.SharePoint.Utilities"
Assembly="Microsoft.SharePoint, Version=14.0.0.0, Culture=neutral,
PublicKeyToken=71e9bce111e9429c" %>
```

```
<%@ Register Tagprefix="asp" Namespace="System.Web.UI" Assembly="System.Web.Extensions,
Version=3.5.0.0, Culture=neutral, PublicKeyToken=31bf3856ad364e35" %>
<%@ Import Namespace="Microsoft.SharePoint" %>
<%@ Register Tagprefix="WebPartPages" Namespace="Microsoft.SharePoint.WebPartPages"
Assembly="Microsoft.SharePoint, Version=14.0.0.0, Culture=neutral,
PublicKeyToken=71e9bce111e9429c" %>
<%@ Control Language="C#" AutoEventWireup="true"
CodeBehind="VisualWebPart1UserControl.ascx.cs"
Inherits="VisualWebPart.VisualWebPart1.VisualWebPart1UserControl" %>
```

VisualWebPart1UserControl.ascx.cs

Between the .ascx control and the .cs codebehind file, this is where you can do your SharePoint magic:

```csharp
using System;
using System.Web.UI;
using System.Web.UI.WebControls;
using System.Web.UI.WebControls.WebParts;
namespace VisualWebPart.VisualWebPart1
{
    public partial class VisualWebPart1UserControl : UserControl
    {
        protected void Page_Load(object sender, EventArgs e)
        {
        }
    }
}
```

You will notice in the Toolbox section of your Visual Studio IDE that you have quite a variety of options to choose from to use in this user control web part. Figure 2–8 highlights a few of these.

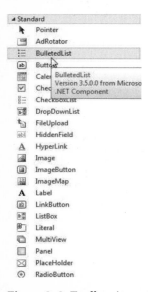

Figure 2–8. Toolbox items in visual web part

Note the highlighted control—the BulletedList. You can see from the mouseover text that the version of BulletedList targets is version 3.5.0.0 of the .NET Framework.

▪ **Note** Recall that as we explained in the first chapter, the SharePoint 2010 release is targeting .NET 3.5. This means your SharePoint development will also need to target .NET 3.5 and you will not be able to use the new features of .NET 4.0 in your SharePoint solutions until SharePoint provides support for it.

Also of note in the code-behind file is that your entire SharePoint object model including API, LINQ to SharePoint, and site elements are right at your fingertips to work with to interact with your SharePoint 2010 web site.

Wrapping ASP.NET Development

As an ASP.NET developer, one of the first considerations you might have is to think about how you might interact with an external database to SharePoint. After all, we want to wrap the features of SharePoint within an ASP.NET application in this book. There are a couple of options for how you might go about this:

- Through external content types and Business Connectivity Services (BCS)
- Directly through the .NET Framework API

Both of these options have tradeoffs and specific approaches that we will cover in detail in later chapters in this book. For now, consider that for simple connectivity to external content types that consist of databases, or even ERP applications such as SAP, BCS is the recommended approach.

▪ **Note** BCS is a feature that is designed for connecting your SharePoint 2010 environment to external systems. We cover BCS in detail in Chapter 7 of the book.

If you have a scenario that involves an ASP.NET application with a more complex database structure, there may be a better way. External content types have a certain amount of overhead and limitations to them in that you will be interacting with a SharePoint list as opposed to a transactional database. In these types of scenarios, it may be a better approach to interact directly with the transactional database from within your SharePoint solution. Going directly through ADO.NET 3.5 and the .NET Framework API is going to involve planning out carefully where we will store database configuration information and ensuring performance planning for the web part. These scenarios and constraints will be detailed out in later chapters in the book.

Coding the Sample Visual Web Part

For now, let's get back to our sample visual web part. We'll add a little bit of code and interact with the SharePoint object model in the SharePoint API. To build SharePoint solutions that contain ASP.NET applications and elements within them, there will be a great deal of interaction in a typical solution with both the SharePoint API and more traditional methods of ASP.NET coding.

For this web part, let's design and code a web part that will list our high-priority tasks from our tasks list. To start, open up the VisualWebPart1UserControl.ascx file, add a header element <h2>, and drag a label from the toolbox below it, as shown in Figure 2–9.

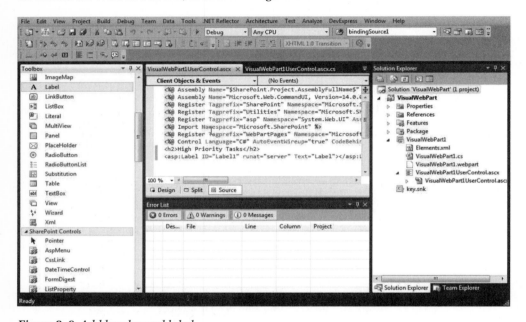

Figure 2–9. *Add header and label*

Next, open up the code-behind file VisualWebPartUserControl.ascx.cs, and add the following code to the Page_Load event:

```
var site = SPContext.Current.Web;
var taskList = site.Lists["Tasks"];
var oQuery = new SPQuery();
oQuery.Query = "<Where><Eq><FieldRef Name='Priority'/>" +
               "<Value Type='CHOICE'>(1) High</Value></Eq></Where>";
var tasks = taskList.GetItems(oQuery);

foreach (SPListItem task in tasks)
{
    Label1.Text = SPEncode.HtmlEncode(task["Title"].ToString())
        + " -- " + SPEncode.HtmlEncode(task["Description"].ToString())
        + "<br>";
}
```

This section of code introduces a number of concepts that are important to discuss in interacting with the SharePoint API.

- SPContext.Current.Web—Managing the creation and disposal of objects is an important topic in SharePoint development. The following MSDN article covers a great deal of information on the best practices for using disposable Windows objects: `http://msdn.microsoft.com/en-us/library/aa973248W.aspx`. You must specifically dispose of objects that you have created in your solution. The two ways I do this are:

  - Utilize the `using` statement: `using()`

  - Utilizing SPContext.Current

  The way I think about these to remember them is that if I am coding something that interacts with the site the code is instantiated on, then I'll use the second option, the SPContext, because my code is contained in the same context. If I am targeting resources outside my immediate area, I will have to create and dispose of the objects, so I use the first option (the `using` statement). The `using` statement automatically wraps resources with a `try/catch` block and disposes of resources created within the brackets. One important tool that is used by many SharePoint administrators to ensure the proper disposal of SharePoint objects is SPDisposeCheck. You can find this tool at `http://code.msdn.microsoft.com/SPDisposeCheck`.

- var—The var keyword was introduced in C# 2008 and is used mostly for returning anonymous types from LINQ queries. It allows you to specify a variable without declaring the type. I use it to save keystrokes.

- `SPQuery` and `GetItems()`—In SharePoint, to filter list items to specified values, a specific type of query is used called a CAML query. CAML is an XML language construct developed for the SharePoint product. It's a good idea to have some basic familiarity with CAML, even though for SharePoint 2010 there are new features enabling LINQ to SharePoint for a more rapid retrieval of list data. We will cover LINQ to SharePoint in a later example. You can find a great resource to get a head start on CAML and how to utilize it in SharePoint development in the SharePoint Foundation 2010 SDK—the article is entitled *Introduction to Collaboration Application Markup Language (CAML)*. You can find the SharePoint SDKs online at the following link, which also offers downloadable options for offline viewing: `http://msdn.microsoft.com/en-us/library/ee557253(v=office.14).aspx`

There is also great further content to build some initial familiarity with the best practices for SharePoint development in the SharePoint Server SDK—the content is entitled *Enterprise Development with SharePoint Server*. You can find this content online at `http://msdn.microsoft.com/en-us/library/ee559285(v=office.14).aspx`.

■ **Tip** The SPQuery class is primarily targeted toward querying individual lists or document libraries. To amalgamate information over a series of libraries and lists that may cross site boundaries, the SPSiteDataQuery class is the recommended approach. SPSiteDataQuery has significantly less performance overhead than an approach of looping through individual site collections to build lists. One excellent resource for seeing SPSiteDataQuery in action is the Codeplex project named Camelot, which you can find at http://camelot.codeplex.com/. Camelot is an application for testing cross site SPSiteDataQueries. There are a number of other SharePoint tools, add-ons, and projects on Codeplex that are of great benefit to SharePoint 2010 development. You are encouraged to make Codeplex a regular stop in your quest for SharePoint resources.

Deploying a Solution

Now that we have added all the code and components we need to the visual web part, it is time to deploy it to the SharePoint environment to see how it looks. For this release of Visual Studio 2010, the VS team put a great effort into making the packaging, deployment, and debugging of SharePoint solutions a much easier experience than with previous product versions. In fact, deploying and debugging SharePoint solutions were one of the primary user stories that the SharePoint Visual Studio team targeted for the 2010 release. Reza Chitsaz, a Sr. Program Manager on the Visual Studio team, says"

> *"For this release we were going after the F5 experience and improving the way you interact with SharePoint as a developer. That was our primary user story."*

To improve the way we interact with SharePoint and produce a coherent F5 experience similar to the one available in ASP.NET development was no small feat.

Examining the Deployment Process

One of the first things that you will notice is some differences in the Build menu in Visual Studio (see Figure 2–10).

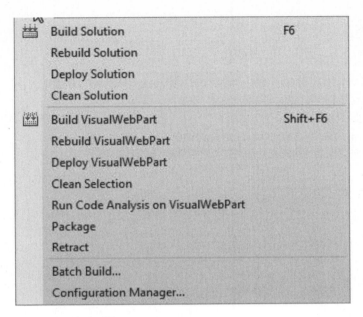

Figure 2–10. Build menu

Notice that we have two new selections—Package and Retract. Packaging solutions is a major feature in VS 2010 and has its own designer. We will go into detail on that later in this chapter. Retract allows the developer to retract a previously deployed SharePoint solution that is in your project from the SharePoint site, removing it.

You can go ahead and press F5 for your visual web part solution and watch the process. To build and deploy the SharePoint solution, we actually need a number of things to take place. You can view each of the steps involved as well as configure custom steps or remove some of the steps in the Deployment Configuration designers. Access these by selecting the Project menu, and the Properties for VisualWebPart1, or any SharePoint 2010 project in Visual Studio 2010. On the SharePoint section, which is all new, scroll to the bottom and select the Default deployment configuration under Edit Deployment Configurations. Then click the View button, which brings you to the View Deployment Configurations designer window, as seen in Figure 2–11.

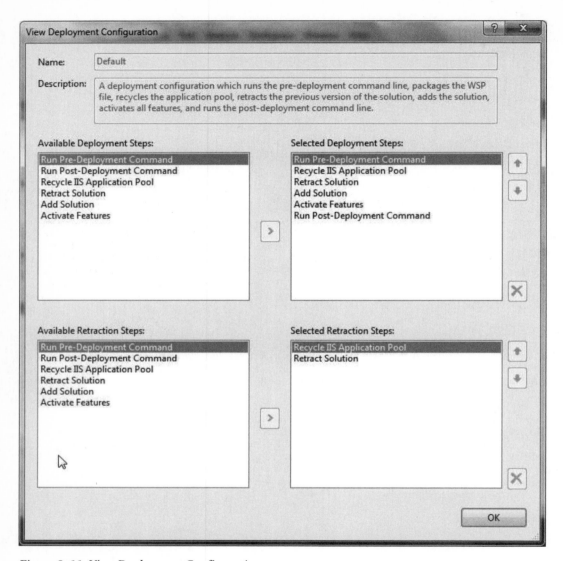

Figure 2–11. View Deployment Configuration

Note all of the steps involved in building a SharePoint solution and installing it in your local SharePoint environment for testing and debugging. The steps are:

1. Run Pre-Deployment Command—This is the opportunity to have a custom build script for necessary things such as running the SPMetal tool to generate LINQ to SharePoint object models to run against.

2. Recycle IIS Application Pool—To activate .dlls installed to the GAC requires recycling the IIS application pool that the SharePoint site is running under. This preserves the F5 one-button experience.

3. Retract Solution—Any previous versions of this solution are retracted from the SharePoint environment.

4. Add Solution—The current SharePoint solution is added to your SharePoint environment.

5. Activate Features—Once the solution is deployed, any features on the SharePoint site are activated so they may be used.

6. Run Post-Deployment Command—This is another touch point for scripting opportunities. You can find a walk-through for creating a custom deployment step at http://msdn.microsoft.com/en-us/library/ee256698(VS.100).aspx.

Once you have completed all of these steps, your previous F5 action will bring up your SharePoint site in a browser window. For your visual web part solution, you will need to place the web part on any page in your environment for it to show up. You can easily do this by interacting with the SharePoint 2010 ribbon control when you have a test page in edit mode. Figure 2–12 shows the ribbon parts that has the command to insert the web part. Note that if you have any breakpoints set in the Page_Load event, the breakpoint will be hit when you instantiate the web part on the page. Figure 2–12 shows the web part instantiated on a page, and Figure 2–13 shows a breakpoint being hit in the debugger.

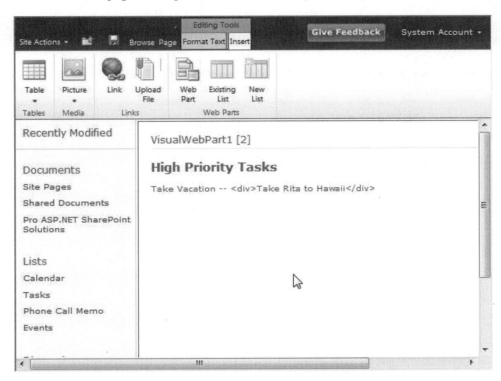

Figure 2–12. Web part on the SharePoint page

There are other tasks in my task list that do not have a high priority, and they are not showing up in my list. This is due to the CAML query selection.

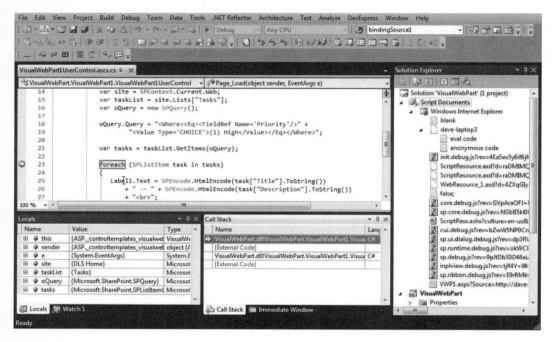

Figure 2–13. *Breakpoint in debugger*

Deploying to a Test or Production Environment

One other important concept to cover in deploying a solution is how to deploy this solution to another web site besides the work environment computer. The F5 experience is tremendous in a development environment, but what about a test or production environment?

One of the features offered with Visual Studio 2010 is the package selection. This selection builds the current configuration and packages it up into a SharePoint solution file (.wsp). You can see the package selection in Figure 2–14.

Build Solution
F6
Rebuild Solution
Deploy Solution
Clean Solution
Build VisualWebPart
Shift+F6
Rebuild VisualWebPart
Deploy VisualWebPart
Clean Selection
Run Code Analysis on VisualWebPart
Package
Retract
Batch Build...
Configuration Manager...

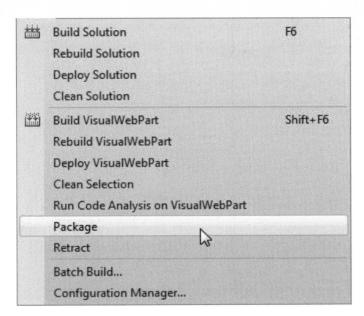

Figure 2–14. Visual Studio package build option

When you build the package, it places the .wsp solution file into the build directory, found at either /bin/Debug for a debug configuration setting, or the /bin/Release folder for a release configuration setting. You can see the files that are produced in Figure 2–15.

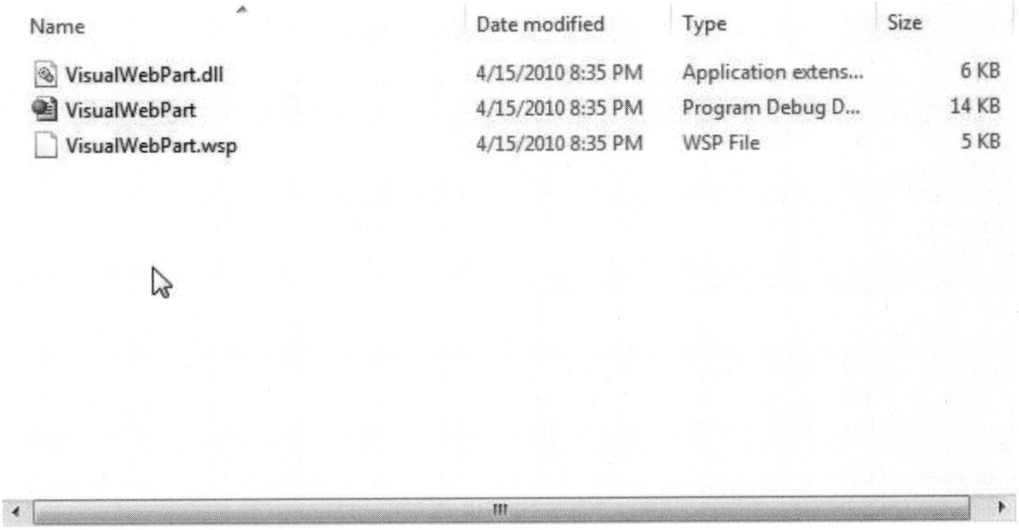

Name
Date modified
Type
Size
VisualWebPart.dll
4/15/2010 8:35 PM
Application extens...
6 KB
VisualWebPart
4/15/2010 8:35 PM
Program Debug D...
14 KB
VisualWebPart.wsp
4/15/2010 8:35 PM
WSP File
5 KB

Figure 2–15. /bin/Release folder contents after package build

You can take the .wsp file from your environment and install it on a test or production server using a PowerShell command.

To install the solution, you first navigate to your production environment and run the SharePoint 2010 Management Shell, as found in the Microsoft SharePoint 2010 Products menu shown in Figure 2–16.

Figure 2–16. SharePoint Management Shell menu selection

This opens up a PowerShell command window as well as runs the SharePoint configuration PowerShell script named sharepoint.ps1. You can find this script in the SharePoint root directory, under \CONFIG\POWERSHELL\Registration directory. The sharepoint.ps1 script registers all of the SharePoint PowerShell commandlets to use to manage your SharePoint environment.

To install or add your solution to a the solution store in your SharePoint environment, run the PowerShell commandlet command Add-SPSolution, which takes one parameter that consists of the path to your .wsp solution file. It looks like the following:

```
Add-SPSolution c:\temp\VisualStudioWebPart.wsp
```

If your solution is a sandboxed solution, you would use Add-SPUserSolution instead of Add-SPSolution. When you run the script, it returns the ID of the solution generated by SharePoint as well as the deployment status of the solution. This PowerShell command adds the solution to your SharePoint environment. The path to your .wsp file needs to be a full one.

Next we need to deploy the solution. Use the following command:

```
Install-SPSolution –Identity VisualStudioWebPart.wsp –WebApplication
   http://yoursite -GACDeployment
```

Now your feature should be available to include in a SharePoint page. To do this, you can edit a SharePoint page, select Insert on the ribbon, select the Web Part icon, and browse to your visual web part, which will be found in the Custom folder. An image of this is shown in Figure 2–17.

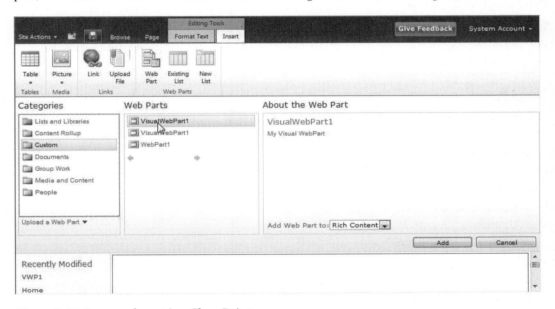

Figure 2–17. Insert web part in a SharePoint page

A couple of other useful PowerShell commands related to managing solution files are:

```
Update-SPSolution –Identity VisualWebPart.wsp –LiteralPath
   c:\temp\VisualStudioWebPart.wsp –GACDeployment
```

This command updates the SharePoint solution. Also:

```
Uninstall-SPSolution –Identity VisualWebPart.wsp –WebApplication
   http://yoursite -confirm
```

This command retracts a solution. The following command removes the solution from the solution store:

```
Remove-SPSolution –Identity VisualWebPart.wsp
```

A great resource to delve further into SharePoint 2010 PowerShell commandlets is the following TechNet resource: http://technet.microsoft.com/en-us/library/ee806878(office.14).aspx.

So this concludes the first project template and type (that isn't just an empty solution) —the Visual Web Part template. We took a little more time on this project to go over very specific windows and areas as well as a little time calling out some of the best practices and techniques for interacting with the SharePoint API. We also highlighted a complete end-to-end solution development cycle, including packaging and deploying a solution to a test or production environment. All of this is important to build a little foundation in some of the standard practices in SharePoint development.

Let's move on to look at some of the important designers, and then some other project type templates that are common to use.

Using Features

One integral feature built into Visual Studio 2010 for SharePoint 2010 development is the way it handles SharePoint features. Features in SharePoint are one of the core building blocks of both the SharePoint product and any customized solution that you will build in SharePoint 2010. Features are added in behind the scenes in most of the SharePoint 2010 project templates. Features are represented by XML files that the SharePoint project interprets and controls.

Features are also the building blocks that are most recommended for deploying customizations to the SharePoint environment. The reason for this is that you can install and uninstall features in a controlled fashion across multiple SharePoint web farm servers and installations. This means that they are the standard way of handling customizations that most SharePoint administrators are used to and comfortable with. This is an important consideration specifically because working with the flow of your SharePoint administrators makes implementations easier, and also there is nothing that is more of an anti-pattern to collaboration than friction between SharePoint developers and administrators on a project.

You may also be activate and deactivate features from the SharePoint administrative web site or site settings sites. This allows the greatest amount of portability for your customization. You can also scope features from the Farm level all the way down to the Site level, which represents the scope of availability for feature activation.

Much of the SharePoint product itself is built and deployed in features. For instance, many of the features available in the SharePoint 2010 Server edition are packaged up in features that are installed along with that product and are not available in SharePoint 2010 Foundation installs. Many third-party tools as well are built within features and activated and licensed on a SharePoint farm or site basis.

As an example of how Visual Studio 2010 templates and SPIs utilize features behind the scenes, let's look again at our VisualWebPart project. Notice the Features folder and the expanded items underneath it in Figure 2–18.

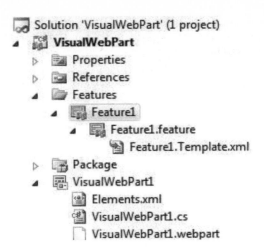

Figure 2–18. Features elements

You can see that below the Features directory there are a number of nodes and/or elements added in. Let's look at them now.

▪ **Note** The Features and Package directories are integral parts to any SharePoint 2010 solution, and developers should not remove them for any reason, even if they are not used. Removing them can cause problems with building, packaging, and deploying your customizations.

Feature.Template.xml

This is the XML file that defines the feature to the SharePoint product when installed. You may open and view this file either by double-clicking on it or by highlighting the Feature node and selecting View Template from the right-click menu.

```
<?xml version="1.0" encoding="utf-8" ?>
<Feature xmlns="http://schemas.microsoft.com/sharepoint/">
</Feature>
```

Feature1.feature and Feature1 Nodes

These are internal nodes that are added automatically to help facilitate the definition, packaging, and deployment of the feature. Double-clicking either of these files or selecting View Designer in the right-click menu with the Feature1 node highlighted brings up the Feature Designer, as seen in Figure 2–19.

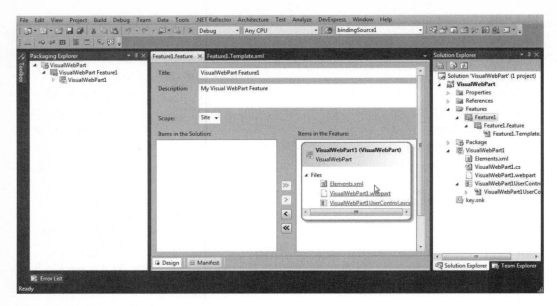

Figure 2–19. *Feature Designer*

The Feature Designer offers the ability to define the title and description of the feature. This is what will show up in the SharePoint environment when selecting features to activate. Also available to define is the scope of the feature. Feature scope has four options:

- Farm—Activates the feature for an entire farm

- Site—Activates the feature for all web sites in a site collection

- Web—Activates the feature for a specific web site

- WebApplication—Activates the feature for all web sites in a web application.

The windows below this are Items in the Solution and Items in the Feature. By default in our VisualWebPart solution, the web part is added to the feature. However, if you have more than one web part, or other SPIs in the solution such as controls, application pages, modules, images, resources, or other constructs, the Feature Designer offers drag-and-drop control over which of these you would like to package together as a feature. The Designer offers great visual interactive control over your SharePoint customizations.

■ **Note** Prior to SharePoint 2010, feature development and deployment was much more archaic. Feature.xml files, .webpart files, and artifacts all had to be packaged up individually by making a packaging file with a .ddf extension, and then running a tool called makecab.exe on the file to package up the files and assemblies into a .wsp solution file for installation in your SharePoint environment. The Feature Designer and Package Designer in Visual Studio 2010 have abstracted away the need for this kind of low-level interaction. These two features have greatly removed the barrier to rapid development in a SharePoint environment.

In the Items in the Feature window, you can expand the Files element to show exactly what is contained within the feature. In our project, we can see that the Elements.xml file, the VisualWebPart1.webpart file, and the VisualWebPart1UserControl.ascx file are all included in the feature. These files represent actual files that will be deployed to the SharePoint environment as part of the feature. You can examine what exactly is deployed by navigating to the SharePoint root and navigating to the \TEMPLATE\FEATURES directory underneath the root. There, you will notice a folder for each of your features that you have deployed, as well as folders for standard features included in the SharePoint product. Examine some of the folders and the exact files deployed underneath them to get an idea of the different items that are available and how they look deployed.

■ **Tip** The SharePoint root is an important location to remember. The SharePoint root is a file directory on your server that SharePoint is installed on that you can find at C:\Program Files\Common Files\Microsoft Shared\Web Server Extensions\14. This is where the SharePoint product installs files on your file system during installation.

Another way to examine what files are packaged in the feature is to select the Manifest tab at the bottom of the SharePoint Feature Designer window. This switches views to a preview of the packaged manifest, as shown in Figure 2–20.

Note that this view also shows the edit options that are available by expanding the Edit Options area. Changes entered into Edit Options through the XML editor will be merged with the automatically packaged elements in the top section. This offers a little more control over including any custom items necessary to deploy with your SharePoint customization.

A final option is available to advanced SharePoint developers. Overwrite generated XML and edit manifest in the XML Editor is a selection that will allow you complete customization control over feature packaging. Here, you can define elements yourself to include if you need or want the absolute control over the feature packaging available.

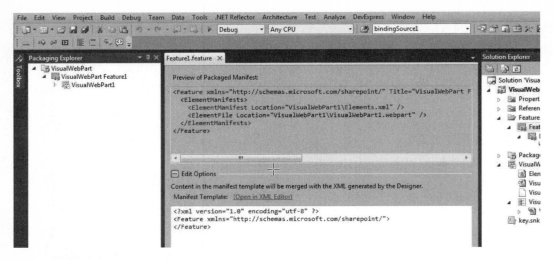

Figure 2–20. *Feature Designer package Manifest view*

■ **Note** If you choose to take full control over the packaging and use the XML editor, the Feature Designer is no longer active and not usable. You can choose to go back to the Designer, but at that point any changes you made in the XML will be lost.

Package Designer

The other main advancement in the Visual Studio 2010 interface for SharePoint development that shows up in every project is the Package Designer. SharePoint project may have many features. But each SharePoint project has exactly one package, which controls how the SharePoint customizations are built into a solution, or .wsp file. Packages for SharePoint can contain multiple features as well as other artifacts, such as modules, which are used as containers for files, applications pages, resources, and other things.

One way to look at it is that the Package Designer is like the Build Manager. You can select which items go into it or stay out. The primary view of the Package Designer for our VisualWebPart project is shown in Figure 2–21.

Notice that the Package Designer view looks somewhat similar to the Feature Designer, in that there is roughly the same layout, with Items in the Solution in the left-hand window and Items in the Package in the right-hand window. The feature appears in the Items in the Package window, with all of the project items as part of that.

The Package.Template.xml file simply is a container file to identify what needs to be built. Double-clicking on the Package or Package.package files, or right-clicking the Package file and selecting Package Designer brings up the Package Designer.

Packages are componentized into features, and each feature contains its own particular SPIs, such as our visual web Part. Similar to the Feature Designer, there is an Advanced view that shows the manifest.xml file and offers the ability to edit this file. This is shown in Figure 2–22.

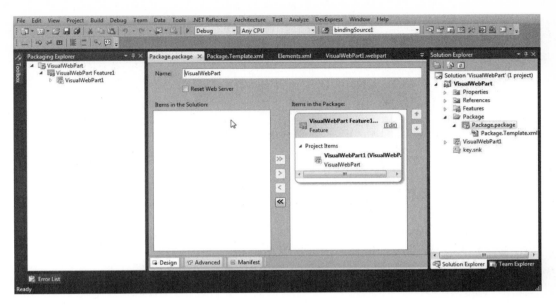

Figure 2–21. Package Designer

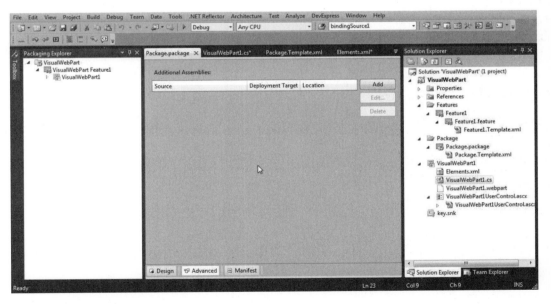

Figure 2–22. Package Designer Advanced view

■ **Tip** The Advanced window of the Package Designer offers the ability to package dependent assemblies that are not already installed on your SharePoint server.

Also offered in the Package Designer is the ability to completely override the designer settings and features and to manually code the manifest.xml file to have complete control over it. This allows you to specifically package up what will appear in the .wsp solution file to be deployed to your SharePoint server. This is shown in Figure 2–23.

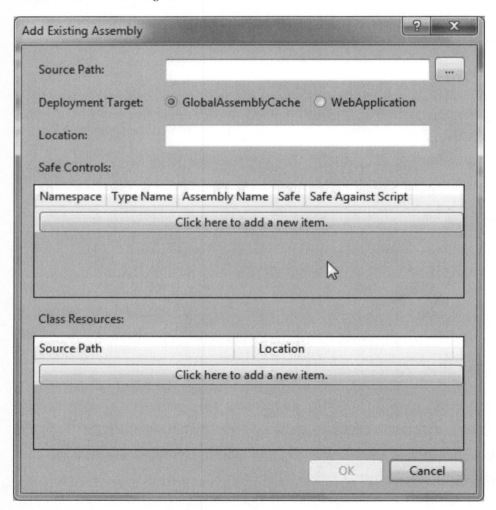

Figure 2–23. Package Designer—Add Existing Assembly

This window allows you the freedom to add an existing assembly that is not currently installed on the SharePoint server. It allows the inclusion of the .dll in the package as well as a directive to deploy the assembly as a Safe Control in the SharePoint environment.

Packaging Explorer

Also of value in working with packages is a new window called the Package Explorer. The Explorer gives you a hierarchical view of all the features and files that are included in your package. You can use it to quickly move files from one feature to another, or to delete features/files from a given package/feature. You can also view all packages within the solution and move features/files from one package to another, add/delete features, and perform other helpful operations on packages. The Packaging Explorer is shown in Figure 2–24, and opens when you select the View Designer selection on the Package right-click menu.

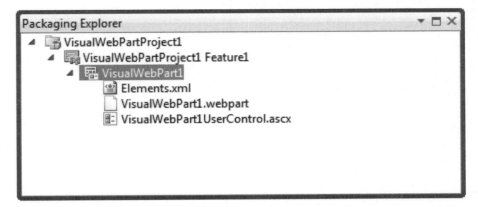

Figure 2–24. Packaging Explorer

SharePoint Project Templates

Besides the Visual Web Part project template, there are many other templates as well as SharePoint project items that are included in Visual Studio 2010. The following sections list brief descriptions of what comes with the standard Visual Studio 2010 installation.

Sequential Workflow

Workflows also are among the most common types of projects that are used in SharePoint 2010 customizations. The workflow template takes advantage of the Windows Workflow product integrated with SharePoint 2010. Workflows are utilized to design features that require business processes, notifications, and steps that require a document of a list to retain information in an offline state. The workflow templates also include a wizard that helps you to define the context within which the workflow will work. The Workflow Customization wizard runs at the beginning of defining a project, right after the configuration for trust levels.

The first step of the Workflow wizard can be seen in Figure 2–25.

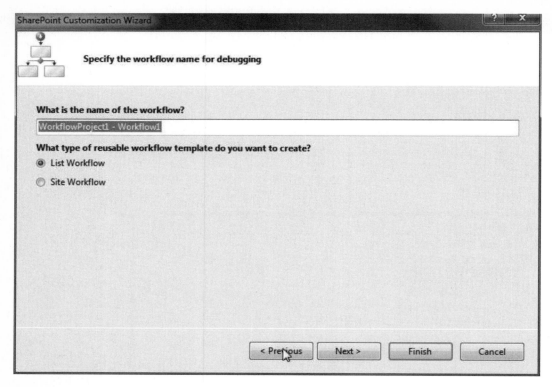

Figure 2–25. Workflow Customization Wizard—workflow context

This step allows you to name the workflow as well as define the context within which the workflow will function. You can design Workflow templates for both the list level or the site level. The site level attachment of a workflow is a new feature in SharePoint 2010. The next step is shown in Figure 2–26.

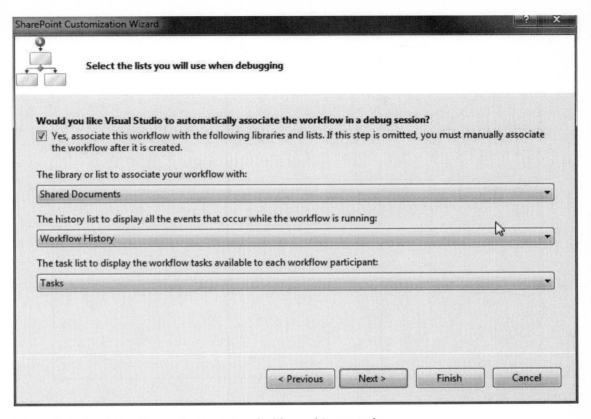

Figure 2–26. Workflow Customization Wizard—library, history, tasks

This step of the workflow configuration allows you to select the document library or list with which the workflow will be associated. Workflows on document libraries can help to define the lifecycle of the document within SharePoint, including defining steps for interaction with different departments or teams. The next step of the workflow wizard is shown in Figure 2–27.

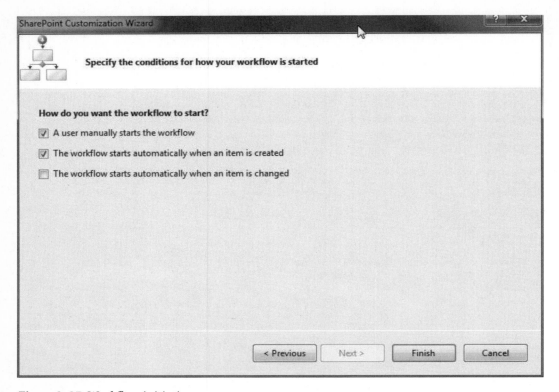

Figure 2–27. Workflow initiation

This configuration step is the final step. It allows you to define when the workflow starts execution. It is available to tie the initiation of a workflow in SharePoint 2010 to a specific action initiated by the user, the addition or a creation of a list item in a list or the addition of a document to a document library, or to the updating of a list or document library.

■ **Tip** You can re-enter this wizard and change values by clicking on the workflow SPI in the Solution Explorer and selecting the builder button for the History List property in the VS property window.

The automatic association of a workflow to common actions such as uploading a document to SharePoint or updating a list item is a very powerful feature. This association adds great depth to document management for SharePoint.

When the Workflow Configuration wizard completes, the SPIs included in the template are added to the project. The Workflow Designer is the next item that opens, and the first touch point is defined in the workflow by default—the onWorkflowActivated action (see Figure 2–28).

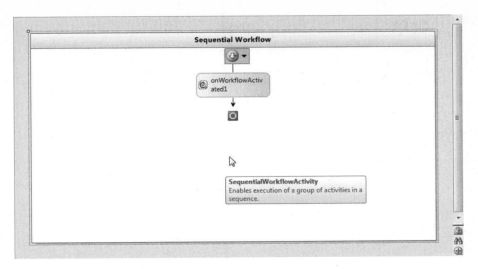

Figure 2–28. Visual Studio 2010 Workflow Designer

There is a whole toolbox full of available actions to implement in a workflow project. The vast majority of the items were implemented in .NET 3.0, but a few are upgrades in .NET 3.5. Figure 2–29 shows a number of these items.

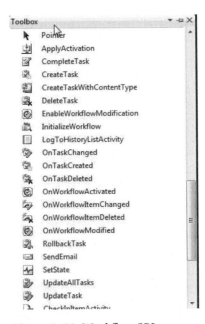

Figure 2–29. Workflow SPIs

Note that SharePoint 2010 Workflow SPIs contain a rich designer experience and interaction with the Workflow Designer that allow for both visual and code-based interaction with the workflow activities. Workflows exist to interact with tasks defined as related to the workflow as well as changes in the workflow associated item.

Visual Studio 2010 also supports project templates for forms that are associated with workflows. You can add .aspx pages for Workflow Association and Initiation forms to control custom actions relating to initiating a workflow of associating a current element with a workflow.

State Machine Workflow

This workflow template contains a mostly similar set of project files as the Sequential Workflow template. It also uses the same configuration wizard at the beginning. The main difference with the State Machine Workflow is that there is an initial state that is defined, and several more SPIs that are related to interacting with the state of the item. Figure 2–30 shows the different Workflow Designer and initial state.

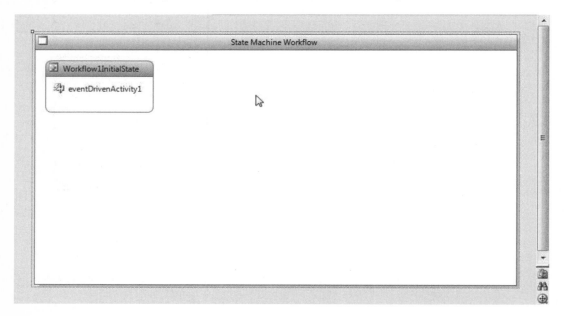

Figure 2–30. *State Machine Workflow Designer*

Events that occur within the SharePoint system can affect the state of the workflow.

Visual Studio 2010 also supports adding Workflow Initiation and Association aspx forms to your workflow projects. Once the workflow project is created, right-click on the SPI and Add Item ➤ Workflow Initiation Form. You can use this form to gather data from the user that you can use within your workflow (to make certain decisions) once the workflow is initiated. You can use the Workflowproperties.InitiationData to get to the values being returned by the Initiation form. An example would be an initiation form that asks for the approval amount of an expense report. Based on the approval amount, you can branch off and do different things within the workflow based on the value entered in the form.

Business Data Connectivity Model

This template provides a model for interacting with external content, which could reside in an external SQL Server database, or an external system that is exposed to SharePoint through a SOA model such as web services. You can rapidly configure BDC projects with the SharePoint 2010 Designer. You can use the templates in .NET to interact programmatically with the external system. BDC model templates include a designer tool as well to interact with entities, as shown in Figure 2–31.

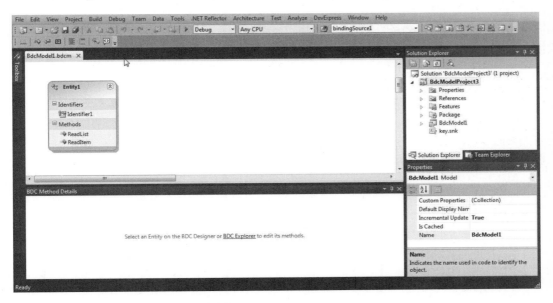

Figure 2–31. Visual Studio BDC model designer

As stated before, BDC models can be useful for interacting with more simplistic aspects of external systems such as single tables and simple associations. However, more complex interactions with external systems will require a different approach that we will cover in a later chapter in this book.

We will also highlight in that chapter some of the additional BDC Designer and Explorer windows in Visual Studio 2010.

Event Receiver

The Event Receiver project template also contains a customization wizard to help define the event that is targeted by the solution. The wizard with some of the selection choices is shown in Figure 2–32.

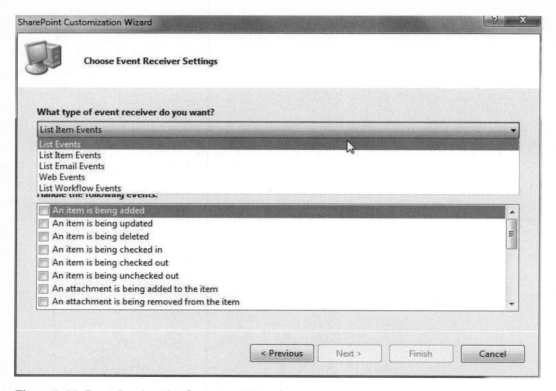

Figure 2–32. Event Receiver Configuration Wizard

The wizard defines the method to override in the project to handle the specific type of event.

List Definition

The List Definition project template also has a new customization wizard that allows you to select the base list from which your custom list will be defined. A view of this wizard is shown in Figure 2–33.

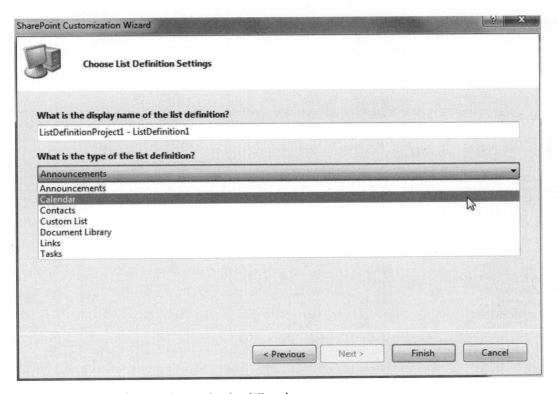

Figure 2–33. List Definition Customization Wizard

The configuration and the template add elements to the project to interact with a custom list definition. The interaction includes a number of artifacts, including element definitions, dialogue forms to interact with the list, and repair and upload pages associated with the list. The SPIs are shown in Figure 2–34.

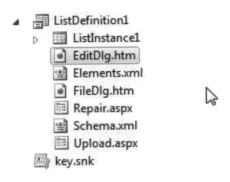

Figure 2–34. List Defintion SPIs

ContentType

The ContentType template is a fairly simple template that offers a customization wizard to define the root content type that the project is based upon, and then adds the proper ContentType ID that SharePoint 2010 can identify the feature by.

The customization step is shown in Figure 2–35.

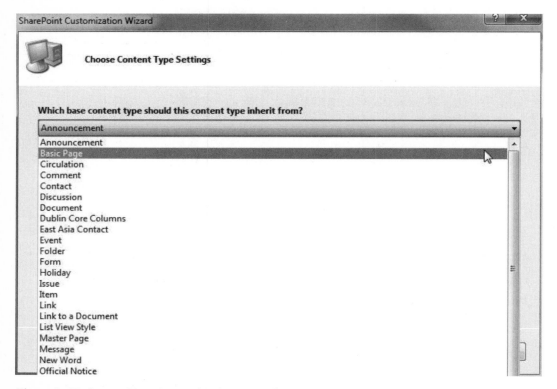

Figure 2–35. ContentType Customization Wizard

Module

A module is a simple container for deploying pages and other content to SharePoint 2010. When you select the template, a Sample.txt file is placed in the module path and configured for deploying to SharePoint as a rough example. If folders are created in Modules, but nothing is deployed to them, then SharePoint 2010 actively decides to not deploy the folders.

Site Definitions

The Site Definition project template in SharePoint 2010 allows you to define the baseline template named onet.xml that allows you to define a complete site template for SharePoint 2010. Site templates are used to define a site that a new site in a site collection can be based upon. The default page to interact with the site is also included as a SPI. Onet.xml files are contained in the baseline SharePoint 2010 product to define the default site definitions that are used to deploy sites in the baseline product. Custom site definitions can be built based upon the core product site definition onet.xml files.

Import Reusable Workflow

This project actually represents a significant advance in another SharePoint product—the SharePoint 2010 Designer. In previous versions of SharePoint, it was much easier to implement a workflow in SharePoint designer than it was to custom code something in Visual Studio. However, in SharePoint 2010, it is possible to export a workflow from SharePoint 2010 Designer and import it in to Visual Studio by way of the Import Reusable Workflow template. This allows you to define and deploy features that represent reusable workflow as opposed to having a SharePoint Designer version that is tied completely to one list in the content database and not available to be utilized anywhere else.

By importing the reusable workflow into Visual Studio, you can extend the workflow that was started by the business analyst or power user by adding custom code activities and using the features of .NET and Visual Studio.

Import SharePoint Solution Package

Reusability is a fantastic feature in a lot of the Visual Studio 2010 feature packages for SharePoint 2010. The Import SharePoint Solution Package feature allows you to select any SharePoint 2010 .wsp file and import it into Visual Studio 2010 to work with it. Portability between toolsets is one major advantage of SharePoint 2010 over many other options available.

After you import solutions, you have the capability to extend the features that were imported in by writing custom code. One example of this would be to bring in a list instance and adding an event receiver to it. After customizations, it is possible to repack the solution and deploy it back out. So Visual Studio 2010 supports a rich lifecycle development story that allows integration with other tools and teams.

Other Visual Studio Templates and Features

Visual Studio 2010 also has other project item templates available based upon what you are working with. In addition to this, Visual Studio 2010 is extensible so that many more project templates and project item templates are being released to forums such as MSDN and Codeplex.

One particularly helpful set of these templates is the CKS Dev Toolkit, which you can find at `http://cksdev.codeplex.com/`. This toolkit includes additional templates such as templates for master pages, site definitions, custom actions and action groups, delegate controls, full trust proxies, and SPMetal projects for interacting with LINQ-to-SharePoint. With the rich extensibility model of Visual Studio 2010, it is recommended to stay current on releases and publications to many of these areas for pre-built tools that are being released ongoing.

Team Development

One concept that comes up when discussing packaging features and .wsp solution files and deploying them to SharePoint servers is "What should a team development environment look like?" While there are a number of options in how to configure an environment of this nature, there is a baseline recommendation in what type of environment to set up, and a few great options to go along with that. As a baseline bare minimum, you will want to have three environments set up for SharePoint development: development, test, and production.

Development

Because SharePoint 2010 offers the ability to set up a development environment on either Windows 7 or Windows 2008 Server, the first component of a SharePoint custom solution environment is a development environment. A developer can configure a local SharePoint installation on a personal machine to be able to perform SharePoint customizations, to immediately deploy them to the local environment through F5, and the ability to test out how changes will look on a SharePoint site. Every SharePoint developer needs some kind of local development environment set up for them. There are three basic options available to set up a SharePoint development environment:

- Local SharePoint Install

- Bootable Virtual Hard Drive (.vhd)

- Server with a Virtual Machine (VM)

Each of these options is viable and the choices that you make have certain tradeoffs in ease of setup, performance, and flexibility. For more information on setting up a local environment, see the MSDN article at `http://msdn.microsoft.com/en-us/library/ee554869(office.14).aspx`.
In addition to the local development environment, if a team has the resources, it is a good idea to set up some kind of a common development environment as a place to deploy common changes to. This can provide a first look and feel for how features work together, and a place to show work in progress.

Test

This is an area that should resemble the production environment in how it is set up. It may not necessarily need the same amount of hardware resources involved, but can be a scaled down approximation of production. The idea of this is that testing on an environment set up like production will help to increase the quality of your change control and deploy better code and better solutions. You can monitor performance issues and set up specific test case scenarios for testing. A good test environment will be owned by the QA department, and many times for quality purposes, will not be under the control of your development team.

Testing software is an art in and of itself, and a career in and of itself. Testing harnesses and automated testing scripts that you can set up to do regression testing are fantastic elements to have in a SharePoint customization environment.

Production

This is your live environment that all of your SharePoint users depend on for document management and collaboration. You will want to keep the availability of this environment as high as possible. This environment is one on which change control should be tracked by some means. Changes to production environments should be scheduled during maintenance windows that are communicated to workers so that they have proper expectations of system availability.

Note that these environments and recommendations are just basic practical considerations for team development with SharePoint 2010. Your particular environment is going to have to scale to the ability and size of your team and organization. As your team gets more mature and you gain more resources, you can develop and increase advanced engineering practices, such as continuous integration, one-click build and deployments, and automated testing. All development should operate under source control of some kind. Microsoft Application Lifecycle Management (ALM) tools offer a great option for development that is tightly integrated with SharePoint—you can set up projects with their own team sites in ALM that have great reporting and collaboration features.

Continuous integration (CI) and automated deployments are supported there as well. Source control, CI, testing (including test driven development), and their interaction with environments are a whole subject on their own. While it's impossible to give complete coverage to them in this short chapter, they are important enough concepts to give you some exposure to so that you can build them into your practices over time.

■ **Tip** If your team is small, or you are doing SharePoint project development on your own, it is still a great idea to utilize the ideas presented for team development by yourself. You can set up a common development environment, a test environment, and a production environment. You can set up continuous integration and automated tests yourself as a fun project. If you take the time to set up a quality environment, even if it takes you a little bit of extra time to do so, the returns in the form of happy users and projects coming in on time with great features are experiences that are tremendously rewarding! Taking the initiative like this will probably mean you won't be doing the work by yourself for long!

SharePoint development is notorious for starting in a concocted development environment and ending in a .wsp file with not a great deal of solid practices wedged in between. With the amount of effort Microsoft has put into making the development environment for SharePoint Visual Studio 2010 solid, it's time for that trend to turn around and for us to see capable and mature SharePoint teams that can do some amazing things!

■ **Tip** There is a great whitepaper that is available from Microsoft on setting up Team Build environments that you can find at `http://msdn.microsoft.com/en-us/ff622991.aspx`, which describes in detail how to set up integrated TFS Team Builds for SharePoint projects.

Summary

In this chapter we have covered advancing the SharePoint development environment with Visual Studio 2010, highlighted the anatomy of a SharePoint development project, including SharePoint SPIs, features, and packages. We walked through a complete SharePoint development cycle by building a simple visual web part, deploying it to our local machine, testing and debugging it, packaging it, and deploying it to our next stage environment. We also discussed same salient points concerning SharePoint best practices for individual developers as well as team development, and delved a little into the PowerShell environment.

We've covered a lot of territory and briefly exposed developers coming from an ASP.NET background who are not familiar with SharePoint to key areas of SharePoint development. For those more familiar with SharePoint, we've detailed out how to perform key development tasks in the Visual Studio 2010 environment and in utilizing the new administrative PowerShell interface to SharePoint 2010.

CHAPTER 3

■ ■ ■

SharePoint, IIS, and the .NET Framework

The higher your structure is to be, the deeper must be its foundation.

Saint Augustine

Now that we have investigated SharePoint as a development platform and highlighted some basic aspects of SharePoint development with Visual Studio 2010, we have the prerequisite information to be able to delve into the nature of what SharePoint really is at the core. This is helpful to do because understanding some of the basic elements and characteristics of SharePoint is critical for making informed decisions about different options that are available when combining ASP.NET applications and SharePoint 2010.

If we can really build a good basic understanding of the core structure of the product, then it frees up our approach and decisions so that we can extend SharePoint 2010 in a fashion that will preserve all of the qualities of the built-in platform, as well as allow us to integrate SharePoint 2010 into outside applications.

Looking at the artifacts that are contained within it, SharePoint 2010 consists of SQL Server databases, Windows services, and files and assemblies that exist on the server's file system.

In this chapter, we will examine SharePoint 2010 from the perspective of its footprint on the Web. We will examine Internet Information Services (IIS) 7 Manager and the functioning of IIS. Then we will cover SharePoint 2010 form a .NET Framework perspective, and examine details of the product from an Internet security perspective, examining Code Access Security. Finally, we will examine a new feature in SharePoint 2010, sandboxed solutions.

SharePoint 2010 in IIS 7 Manager

One way to examine SharePoint, with respect to its relationship to ASP.NET, is to examine how SharePoint is set up within IIS. Figure 3–1 shows the result of a SharePoint 2010 Server installation after running the installation and configuration of SharePoint, with two web applications created.

Figure 3–1. *IIS 7 Manager showing SharePoint web sites*

■ **Note** In this chapter, we will refer to IIS 7 by the major release version number, as opposed to the minor version. This is because IIS 7.0 is the service that is packaged with Windows Server 2008, and IIS 7.5 is the service that is packaged with Windows Server 2008 R2. While there are slight differences, the SharePoint product works the same overall, in either minor version.

The main web site set up by the SharePoint installation is the SharePoint Central Administration v4 site. This site is basically an ASP.NET web application. Its purpose is to perform the administrative tasks related to SharePoint 2010 in a web farm, which includes managing services, starting and stopping them, setting farm accounts and passwords, and provisioning other web sites and site collections. If you are familiar with ASP.NET web sites, you can see several familiar artifacts in the application directory of Central Administration, including a global.asax file, which is used for application startup and base-level interaction, and a web.config file, used for settings for the web site.

IIS and .NET Fundamentals

While drilling down to the protocol level in the interactions between SharePoint 2010, IIS 7, and the .NET 3.5 Framework is probably a little too granular for the purposes of this book, it is important to know a little bit about how these pieces fit together, both for an ASP.NET web application as well as a SharePoint 2010 site.

In this chapter, we will strive for a fairly deep understanding of the interaction between SharePoint 2010, IIS 7, and .NET 3.5, in order to better understand how these products work together to serve up a collaboration platform for a user through a web browser.

IIS 7 is a role that you can install on your server to provide hosting facilities for Internet or intranet applications. A view of this role shown in Figure 3–2.

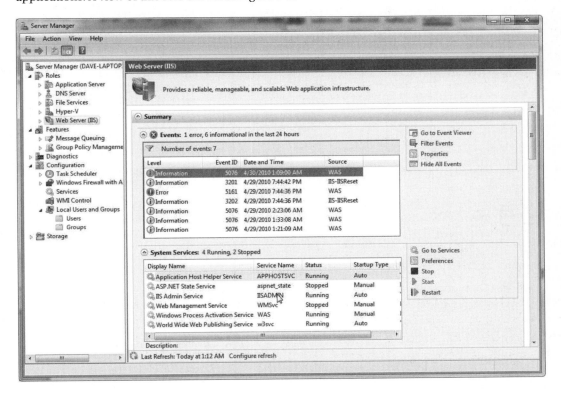

Figure 3–2. IIS and the web role

As you can see in the figure, there are six services that are installed as part of the Web Server role that comprise the feature. One of the central services involved is the w3svc.exe service, or the World Wide Web Publishing Service (WWW Service). This service is what provides web connectivity and management through IIS 7.0.

HTTP.sys Protocol Listener

One of the basic-level components of IIS 7 is a protocol listener called HTTP.sys, which is a kernel-mode device driver, the primary responsibility of which is to listen for HTTP and HTTPS requests and pass them along to IIS 7 for processing. One of the benefits that HTTP.sys provides for serving up web applications is kernel-mode caching, which caches responses at a low level, without having to switch to user mode. It also handles overhead by queuing requests at the kernel level as well. Another benefit is that it handles request pre-processing as well as security filtering.

WWW and WAS Services

IIS 7 has a new service that comes into play when serving up web requests—the Windows Process Activation Service (WAS), or WAS.exe. Previously, the WWW Service, or w3svc.exe alone, handled passing the requests along from the HTTP.sys protocol listener to the application pool worker processes. However, now in IIS 7, the WWW Service no longer manages worker processes. Instead, its primary function has migrated to being a listener adapter for HTTP.sys, managing configuration changes back to HTTP.sys and passing along request notifications from HTTP.sys to WAS. WWW also continues to handle performance counters for web sites.

WAS now manages the application pool configuration as well as the worker processes in IIS 7. WAS has plug-ins available for both HTTP as well as non-HTTP communications, meaning you can communicate with a web service through a WCF endpoint set up over a different protocol, such as NetTcp. That type of setup could completely bypass the WWW service and HTTP.sys protocol listener.

■ **Note** SharePoint 2010 uses WCF Services to expose information to outside entities. However, the endpoints are configured as standard HTTP endpoints and so function in the same fashion as the web applications.

When the WAS service starts up, it reads information from the ApplicationHost.config file, which contains configuration information for the server where it is installed. This configuration file contains global information, as well as application pool configuration and site configuration information. WAS manages the application pools, as well as worker processes for HTTP and other requests. Here's the process in full:

1. A browser request comes in to the server over HTTP or HTTPS.

2. The HTTP.sys protocol listener picks it up.

3. The WWW service notifies the WAS service of the request.

4. The WAS service reads the application pool information of a web application and determines if it already has a worker process started to service requests.

5. If there is a worker process, WAS passes the request to the worker process, and if not, WAS starts one before passing on the request.

6. The worker process invokes an ISAPI filter to activate the .NET Framework to execute code to service the request and formulate a response.

7. In a Web Application, the first step in the .NET Framework where the request is passed is the HttpApplication (in the case of a regular .NET web application). In the code executed is the SharePoint 2010 product as well as any customizations that you may have developed and installed.

ISAPI Filters

IIS routes incoming requests to different URLs that are mapped to your server in a number of ways. One of these ways that is pertinent to how .NET code is executed on the server is through ISAPI filters. The ISAPI programming model allows configuration of a web site to trigger the running of custom code under the frameworks that are set up in IIS. Figure 3–3 shows several ISAPI filters installed on a Windows Server 2008 R2 machine that allows for the execution of .NET code.

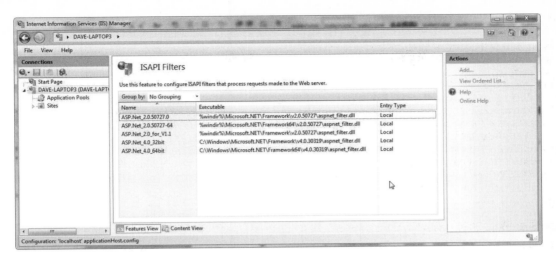

Figure 3–3. IIS 7.0 ISAPI filters

As you can see in the figure, depending on how a particular Web application is set up, the requests coming in to the Web Application will be routed to the appropriate ISAPI filter for the version of .NET that the Web Application is set up to utilize.

■ **Note** Installing Visual Studio 2010 on a development machine will also install the ASP.NET 4 Framework. This framework, unlike the 3.0 and 3.5 .NET Frameworks, is a completely re-written .NET application framework, from the ground up, which drills all the way down to the ISAPI level. SharePoint 2010 web applications do not run under .NET 4. SharePoint 2010 takes advantage of the previous version features in .NET 3.5, which was not a complete re-write of the framework, but rather add-on features onto the .NET 2.0 Framework. SharePoint 2010 Applications will run under ASP.NET 2.0 ISAPI filters. This is not a huge concern, as the .NET 2.0 Framework is a proven production web environment that will easily accommodate the necessary features for a SharePoint 2010 installation. Look for the next version of SharePoint coming out in the Office 15 cycle in approximately 3 years to take full advantage of the .NET 4 Framework.

ISAPI filters route requests from an IIS 7 application pool worker process to the appropriate .NET Framework, in order to handle the code execution. The .NET Framework runs in an integrated fashion with IIS 7, and passes off the request to code executing within the application. For a Web Application, this initializes an HttpApplication, which is the framework .NET application for managing web-site code. SharePoint itself has a customized version of this, called the SPHttpApplication, which adds a few more features to handle end events, thread, and cache options. HttpApplications also have the ability to load built-in modules, such as SharePoint request handling modules and the main SharePoint14Module, to integrate the SharePoint product into a Web Application.

IISReset.exe

One thing you will notice in Visual Studio 2010 and SharePoint 2010 development is that one of the deployment steps for a solution is to run IISReset.exe. This program restarts an application pool's worker process. The reason that this is necessary is that SharePoint has caching mechanisms built internally into the product, for performance reasons. This caching is not aware of new feature XML element definition files that are deployed to the SharePoint root, unless you recycle the IIS application pool worker process. One way to do this is to run the IISReset.exe command from a command line. This, however, restarts the application pools and processes for the entire IIS server, as opposed to just the individual application pool. An alternative to this, for production servers, is a tool called the Windows PowerShell Snap-In, which you can find at `www.iis.net/download/PowerShell`.

This plug-in has cmdlets named Stop-WebItem and Start-WebItem that handle this task. Alternatively, you can simply use the IIS 7 management console to start and stop a particular application pool, as shown in Figure 3–4.

Figure 3–4. *Starting and stopping a web site through IIS Manager*

Simply select the Restart option under "Manage Web Site" to recycle the application pool for that web site only.

Modules

One of the new features in internal architecture introduced in IIS 7 is a new web server engine that allows you to add or remove components, called modules, to your web site. Modules themselves are nothing more than simple constructs in .NET, sed to add feature sets to an HttpApplication. Many modules are involved in standard ASP.NET web sites, and SharePoint has a number of modules as well, for specific SharePoint 2010 feature integration.

You can see a number of the default modules in IIS 7 to manage .NET Web Applications in Figure 3–5.

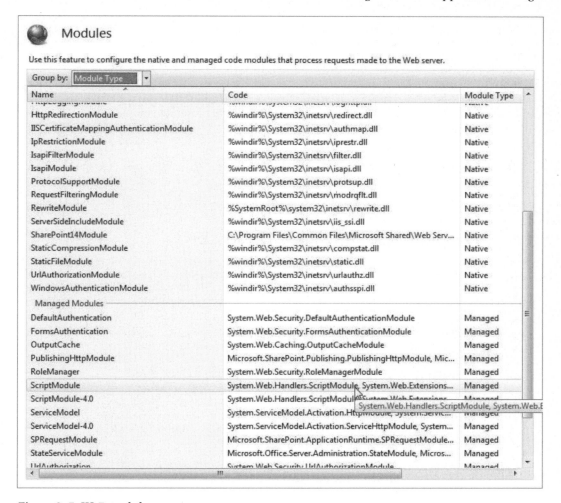

Figure 3–5. *IIS 7 modules*

Module types can be native or managed, and, as you can see by the Code path in the Figure 3–5, many modules are standard IIS 7 modules for interacting with any type of Web Application. However, some of the modules in the figure are SharePoint-specific:

- You can see the SharePoint14Module, which is part of the SharePoint ISAPI DLLs, and is responsible for the main interaction of the Web Application and the SharePoint product.

- Also visible in the Figure 3–5 are a couple more SharePoint modules, the SPRequestModule, which is the SharePoint module that helps to route requests within calls to a SharePoint application, and the StateServiceModule that functions to release request states.

- The final SharePoint module visible in the figure is the PublishingHttpModule, which is primarily used within SharePoint publishing sites for caching. These are just an example of the many modules that work together to provide a .NET Web Application, as well as SharePoint-specific modules that interact with the SharePoint product.

Now that we have drilled down into some of the basic workings of IIS 7 and how it interacts with SharePoint, let's look at some of the SharePoint-specific elements that interact with IIS.

■ **Tip** For more detail about the inner workings of IIS 7, the web site `http://learn.iis.net` is an outstanding resource.

SharePoint 2010 File System Folders Under IIS

The virtual directories and folders described in this section will appear in each of the SharePoint sites, including a number of virtual directories and folders beneath the top-level site. The folders are actually in the IIS folders for the SharePoint web sites, and are typically found in the c:\inetpub\wwwroot\wss folder. This folder is typically referred to as the "WSS" folder in SharePoint terminology. These folders contain the following:

- *_app_bin:* This directory contains navigation sitemaps (.sitemap), as well as compiled libraries (DLLs) related to SharePoint that are used in the site.

- *_vti_pvt:* This area is for configuration files related to versions of XML and SharePoint. They are not used except internally by SharePoint.

- *App_Browsers:* This folder houses XML browser compatibility files (.browser) that instruct SharePoint 2010 how to render certain controls for different browsers. This is part of the product feature that enables SharePoint to support mobile browsers out-of-the-box.

- *App_GlobalResources:* This directory contains .NET Managed Resources files (.resx) that are used for messaging and as a primary way for localization and language packs to render content in a native language. In developing SharePoint solutions, it is a best practice to use .resx file resources for strings or messages that have the potential to be translated to a different language.

- *Aspnet_client:* This folder is used by the .NET framework for client-side interaction.

- *Bin:* Like ASP.NET applications, the bin directory would contain custom compiled .NET libraries (DLLs) that represent SharePoint customizations deployed to the Web Application level.

- *Wpresources:* This is the directory used to store .NET Managed Resources files
(.resx) for customized web parts. It is also used for resources including localization
in web part customization.

The SharePoint virtual directories seen under the main web site actually point back to the main
installation directory of the SharePoint product. This is generally found at `c:\Program Files\Common`
`Files\Microsoft Shared\Web Server Extensions\14`. This location is referred to in more modern
references as the "SharePoint Root."

■ **Note** You may also see, in older documentation, references to what is called the "12 hive," as the previous
SharePoint product was stored in the `Web Server Extensions\12` folder, as opposed to the `Web Server`
`Extensions\14` folder.

SharePoint 2010 Virtual Directories

These virtual directories contain the following:

- *_admin*: This includes ASP.NET pages (.aspx), ASP.NET user controls (.ascx), and
XML documents (.xml) for web-site pages related to administration (SharePoint
Central Administration v4 site only).

- *_controltemplates*: This folder contains user controls (.ascx) used in web-site
collection page control templates. These templates will come up later in this
chapter.

- *_layouts:* This area includes ASP.NET master pages (.master), ASP.NET pages
(.aspx), JavaScript files (.js), CSS files (.css), and images, used in the site, as well as
many other artifacts. This directory contains main elements for many of the
SharePoint 2010 features available.

- *_vti_bin:* This directory contains files related to web services SharePoint 2010
exposes. These will become more familiar later in the book, in the section on the
Client Object model and connecting to SharePoint from external applications.

- *_wpresources:* This is an alternative folder location in the SharePoint root, which is
used for .NET Managed Resources files (.resx) used in messages or localization.

This listing gives us one dimension of a picture of a SharePoint web application.

To look at SharePoint 2010 from a strictly ASP.NET perspective, the Central Administration v4 web
site is an ASP.NET Web Application that exists to configure the product and to bring up other ASP.NET
Web Applications. All of this is done through an administrative web interface. Figure 3–6 shows one of
the screens used to create Web Applications in SharePoint 2010.

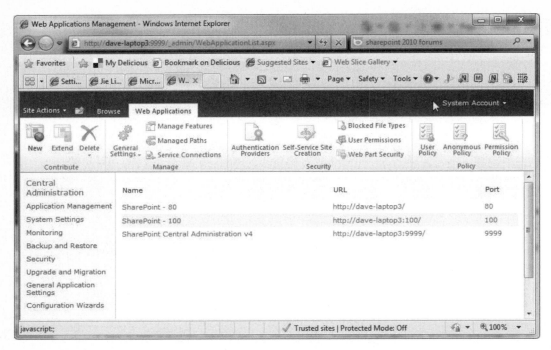

Figure 3–6. *SharePoint 2010 central administration web applications*

Note the SharePoint ribbon at the top part of the screen. The ribbon contains the new Microsoft Office 2010 style of ribbon interaction for your tasks. This is a little different style than applications have been in the past, so it may take a little adjustment before you are completely accustomed to it. However, with recognizable icons and clear titles, after an adjustment period, you should become more proficient with this style of ribbon.

You can create Web Applications through this interface by clicking the New button, which brings up a dialog box to define certain characteristics of the web site; they can be extended, which is a mechanism to expose the same content in a Web Application to different types of users by using separate URLs to access the content or separate authentication methods. You can extend web sites to up to five different network zones (Default, Intranet, Internet, Custom, and Extranet). A common use for this functionality is exposing a Web Application to internal users in a company as well as users external to the company.

There are also a number of different aspects to a web application with respect to SharePoint that you can modify through this interface. You can activate or deactivate SharePoint Features for the application, and modify Managed Paths, allowing you to define URLs for different areas of web sites. You can set up authentication providers for different zones, and turn on the ability for users to create their own sub-sites. Also, you can maintain the file types that are allowed to be uploaded into a document library, or attached to a list, as well as specific permissions and security settings, with respect to users and web parts. You can add, edit, and delete users through this interface, and modify policies to allow anonymous access. Additionally, you can define the default permission levels for content below the web application level.

Web Applications in SharePoint 2010 is the highest level of logical definition available for the containment of all site content. The next logical step in building out SharePoint sites is to create a site collection. *site collection* is a somewhat different term coming from an ASP.NET background. However, the term is very accurate and descriptive. You create a Site Collection from specific types of SharePoint templates, which define the look and feel of the site and the features available.

Figures 3–7 and 3–8 show the creation of a new Site Collection.

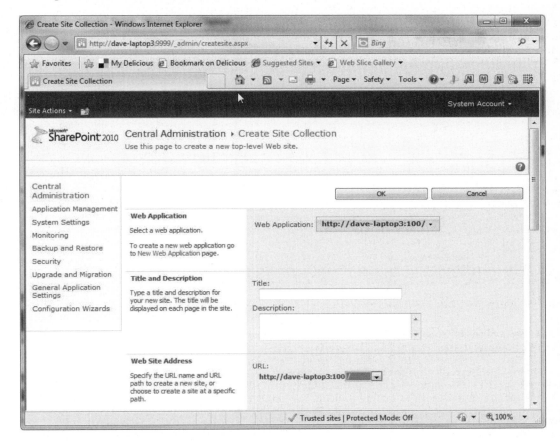

Figure 3–7. *Creating a Site Collection—top of page*

You can create the Site Collection under a specific Web Application. This will cause the content under this Site Collection to be set up in the database provisioned in the web application. It will also allow you to define a specific title and description for the Site Collection, as well as to define the URL of the collection.

■ **Note** The drop-down list for the site collection URL contains a built-in Managed Path named "sites." If you want to organize your Site Collections by some other URL name, first create a Managed Path, then select it in the drop-down menu. This is a common way site collections are organized under a web application.

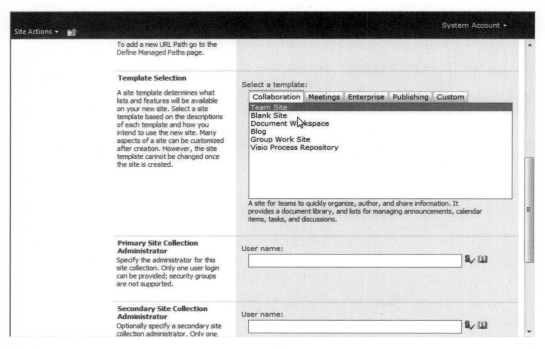

Figure 3–8. *Create Site Collection–bottom of page*

In Figure 3–8, we see that we can select a specific site template on which to base the Site Collection. Two very commonly used site templates are the Team Site, for intranet site collections, and the Publishing Portal, for extranet site collections. Templates determine what features are present on the Site Collection. For example, the Team Site template includes a document library named "Shared Documents," and lists for announcements, calendar items tasks, and discussions, all lists commonly used in a team environment. On the other hand, a Publishing Portal includes a home page, a sub-site for press releases, a search center, and a login page. Web pages are set up to be published through approval workflows. Other built-in standard SharePoint templates include:

- *Blank Site:* This is an empty site, which allows for complete customization.

- *Document Workspace:* This has features for a team to work on a document, with a document library, tasks, and a links list.

- *Blog*: This one is for a site for a single person, or team, to post blog entries.

- *Group Work Site*: This is a template for teams to share information, with a group calendar, circulation, a phone-call memo, and a document library.

- Visio Process Repository: This is a site for sharing Visio process diagrams.

- *Meeting Workspace:* Here are five built-in templates for managing meetings, everything from a basic meeting to a social meeting.

- *Enterprise Templates:* With SharePoint 2010 Enterprise, there are a number of templates to set up sites based upon features in the Enterprise version of SharePoint 2010:

    - Document Center: This is a template for managing enterprise documents.

    - Records Center: This provides for document management, including routing and delete rules.

    - Business Intelligence: A complete set of features are here, including Excel Services, Visio Services, PerformancePoint, Report Builder, and Reporting Services, as well as tools for solutions, including Key Performance Indicators (KPIs), custom reports, and data mining.

    - Enterprise Search: This site is set up for delivering searches, both on content and people.

    - My Site Host: This is a template used for personal sites and People Profiles.

    - Basic Search Center: This site is for basic and advanced search results.

    - FAST Search Center: This template is a site for delivering the FAST search experience, which is Microsoft's new search project that delivers highly visual results.

- *Enterprise Wiki:* This is a site built to rapidly collect and share knowledge across an enterprise, with rapid content editing and page creation.

This list covers the basic built-in site collection templates that are available to use out of the box. For an extensive list of site templates, as well as sub-site templates and a downloadable .zip file containing screenshots of each home page, see the blog post *Which SharePoint 2010 Site Template Is Right For Me*, by Todd Baginski at
`www.toddbaginski.com/blog/archive/2009/11/20/which-sharepoint-2010-site-template-is-right-for-me.aspx`

After SharePoint 2007 was released, there were also subsequently 40 templates released covering many varied scenarios including an Absence Request and Vacation Schedule Management template, as well as a Sales Lead Pipeline. You can obtain information about these templates in the article, *Application Templates for Windows SharePoint Services 3.0:*, by TechNet, found at:
`http://technet.microsoft.com/en-us/windowsserver/sharepoint/bb407286.aspx`

While these templates have not yet been upgraded to SharePoint 2010, it is highly likely that either Microsoft, or one of the enterprising CodePlex users, will undertake this endeavor before the SharePoint 2010 product has been released for too long.

It is also possible for developers to create their own site templates, or to save a particular site as a template. Visual Studio 2010 has a project type for this, and you can use it to customize a template for specific business requirements. This feature has quite a powerful extensibility.

So far, in this chapter, we have learned how SharePoint sites are set up in IIS, as well as covered a little more detail about how SharePoint is extended to multiple site collections and sites under a particular web application. Next, we will dig into SharePoint's integration with the .NET Framework, and several aspects of this that are important, with respect to SharePoint customizations and integration with other ASP.NET applications.

SharePoint 2010 and the .NET Framework

The next step in exploring the SharePoint 2010 product is to examine it with respect to its interaction with the .NET Framework. One of the prerequisites that is necessary to install on a server or workstation, prior to installing SharePoint 2010, is the .NET 3.5 Framework SP1. The baseline SharePoint 2010 product was built to target the .NET 3.5 framework.

WSS web.config File

A very simple way to start to identify the SharePoint touch points with .NET is to examine the web.config file found in the WSS directories for your SharePoint sites. While we will not examine all of the settings included in this file, there are certain key areas that are vital to understand when building a picture of how SharePoint 2010 interacts with the .NET Framework.

Assemblies

One of the first places to start in examining the web.config file is to see which assemblies SharePoint 2010 loads by default in every SharePoint Web Application. Listing 3–1 shows this.

Listing 3–1. SharePoint 2010 web.config Assemblies

```
<assemblies>
    <add assembly="Microsoft.SharePoint, Version=14.0.0.0, Culture=neutral,
            PublicKeyToken=71e9bce111e9429c" />
    <add assembly="System.Web.Extensions, Version=3.5.0.0, Culture=neutral,
            PublicKeyToken=31bf3856ad364e35" />
    <add assembly="Microsoft.Web.CommandUI, Version=14.0.0.0,
            Culture=neutral, PublicKeyToken=71e9bce111e9429c" />
    <add assembly="Microsoft.SharePoint.Search, Version=14.0.0.0,
            Culture=neutral, PublicKeyToken=71e9bce111e9429c" />
    <add assembly="Microsoft.Office.Access.Server.UI, Version=14.0.0.0,
            Culture=neutral, PublicKeyToken=71e9bce111e9429c" />
    <add assembly="Microsoft.SharePoint.Publishing, Version=14.0.0.0,
            Culture=neutral, PublicKeyToken=71e9bce111e9429c" />
    <add assembly="Microsoft.Office.Server.Search, Version=14.0.0.0,
            Culture=neutral, PublicKeyToken=71e9bce111e9429c" />
</assemblies>
```

Let's look at them each in turn:

- Of these assemblies, the Microsoft.SharePoint assembly is by far the largest and most pervasive. It contains over 700 classes and consists of the core SharePoint product.

- System.Web.Extensions contains the libraries for most of the client-side AJAX interaction.

- Microsoft.Web.CommandUI contains internal classes SharePoint 2010 uses to interact with the ribbon.

■ **Tip** To interact with the ribbon in customizations, instead of using Microsoft.Web.CommandUI elements, use the SPRibbon object in Microsoft.SharePoint.WebControls. That's the public-facing interface for the ribbon.

- Microsoft.SharePoint.Search are libraries for SharePoint 2010 Foundation Search.

- Microsoft.Office.Server.Search is the SharePoint 2010 Server Search, which includes more features such as the ability to crawl external sites.

- Microsoft.Access.Server.UI is used with SQL Server Reporting Services (SSRS) in some of the Enterprise licensed BI features.

MergedActions

Another area of interest in the web.config file is the MergedActions section, shown here:

```
<MergedActions>
        <Action id="813d46d1-4342-4d45-b58c-439292cd454d" sourceFile="C:\Program Files\Common
Files\Microsoft Shared\Web Server Extensions\14\config\WEBCONFIG.ACCSRV.XML" />
```

MergedAction configuration files allow SharePoint 2010 to load up additional elements for parts of the product, such as Access Services in this example. They also allow for upgrade configurations, mapping many of the MOSS 2007 assemblies into the new version 14 libraries for upgraded and imported features. They also add many of the required assemblies for product parts to the SafeControls section.

Modules

We touched upon the function of modules earlier in the chapter with respect to how they interact with an HttpApplication and how they are pluggable into the IIS 7 framework. In the web.config file for a SharePoint application, several of the standard IIS 7 modules are removed and replaced with other SharePoint-specific modules. These are as follows:

```
<modules runAllManagedModulesForAllRequests="true">
        <remove name="AnonymousIdentification" />
        <remove name="FileAuthorization" />
        <remove name="Profile" />
        <remove name="WebDAVModule" />
        <remove name="Session" />
        <add name="SPRequestModule" preCondition="integratedMode"
                type="Microsoft.SharePoint.ApplicationRuntime.SPRequestModule,
                Microsoft.SharePoint, Version=14.0.0.0, Culture=neutral,
                PublicKeyToken=71e9bce111e9429c" />
        <add name="ScriptModule" preCondition="integratedMode"
                type="System.Web.Handlers.ScriptModule, System.Web.Extensions,
                Version=3.5.0.0, Culture=neutral, PublicKeyToken=31bf3856ad364e35" />
        <add name="SharePoint14Module" preCondition="integratedMode" />
        <add name="StateServiceModule"
                type="Microsoft.Office.Server.Administration.StateModule,
                Microsoft.Office.Server, Version=14.0.0.0, Culture=neutral,
```

```
                PublicKeyToken=71e9bce111e9429c" />
       <add name="PublishingHttpModule"
            type="Microsoft.SharePoint.Publishing.PublishingHttpModule,
            Microsoft.SharePoint.Publishing, Version=14.0.0.0, Culture=neutral,
            PublicKeyToken=71e9bce111e9429c" />
</modules>
```

As we can see in this section of the web.config file, five standard modules are removed, and five others are added. The reason the five modules are removed is that SharePoint 2010 handles the features that are contained within the modules on its own within the product. Anonymous identification and access to the site is handled internally by SharePoint 2010 settings, as are file authorizations, profile management, access to content such as can be found in document libraries, and session information. Of the modules added, the ScriptModule is the only one that is not specific to SharePoint. This is added in to offer AJAX features on a SharePoint site. The basic function of the SharePoint modules are:

- *SPRequestModule:* This module handles routing requests to specific areas of the SharePoint product, which is somewhat differently constructed than a standard ASP.NET Web Application.

- *SharePoint14Module:* This is the workhorse module of the SharePoint product. It handles rendering page content, interacting with lists and libraries, and many other staple functions of SharePoint.

- *StateServiceModule:* This module functions mainly to release request states.

- *PublishingHttpModule:* This module is part of the Publishing sites and mainly is used for caching.

SafeControls

This section of the web.config file has to do with Code Access Security in SharePoint, and is a good transition point to talk about permissions and security within the SharePoint product and custom code.

Safe controls are a means to indicate, within the web.config file, that a control or assembly is allowed to be executed within SharePoint's partial trust environment. The SafeControls section in web.config sets specific trust levels for controls—both standard built-in .NET controls as well as your own custom controls. An example of an entry in this section is as follows:

```
<SafeControls>
    <SafeControl Assembly="System.Web, Version=1.0.5000.0, Culture=neutral,
        PublicKeyToken=b03f5f7f11d50a3a"
        Namespace="System.Web.UI.WebControls" TypeName="*" Safe="True"
        AllowRemoteDesigner="True" SafeAgainstScript="False" />
```

This assembly sets permissions to allow all of the standard ASP.NET WebControls to be used in SharePoint in custom development solutions. The SafeControl indication covers the assembly named, whether it is deployed to the General Assembly Cache (GAC) or to the Web Application.

■ **Note** Visual Studio 2010 will automatically add your DLLs from SharePoint customizations into the SafeControls section of the web.config file when you deploy it. This occurs by marking your assembly's manifest.xml file with a SafeControls tag.

Code Access Security

Code Access Security(CAS) refers to the security restrictions placed upon code executing in a partially trusted domain. SharePoint 2010 provides an environment that contains access restrictions that allow code to access only the level of security necessary for operations. This prevents SharePoint 2010 customizations from being compromised by other applications.

SharePoint 2010 CAS policies are direct modifications to standard ASP.NET security policies. You can define these policies or trust levels in the web.config file with built-in settings of Full, High, Medium, Low, and Minimal. These trust levels reflect varying degrees of restriction and resources available to code in an ASP.NET environment. You can find these security policy files in the following directory on a 64-bit machine (for a 32-bit machine, the path includes Framework instead of Framework64):

```
c:\Windows\Microsoft.NET\Framework64\v2.0.50727\CONFIG
```

In SharePoint 2010, there are two main trust levels that are provided for CAS. These levels are WSS_Medium and WSS_Minimal, which you can find in the following web.config section:

```
<securityPolicy>
        <trustLevel name="WSS_Medium" policyFile="C:\Program Files\
            Common Files\Microsoft Shared\Web Server Extensions\14\config\
            wss_mediumtrust.config" />
        <trustLevel name="WSS_Minimal" policyFile="C:\Program Files\
            Common Files\Microsoft Shared\Web Server Extensions\14\config\
            wss_minimaltrust.config" />
</securityPolicy>
```

By default, the SharePoint 2010 web application is set up with the WSS_Minimal trust policy. If you search through the web.config file for the "trust" setting, you will see the only entry is the following:

```
<trust level="WSS_Minimal" originUrl="" />
```

This setting provides for the most security in your SharePoint 2010 web application, ensuring the highest level of protection against malicious code. With the WSS_Minimal setting, very little is permitted of the code. Access to minimal levels of AspNetHostingPermission settings, execution of code within a security sense, and permissions for web parts to talk with other web parts on a page are among the few things permitted. Things that are not permitted include modifications to the environment, FileIO, IsolatedStorage, reflection, registry access, controlling other security elements such as the principal identity or threading, sockets, SqlClient or OleDB interaction, DNS access, or printing are among the few that are restricted.

There is also a third trust level that is defined within the SharePoint 2010 product that was not there in 2007 versions. This file is the wss_usercode.config file, and is found also in the SharePoint root \config folder. However, web applications do not use this file directly, as this file is related to sandboxed solutions. These permissions are used by the User Code Service that implements the features of Sandboxed solutions, as well as handling resources.

■ **Note** If you find that the code restrictions are too restrictive for your particular environment, you can comment out the trust node, which will leave the WSS_Medium trust level intact for your Web Application.

Custom Trust Level Configurations

It is possible to define your own trust level configuration, so that it contains different permission settings than either of the product configurations WSS_Minimal or WSS_Medium. The recommended process when doing this would be to pick the trust configuration file that has the greatest number of permissions that are higher than what you are looking to configure, and remove some of them. So, for example, if you look through the WSS_Medium policy file and find that it is 90% of what is necessary for your environment, except for some specific restrictions that need to be put in place unique to your environment, copy the wss_mediumtrust.config file to a unique name such as wss_mycompany.config in the same SharePoint root \Config directory (full directory is in the <trustLevel node). Then, in your Web Application root directory, make a backup copy of your web.config file, then edit the <trust/> element to refer to your custom trust level.

The final XML nodes in your web.config file would look similar to the following:

```
<trustLevel name="WSS_MyCompany" policyFile="C:\Program Files\
        Common Files\Microsoft Shared\Web Server Extensions\14\config\
        wss_mycompany.config" />
<trust level="WSS_MyCompany" originUrl="" />
```

■ **Tip** You can edit your web.config file in any text editor, including Visual Studio 2010. It is advisable to make changes to any production configuration files first on a test system, with ample time to test the changes, and then automate any kind of push to a production environment. If you do not have tools built to accommodate that, you can use PowerShell to build some simple tools for this purpose. Also, changes of this nature to a production system should be done within a maintenance window when users are not actively connected to your SharePoint site collections. The reason for this is that mistakes made to configuration files can result in a SharePoint 2010 site not being accessible or throwing an error. It is advisable to control your touchpoints to production systems so that they are as few and as automated as possible.

It is also possible to modify policy definitions during the deployment of your assembly. This is one way to package up everything that is required within your custom solution, including security needs, so in one sense it is an attractive solution. Doing this would involve the Advanced Package Editor in Visual Studio 2010 merging XML elements into the deployment package for security. You can see a picture of this happening in Figure 3–9, and the XML entered in Listing 3–2.

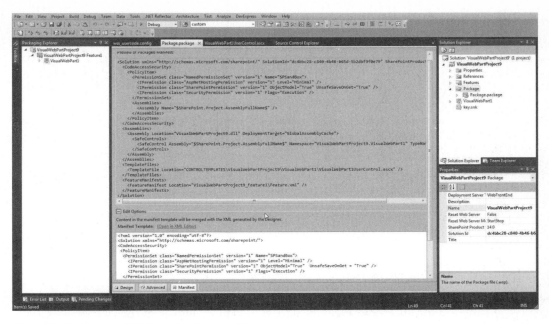

Figure 3–9. *Advanced Package Designer editor*

Listing 3–2 shows the XML entered into the lower window of the editor that will be merged with the rest of the package. With respect to what these security entries represent, this particular segment will place the same trust levels on my Visual Web Part as would be placed on a sandboxed solution.

Listing 3–2. *The XML that Will Be Merged with the Rest of the Package*

```xml
<?xml version="1.0" encoding="utf-8"?>
<Solution xmlns="http://schemas.microsoft.com/sharepoint/">
<CodeAccessSecurity>
 <PolicyItem>
  <PermissionSet class="NamedPermissionSet" version="1" Name="SPSandBox">
    <IPermission class="AspNetHostingPermission" version="1" Level="Minimal" />
    <IPermission class="SharePointPermission" version="1" ObjectModel="True"  UnsafeSaveOnGet
= "True" />
    <IPermission class="SecurityPermission" version="1" Flags="Execution" />
  </PermissionSet>
  <Assemblies>
    <Assembly Name="$SharePoint.Project.AssemblyFullName$" />
  </Assemblies>
 </PolicyItem>
</CodeAccessSecurity>
</Solution>
```

Strong Name Signing Assemblies

One aspect of the security in SharePoint 2010 is that assemblies that are deployed to SharePoint must be signed with a strong name. This is accomplished by generating a strong name key using the SN.exe tool. The SharePoint 2010 project templates actually handle creating the strong name key for you, adding a key.snk file to the project. This ensures that the assembly has not been tampered with since deployment.

One thing to note in the overall security approach that you have for SharePoint customizations and custom code that is running in your SharePoint environment is that this trust level only applies to DLL assemblies that fall under the boundaries of the web application. However, the default setting in Visual Studio 2010, when you select the "deploy as a farm solution" option in your project definition wizard, is to deploy any DLL assemblies to the Global Assembly Cache (GAC). Deploying assemblies to the GAC ensures that they will run in the highest trust fashion possible on your server. This also means they will run with the least amount of security constraints possible.

In general, it is a very common practice for SharePoint developers to deploy assemblies to the GAC and have security checks in place around their code, such as running the SPDisposeCheck utility on their assemblies. However, in reality, this scenario offers a little less security than deploying to the web application. In fact, one of the newer features in SharePoint 2010, sandboxed solutions, probably arose out of these common types of practices and the instability factor, over time, that multiple assemblies deployed to the GAC had on production environments. This relatively common occurrence led to common destabilization of SharePoint environments and, hence, a new feature to protect against this.

While sandboxed solutions can be ideal in certain scenarios, another approach can be to simply deploy assemblies to the web application. This way, they inherit all of the CAS settings that are common to the rest of your SharePoint 2010 deployment. Web parts, workflows, and other similar site-collection–related assemblies really don't have a global need to be deployed to all Web Applications in your farm. You can change the target of your deployment from the GAC to the web application simply through a drop-down in your Visual Studio product. Highlight the project itself, and modify the project properties in the Properties window, as seen in Figure 3–10.

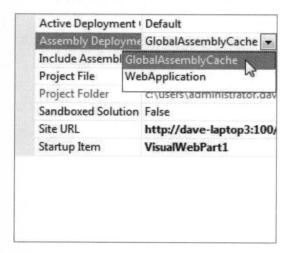

Figure 3–10. Properties window—Changing the target of your Assembly Deployment

As you can see, targeting the Web Application for deployment is made much simpler with the changes to SharePoint 2010 features in Visual Studio 2010.

Sandboxed Solutions

Another topic to cover, with respect to security within the SharePoint 2010 product, is sandboxed solutions. This product feature involves a more complex way to manage assemblies and features in a SharePoint environment. Sandboxed solutions were created in response to an overwhelming number of requests from SharePoint administrators, who wanted a better way to be able to control their environments with all of the customizations flowing into them. As mentioned previously, assemblies that are deployed to the GAC can have a dramatic impact upon a SharePoint farm, and, in some instances, can even quickly overwhelm the available resources in a farm, effectively taking it offline.

When problems of this nature occur, it is very difficult to be able to trace what is happening back to the offending code. Universal Log (UL) files have to be examined in detail, as well as application and system event logs, and change control processes need to be examined. Because of this difficulty, the potential for downtime with code deployed to the GAC is higher.

The solution to these types of administrative functions in SharePoint 2010 was to introduce a feature called sandboxed solutions. One of the fundamental differences between sandboxed solutions and farm solutions is where they run. All farm solutions outside of sandboxed solutions, regardless of the security policies set for them, run in the same IIS 7 application pool that runs the SharePoint Web Application. Sandboxed solutions do not run in this application pool. Instead, they have a completely separate service that runs on the server, whose responsibility it is to spin up worker threads to execute the code in sandboxed solutions. This service is called the Windows SharePoint Services User Code v4 service. This service, in addition to handling the proper threading to execute user code, also maintains a history of resource usage for the code. It checks the code against a certain threshold of resource quotas, and if it finds that a particular assembly or offending solution consumes over its quota of resources, it will disable it. So potentially, a user could be viewing a web part, the part could go over its resource limit, and then the next time the user returns to the page, the web part will not render. You can see the Solutions Gallery where the sandboxed solutions are managed in Figure 3–11.

Figure 3–11. Sandboxed solutions

As you can see in the figure, there is one SandboxedWebPart1 solution that is deployed to the site collection named Dave Home. The resource quota is 300 server resources, and this particular web part has not used any resources to date.

The resources that are tracked consist of some very specific measurements related to CPU, I/O, threading, and abnormal process termination. To examine each of the local resources that are tracked, we can open up a SharePoint 2010 Management Shell (PowerShell console) and type the following in:

```
[Microsoft.SharePoint.Administration.SPUserCodeService]::Local.ResourceMeasures | more
```

This will output the SharePoint user code service resource measures and pipe the output into a paging function, so that you can view them. Figure 3–12 shows the output of this command.

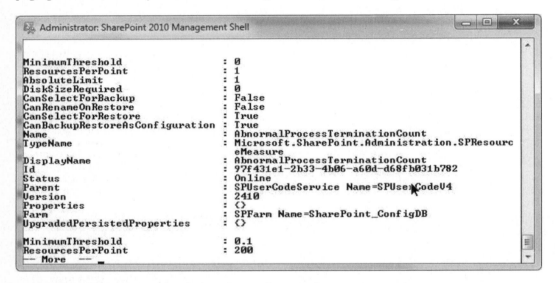

Figure 3–12. *PowerShell output looking at sandboxed solutions resources*

As you can see in the figure, the name of this local resource measure is "AbnormalProcessTerminationCount", and the ResourcesPerPoint setting is set to 1. This means that every time a particular sandboxed solution ends with an abnormal process termination, it is measured at 1 point. 299 more points and it will be throttled and disabled. There are 14 other local resource measurements and points, or measurements, that consist of one resource point:

- AbnormalProcessTerminationCount: 1

- CPUExecutionTime: 200

- CriticalExceptionCount: 10

- IdlePercentProcessorTime: 100

- InvocationCount: 100

- PercentProcessorTime: 85

- ProcessCPUCycles: 100000000000

- ProcessHandleCount: 10000

- ProcessIOBytes: 10000000

- ProcessThreadCount: 10000

- ProcessVirtualBytes: 100000000

- SharePointDatabaseQueryCount: 400

- SharePointDatabaseQueryTime: 20

- UnhandledExceptionCount: 50

- UnresponsiveprocessCount: 2

Also, for each of these measurements, there is an AbsoluteLimit number. If the solution goes above it during any one execution, it will trigger disabling of the assembly.

Site Collection Administrator Deployed

Another key point to understand about Sandboxed Solutions is that to deploy these types of solutions, you now no longer need IT personnel. A site collection administrator can deploy a sandboxed solution to the site collection they are in charge of. They can browse to a solution .wsp file, upload it, and activate it all through the Site Settings administrative pages of their site collection. This, in addition to the security it provides, also follows the pattern of rolling out responsibility for individual site collections and sites, from a central IT administration department to trained users that are able to manage their respective areas.

Security

To wrap up this section on CAS, Table 3–1 contains a few highlights of security within SharePoint 2010 as well as ASP.NET 2.0. For further study related to security, see the following Microsoft patterns and practices article entitled "Security Practices: ASP.NET 2.0 Security Practices at a Glance":

`http://msdn.microsoft.com/en-us/library/ms998372.aspx`

Table 3–1. SharePoint 2010 Security Options

Security Option	Benefits	Drawbacks
Sandboxed solutions	• Fully developed feature • Resource throttling • Farm is protected	• Can't use out-of-box with Visual Web Parts • Lower levels of trust and access • Less you can do
Configure trust policy definition and deploy with assembly	• Finer-grained control over security • Impact is limited to one assembly • Will automatically configure test and production servers with deployment	• Requires the most effort on the development and testing end • Potential for varying permissions in a farm. • Administrator deploying the .wsp package can see the policies before deploying
Modify trust level in web application	• Easy to configure once for many assemblies • Increased testability • Impact is restricted to one web application	• Not as secure • Trust level also needs to be deployed to test and production servers • Affects all assemblies in Web application
Deploy assembly to GAC	• Assembly is fully trusted • Easy to deploy • Can do more in code	• Less secure • Potential to impact whole farm

So as we can see in Table 3–1, there are four options available to you in managing security within SharePoint 2010 customizations. Each of these options offers specific benefits, and each also has limitations or drawbacks to the approach. It is also certainly possible to blend certain options, such as deploying administrative assemblies to the GAC, utilizing sandboxed solutions for certain assemblies, and choosing an option for web application deployment. When it comes down to making these decisions, your particular SharePoint 2010 environment, including users, availability, and corporate culture, may dictate which of these options is best for you.

Summary

In this chapter, we have looked at SharePoint 2010 in relation to IIS 7 and the .NET 3.5 Framework. We have covered fundamental concepts relating to IIS 7 and .NET to help build an understanding of the underlying environment SharePoint 2010 runs on, including such concepts as HTTP.sys, the WWW and WAS services, ISAPI filters, IISReset, and Modules. We have examined what exactly is deployed to IIS with a SharePoint web application, as well as looked at some of the virtual directories that point back to the SharePoint product root.

We have broken down many elements in the ASP.NET web.config file to see specific assemblies that SharePoint 2010 uses. We've looked at merged actions. We have also touched upon SharePoint 2010 modules, and the modules concept in IIS 7. We have examined SafeControls with respect to the SharePoint environment. We then delved into the topic of CAS, and covered fundamental elements of handling security for your code in a SharePoint 2010 environment. We talked about the default trust levels that reside within ASP.NET as well as the custom trust levels within the SharePoint 2010 product. We discussed the security aspects of applying a strong named key to assemblies that are deployed to a SharePoint 2010 environment, and finally, we've looked into the options that are available to us within SharePoint 2010 for configuring security. Next, we will be ready to dig into the nature of the SharePoint product even more deeply.

CHAPTER 4

■ ■ ■

SharePoint Architecture–File System, Database, and the Provider Pattern

All our knowledge has its origins in our perception.

Leonardo da Vinci

■ **Reading Tip** This chapter is helpful for building more depth in understanding the components that make up SharePoint 2010.

The next step in building our understanding of SharePoint as a product is to get into details regarding artifacts of SharePoint 2010 that work together to comprise the product itself. While we have already introduced some of these concepts in previous chapters, in this chapter, we will endeavor to take a cross-section of the SharePoint product, looking at it from a more traditional ASP.NET understanding. We'll examine files in the file system, study SQL Server databases, and scrutinize a software development design pattern that has grown into one that is prevalent throughout .NET software development and the ASP.NET framework, the Provider pattern.

The goal of this chapter is to present another piece of the puzzle from a slightly different perspective, putting together a clear picture of SharePoint 2010 as a product. The reason this is important is that understanding the construction of SharePoint 2010 will help you to identify touchpoints that are exposed in the SharePoint 2010 product, for you to be able to accomplish your goal of architecting and developing blended ASP.NET and SharePoint 2010 solutions.

The reason that different perspectives of SharePoint 2010 are important is because there are certain things that we pick up on as clear and obvious when looking at the product from a certain vantage point, which are neither clear nor obvious, when looking from a different perspective. For example, viewing SharePoint 2010 as a modified IIS ASP.NET application helps us to see virtual directories for central administration, web applications, and web service site hosting. We can see the security involved from the IIS and ASP.NET perspective as present in the web.config files in each of these web applications. We can understand certain aspects of performance constraints through an understanding of IIS Application Pool threads and the context within, which SharePoint 2010 runs.

In a similar fashion, we can pick up valuable understanding from viewing SharePoint 2010 through the perspective of the file system and the database, and by understanding the Virtual Path Provider pattern that underlies both. We can see where the touchpoints are for modification in the SharePoint product in the file system as well as the database, and begin to understand how we can construct solutions to deploy customizations to both of these areas.

First, in this chapter, we will highlight the architecture of SharePoint 2010 from the file system perspective. With this vantage point, we will learn some of the basics about what files and directories are used by SharePoint for what purposes. This first section of the chapter will be useful as we identify the location of areas of the product, and where to find files.

Next in the chapter, we will discuss the architecture of SharePoint 2010 from a database perspective. Although direct interaction with the SharePoint 2010 database is not a supported path for SharePoint 2010 customization and interaction, except for the report server and WSS_Logging databases, which were modified to support interaction in 2010, highlighting the different tables and structure of the databases in general will help you understand the SharePoint 2010 product more clearly.

Finally, we will examine particular principles of software design that are included throughout the SharePoint 2010 product design pattern, called the *Provider* pattern, and its relationship to SharePoint 2010 customizations, as well as the underlying architecture.

SharePoint 2010 and the File System

The first and most obvious area where SharePoint 2010 is implemented is evidenced by the .NET files that are installed in the file system.

SharePoint Root

The SharePoint root is located at:

```
c:\Program Files\Common Files\Microsoft Shared\Web Server Extensions\14
```

This directory is the primary location of the files related to the SharePoint 2010 product in the file system. We can see the sub-folders under the SharePoint root in Figure 4–1.

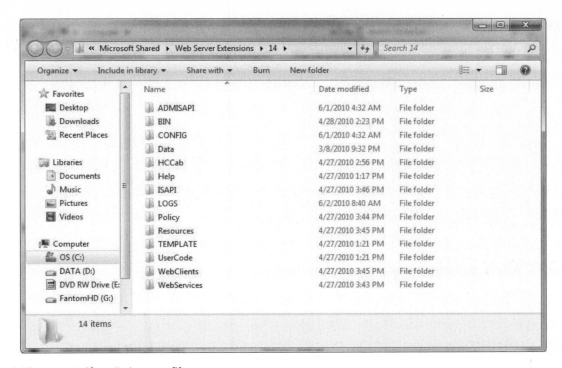

Figure 4–1. SharePoint root file system

This directory, at the SharePoint root, represents most of the file system installation for the SharePoint 2010 product, as it relates to files used by SharePoint web applications. We will drill into these folders directly to dissect what they specifically contain, after we examine a few other high-level SharePoint installation folders.

ADMISAPI

This directory contains two very important web services. The first is the Admin web service, which supports the ability to create and delete sites, to get languages, and to refresh the configuration cache. The other is the Content Deployment Remote Import web service, which is a feature that enables you to import content from other SharePoint farms. As web services, these are interfaces provided for other applications to interface with the SharePoint 2010 product. Both of these web services, as well as this folder, are exposed through IIS and the Central Administration Application, under the _vti_adm directory.

Bin

The Bin directory hosts many of the core dynamic link libraries (DLLs) that the SharePoint 2010 product hosts. This directory hosts applications that are services, such as the OWSTimer application, and product tools, such as PSConfig, which is the product setup wizard that runs after install. This directory is not the main storage point for most of the SharePoint product libraries (that is the ISAPI folder). The distinction between the two directories is that most of the API-related functionality for SharePoint 2010 is stored in ISAPI, while peripheral libraries, utilities, and other DLLs are stored in Bin.

CONFIG

As the title of the directory indicates, this is the storage location for many of the core configuration files for SharePoint. The vast majority of these configuration files are XML documents or XML configuration files. Also housed here are the three Code Access Security (CAS) files, mentioned previously, that control security over SharePoint, the wss_mediumtrust, wss_minimaltrust, and wss_usercode configuration files.

Data

This directory holds data-related files, including stop word files. Stop words, or noise words, are words that the search system will ignore. They are designated as such due to their frequent occurrence in a language to the point that they would be of little value in narrowing down search results. These files are named with a prefix of "noise". Also present are thesaurus files that a search administrator can use to specify replacement sets for words in a search query. These files must be edited before use. When a Search application is set up, these files will be copied to the Program Files\Microsoft Office Server\Data directory for use in Search. These files start with the prefix "ts".

■ **Note** The Program Files\Microsoft Office Server directories are covered later in the chapter.

HCCab

The HCCab directory stores cabinet-compressed files that consist of the help documentation for SharePoint 2010. These files are served up dynamically through the _layouts/helpContent.aspx page and the _layouts/help.aspx pages.

Help

The Help directory contains a compiled help file that is language-specific for the PSConfig utility, called PSConfig.chm.

ISAPI

The ISAPI directory is the primary storage location for all of the elements that make up the SharePoint 2010 API, including ASP.NET server pages, WCF web services, DLLs, and XML configuration documents. If you are looking for a library reference to add into a Visual Studio 2010 project, to take advantage of interacting with SharePoint, with a few notable exceptions, you can expect to find your DLL in this directory.

LOGS

This directory contains all of your log files that are stored on the file system for the SharePoint 2010 product, including ULS logs, usage logs, PowerShell configuration diagnostics, PSConfig diagnostics, and upgrade logs. There are other categories of logging, which are logged to SharePoint databases, which we will cover in the next section of this chapter.

Policy

This directory contains DLLs and configuration files related to group policies and security in SharePoint 2010.

Resources

The Resources directory contains all of the core language-specific resource (.resx) files that are used for localization and string interaction in the SharePoint 2010 product.

■ **Note** Resource files with which you will be interacting may be found here, as well as in the Application root\App_GlobalResources directory.

TEMPLATE

This file folder is one of the most important from a customization perspective. This folder is where the templates, pages, and master pages for SharePoint 2010 sites reside. The breakdown of the directory is shown in Figure 4–2.

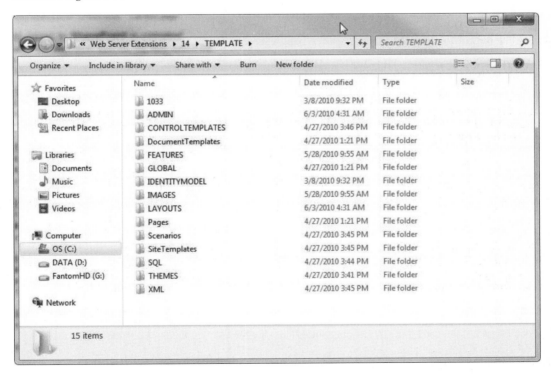

Figure 4–2. The TEMPLATE directory

Each of the directories in the TEMPLATE directory are covered in the following pages.

■ **Note** Your touchpoint for the integration of SharePoint application pages and master pages will be the LAYOUTS directory, and most of the strategies covered later in the book for integrating ASP.NET and SharePoint 2010 involve this directory.

- *1033:* This sub-directory contains templates for various documents, XML files, and workflows. This number corresponds to the language localization for English. If SharePoint is installed with other languages being primary, the number will be different.

- *ADMIN:* The ADMIN sub-directory contains ASP.NET server pages that correspond to administrative tasks. You may access the majority of them through the Central Administration web site.

- *CONTROLTEMPLATES:* This sub-directory contains ASP.NET user controls that are utilized by SharePoint. Also housed here are folders that represent SharePoint customizations deployed to the default setting. For example, visual web parts and site definition projects will be deployed as folders in this sub-directory.

- *DocumentTemplates:* The only thing stored in this directory is the standard ASP.NET server page for wikis.

- *FEATURES:* The FEATURES sub-directory contains approximately 250 folders, which represent the core features of SharePoint 2010. Each of these folders contain a Feature.xml file, which identifies to SharePoint 2010 several characteristics such as the identity, scope, resources, and manifest location of the feature. SharePoint customizations deployed as features will be deployed to this sub-directory, alongside built-in features.

- *GLOBAL:* This sub-directory houses the standard ASP.NET master pages that deploy with SharePoint 2010, such as the v4, default, and minimal master pages. Also here are global templates for site definitions, views, and schema for list templates.

- *IDENTITYMODEL:* Housed in this sub-directory are the default login pages for the different types of authentication models, such as Forms, Windows, Trust, and Card. Also here is the Authentication Method selector that allows choice of login methods if more than one is configured for the same site collection.

■ **Tip** These pages are the ones that you will customize to modify the user authentication experience.

- *IMAGES:* This sub-directory houses all of the standard images for the SharePoint product. If you have images deployed as part of customized solutions, by default they will be deployed as sub-folders of this sub-directory.

- *LAYOUTS:* The LAYOUTS folder is the folder that contains a large portion of the ASP.NET server pages that are used in the SharePoint product. You can reference this directory from within a SharePoint site by using a format similar to the following:

```
http://mysite/_layouts/MySolutionFolder/mypage.aspx
```

The LAYOUTS folder will be one of which full use is made with the strategic suggestions in the later chapters of this book on how to integrate ASP.NET applications with SharePoint.

- *Pages:* Only 3 ASP.NET server pages are stored in this folder, named form, viewpage, and webfldr.

- *Scenarios:* This sub-directory contains wizard-style pages, used in some of the different services with greater complexity, such as BCS, ProfileServiceApplication, and joining the farm with a particular web server.

- *Site Templates:* This sub-directory contains the site templates for the different built-in SharePoint 2010 web templates.

- *SQL:* This sub-directory contains SQL table creation scripts for tables associated with various types of SharePoint 2010 databases. Many of the services database creation scripts are here, such as the UsageDB, the Diagnostics DB, and Configuration DBs. Also stored here are upgrade scripts to upgrade from a SharePoint 2007 solution to a SharePoint 2010 solution.

- *THEMES:* This sub-directory houses the 23 built-in themes or looks that are installed with SharePoint 2010.

- *XML:* The XML sub-directory contains XML schema and document files related to various configurations in SharePoint.

UserCode

The UserCode directory houses the services, libraries, and processes related to sandboxed solutions.

WebClients

The WebClients directory contains files for configuring WCF endpoints to the various services in SharePoint 2010.

WebServices

This directory houses web services for the BDC, root web, secure store, security token, subscriptions settings, and topology. In IIS, these services can be seen in the SharePoint Web Services application.

Program Files\Microsoft Office Server

You can find one of the other primary folders that is used in the SharePoint product at:

```
c:\Program Files\Microsoft Office Servers\14.0
```

This location generally houses file locations specific to the operation of SharePoint 2010 as an Office Server product, as well as various client applications that connect with SharePoint 2010, including Microsoft Office clients. The folders underneath this can be seen in Figure 4–3.

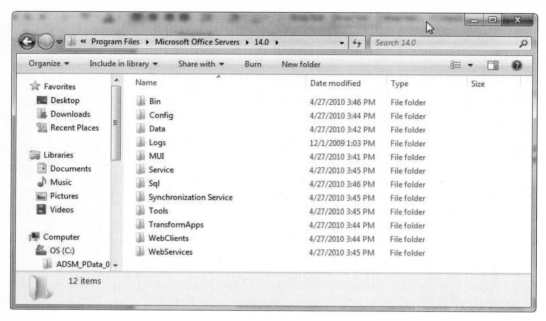

Figure 4–3. Program Files—Microsoft Office Servers directory

Following is a list of several of the more important directories and an overview of what they store.

Bin

The Bin directory houses DLLs associated with several SharePoint 2010 features, including document conversion, InfoPath, BDC metadata management, and web analytics.

Config

This directory holds configuration files for WSRP producers and SAP host connectors. WSRP producers and web parts are web services for remote portlets, which are web service interface specifications developed by the OASIS technical committees for the express purpose of providing producers and consumers with technology non-specific web service interaction.

Data

The Data directory contains data-specific files for product interaction. Some of the databases involved are instances of SQL Express, if that type of installation is chosen for SharePoint. Also present is data related to Notes attachments, Office Server data, and configuration and Visio Server data. These directories represent specific data stores that the SharePoint 2010 product uses internally in its own services.

Logs

These directories are primarily crash logs and web application companion logs.

MUI

This directory houses application-specific files dealing with the Multilanguage User Interface and internationalization in SharePoint 2010.

Service

This directory houses libraries associated with features such as Identity Management, Metadirectory, and Resource Management.

Sql

Sql contains queries related to some of the analytics features, such as Web Analytics. These are used in reports and SharePoint 2010 features.

Synchronization Service

This directory contains files related to the User Profile Synchronization Service feature in SharePoint 2010, which allows external user-related data stores, such as Active Directory, to synchronize user information with SharePoint 2010.

Tools

Tools contains applications related to making and managing certificates, as well as resource management configuration.

TransformApps

This directory contains applications and configuration files related to document converters in SharePoint 2010. This feature is related to document management in SharePoint. Document converters are set up to convert one type of document to another, such as a Microsoft Word 2010 file to a web page, or an InfoPath form to a web page.

WebClients

WebClients contains configuration files related to managing web client metadata.

WebServices

This directory houses web services for interaction with Lotus Notes, metadata, profile services, root certificates, Search, and Word Server.

The Program Files directories and SharePoint installation are not widely used or interacted with. However, a good basic-level exposure to what is there helps build a fundamental understanding of the SharePoint 2010 product. This exposure also helps to understand what is deployed where with product upgrades and fixes, and also provides a level of confidence in interacting with SharePoint.

This rounds out the section on the file system. Next, we will get into the other major component of the SharePoint 2010 product, the SharePoint 2010 databases.

WSS Folders

The SharePoint 2010 sites themselves are deployed to the file system when web applications are created through Central Administration or PowerShell. These directories are located at c:\inetpub\wwwroot\wss\VirtualDirectories. There will be a directory for each of your SharePoint sites. For example, for a

95

main portal site deployed to port 80, the folder might be named portal80. A mysites site also deployed to port 80 might be named mysites80. These folders will contain sub-folders and files such as depicted in Figure 4–4.

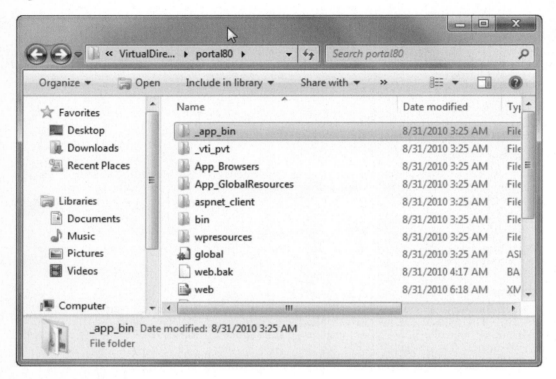

Figure 4–4. *The WSS VirtualDirectory contents*

As seen in Figure 4–4, there are several small directories that appear under the WSS VirtualDirectory folder, which provide for things like localization, DLLs for application pages, resources, and a web.configuration file that helps to define the particular web application installed.

SharePoint 2010 Databases

Another major area of SharePoint 2010, with respect to the product installation, is the database component. As we see later on in the chapter, in the section on the Virtual Path Provider, utilization of that development in serving up content for ASP.NET has provided a wide open field for storing ASP.NET content in a SQL Server database. SharePoint 2010's use of databases is vastly expanded over the SharePoint 2007 product line, and much of this is directly due to enhancements in SharePoint 2010's performance. With the new implementation of services in the a-la-carte fashion, as opposed to Shared Service Providers, one of the advantages inherent there is that each service can be split out to its own database, for performance reasons, and services that are not activated can preserve the space not creating a database.

For a baseline overview of the databases installed along with the SharePoint 2010 product, see Figure 4–5.

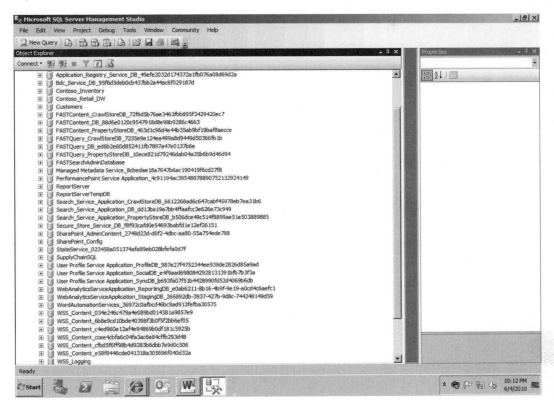

Figure 4–5. *SharePoint 2010 databases—part 1*

The databases that are shown in Figure 4–5 represent the installed databases in a downloadable demo virtual machine available from Microsoft, called the 2010 Information Worker Demonstration and Evaluation Virtual Machine (RTM). The link for this follows. This downloadable virtual machine (VM) has the following configuration of products.

Virtual machine "a" contains the following pre-configured software:

- Windows Server 2008 R2 Standard Evaluation Edition x64, running as an Active Directory Domain Controller for the "CONTOSO.COM" domain with DNS and WINS

- Microsoft SQL Server 2008 R2 Enterprise Edition with Analysis, Notification, and Reporting Services

- Microsoft Office Communication Server 2007 R2

- Visual Studio 2010

- Microsoft SharePoint Server 2010 Enterprise Edition

- Microsoft Office Web Applications

- FAST Search for SharePoint 2010

- Microsoft Project Server 2010

- Microsoft Office Professional Plus 2010

- Microsoft Visio 2010

- Microsoft Project 2010

- Microsoft Office Communicator 2007 R2

Virtual machine "b" contains the following pre-configured software:

- Windows Server 2008 R2 Standard Evaluation Edition x64, joined to the "CONTOSO.COM" domain

- Microsoft Exchange Server 2010

You can download the VM from: www.microsoft.com/downloads/details.aspx?FamilyID=751fa0d1-356c-4002-9c60-d539896c66ce&displaylang=en

This VM represents a relatively full-featured SharePoint 2010 installation, so we will take the time to drill into the different databases installed, that are specific to the SharePoint 2010 product or tie in to this installation of SharePoint 2010 and the corresponding features setup. Also note that in the full names of many of the databases, a GUID or unique identifier is appended on to the end of the database name. This is to ensure uniqueness in larger server installations, which could potentially contain many similar SQL Server databases. For our purposes, we will leave off the GUID in discussing these databases for the sake of clarity of typing.

AdventureWorksDW

This database houses the data warehouse for AdventureWorks. The VM SharePoint install is using this to provide back-end data warehousing for Excel spreadsheets that are stored in SharePoint 2010, to look up information, and present graphs and slices of current business.

Application_Registry_Service_DB

This database, and the corresponding Application Registry Service, allows users to search for and collaborate around business data.

BDC_Service_DB

This database, and the corresponding BCS Service and feature set, enables integration of SharePoint lists with an external line of business databases or systems. In the VM setup example here, there is an external list called Supplier Information, which maps to the SupplyChainSQL database installed in SQL Server. This database is external to SharePoint 2010, but, through BCS Services, it can be read from, inserted to, updated, and deleted from, just like a regular SharePoint List, except that the back-end data is stored in a SQL Server table external to SharePoint. You can see the database in Figure 4–5, and the external list in Figure 4–6.

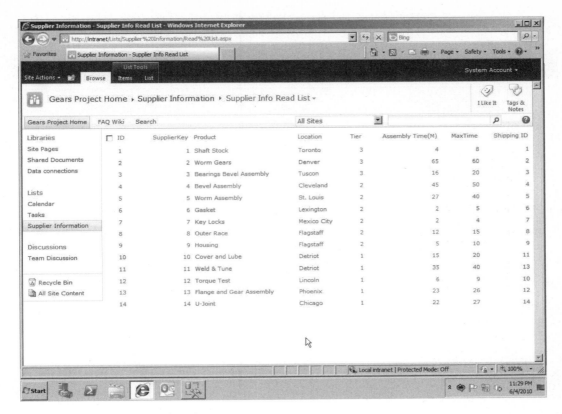

Figure 4–6. – External supplier List

While this list looks very similar to other SharePoint lists, it is directly wired up to an external SQL Server database.

■ **Tip** BCS Services is one key way to integrate external applications into SharePoint 2010. The ability to directly expose one of your database tables in SharePoint as an external list offers a good integration point for applications, and is one of the tools in our toolchest for being able to do application integration into SharePoint 2010 from an ASP.NET application. We will cover more on this in later chapters.

Contoso_Inventory, Contoso_Retail_DW, and Customers

These three databases are external to SharePoint, but are used in the Excel documents that are shared in the Shared Documents library. Also installed in this environment is Microsoft Office Web Applications, which enables SharePoint 2010 to display spreadsheets without opening Microsoft Excel. An example of this is shown in Figure 4–7.

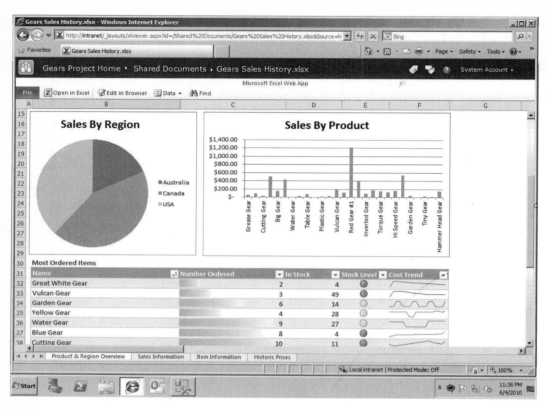

Figure 4–7. Excel spreadsheet shown in Excel web app

FAST Databases

The FAST databases are set up with the FAST Search Service. This service is an advanced Search feature that features item categorization, thumbnails, and previews. An example of FAST Search is shown in Figure 4–8.

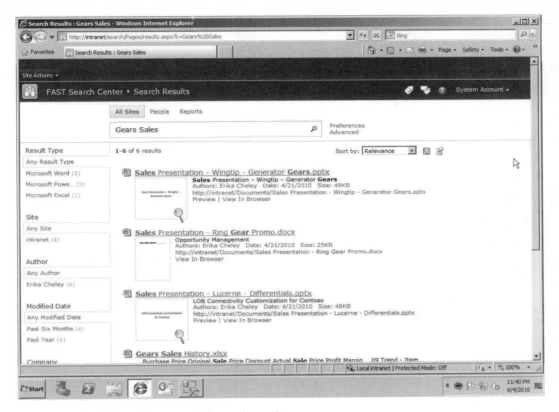

Figure 4–8. FAST Search Center with search results

Quickly going over some of the key advantages with FAST: As you can see in Figure 4–8, the search results with images look a lot better, and offer several key information points about each result, such as the file name, document title, authors, date, size, URL link to the document, and a View In Browser option. Also for PowerPoint presentations, there is a Preview option one can click via the magnifying glass or the Preview link, which drills down into the presentation for browsing it to determine if the search result is the one we are looking for without leaving the FAST Search Center Search Results page. Also of note, the default sorting is by relevance, but there are also options to sort the search results by date. There is also an RSS syndication subscription option to this search result, as well as an option to save this search and investigate it later using Windows Explorer.

On the left-hand navigation side, we see that there are built-in filters available to filter the results data for us, including by result type (the type of document), site on which it originates, author, date modified, and company. Each of these built-in filters works with a single click to narrow down search data. All in all, FAST Search is a very powerful addition to the SharePoint 2010 environment. It is fast, visual, powerful, and can index a wide variety of content.

FAST uses, primarily, seven databases to produce these results. While we won't go into minute details about each of these databases, they are as follows:

- FASTContent_CrawlStoreDB

- FASTContent_DB

- FASTContent_PropertyStoreDB

- FASTQuery_CrawlStoreDB

- FASTQuery_DB

- FASTQuery_PropertyStoreDB

- FASTSearchAdminDB

Managed Metadata Service Database

The Managed Metadata database and service allows individual groups to manage separate taxonomies, hierarchies, keywords, and social tagging, along with the ability to share these items across multiple site collections, as well as web applications.

PerformancePoint Service Application database

The PerformancePoint service and database is a powerful center for central consolidation of data, which allows the creation of balanced scorecards and dashboards that can pull data from multiple data sources and objects, providing a single slice view of the business.

ReportServer, ReportServerTempDB

These databases are related to SQL Server Reporting Services (SSRS), and store information relating to SharePoint 2010's integration with SSRS.

Search Service Databases

These databases correspond to the Enterprise Search Feature, which is the built-in search service that comes with SharePoint 2010.

Secure_Store_Service_DB

The Secure Store Service and DB allow users to store data and associate it to a specific identity or group of identities. This is a secure storage option for users.

SharePoint_AdminContent

This database houses the content for the SharePoint 2010 Central Administration web application.

SharePoint_Config

This database is among the first ones installed when installing SharePoint 2010 as a product. It holds information relating to the web farm, as well as specific configuration settings for SharePoint.

StateService

The State Service, along with its database, temporarily stores user session information related to SharePoint 2010 components. Several other features in SharePoint 2010 depend upon this service running.

SupplyChainSQL

This database is an external database to SharePoint, but linked in through BCS, as shown in the external list image in Figure 4–6.

User Profile Service Application_ProfileDB

The User Profile Service manages detailed information about an organization and the individuals in the organization.

User Profile Service Application_SocialDB

The User Profile Service SocialDB is related to a new feature in SharePoint 2010, which allows users to add social tags to documents, web pages, blog posts. Users can also leave notes on other users My Sites pages as well as other SharePoint web pages.

User Profile Service Application_SyncDB

One aspect of User Profile Services is the feature that allows for synchronizing user profiles, groups, and organization information from within SharePoint 2010 Server, with profile information stored in Active Directory across the enterprise.

WebAnalyticsServiceApplication_ReportingDB, WebAnalyticsServiceApplication_StagingDB

Web Analytics collects usage data of users, including their browsing patterns, search engines used, and keywords that a user types in to find sites.

WordAutomationServices

Word Automation Services is a new service in SharePoint 2010. It provides a userless interface for server-side conversion of Word documents into .pdf and .xps formats. It is used for document conversion.

WSS_Content Databases

WSS Content databases are the databases that store the site content for SharePoint sites.

WSS_Logging

This is a new database in SharePoint 2010, which contains diagnostic logging information. Each of the tables in the database are basically partitioned for performance purposes, and the views that are provided are for interacting. This database is meant to be directly accessed, and one of the existing tables in the database is the ULSTraceLog. This means that the ULS logs that are of great use in diagnosing SharePoint issues are now no longer text-based logs on the file system, but in the database, and can be accessed remotely much easier.

This section has provided us with a basic view of SharePoint 2010 from a database perspective. We have seen that many of the databases correspond directly to a SharePoint 2010 service, and we've seen how the SharePoint product has touchpoints to external databases through BCS and Excel Business Analytics pieces.

For specific and more detailed information regarding the databases in SharePoint 2010, including specifics regarding read/write intensity, sizing, and placement, see the TechNet article here:

http://technet.microsoft.com/en-us/library/cc678868.aspx

Next, we will delve into an underlying concept of how SharePoint works.

SharePoint 2010 and the Virtual Path Provider Pattern

One of the first things to understand about the architecture of SharePoint originates in developments surrounding the ASP.NET 1.1 release, which was first released to production on April 23, 2003. The 1.1 release of ASP.NET introduced a new design pattern utilized broadly throughout the .NET release, called the Provider Pattern. The introduction of the Provider Pattern introduced to .NET functionality that offered a pluggable modularity to designs. This pattern vastly increased the ability of both internal Microsoft developers and external developers in corporations and open source projects to "plug modules in" to ASP.NET. To understand the significance of this pattern, and its impact on SharePoint 2010 development, let's take a little time to develop some basic background on software design principles as they apply to SharePoint development. The benefit for you is to gain a deeper understanding of the architectural design principles behind SharePoint 2010, as well as be able to clearly recognize the Provider Pattern, and easily plug your own custom modules into your SharePoint 2010 development projects.

Object-Oriented Architecture

One of the problems in design with modularity is flexibility. In older designs, in many languages, APIs were published in a series of compiled libraries with detailed documentation of the classes, properties, and methods that the libraries provided to interact with the API.

Methods within an API offer a fixed number of arguments or options to take advantage of. The choices that are available when interacting with an API are chosen by the API provider. This leads the design down a restricted path where the options are tightly controlled. This type of an approach to object-oriented software design also leads toward problems, such as rigidity.

Rigidity problems present symptoms such as software becoming more and more locked in to a certain path, with characteristics becoming harder and harder to change. As designs become more complex, and code increases over time, the interactions between classes also increase. A design becomes locked into a particular direction, and changes become more and more difficult. This leads to a secondary problem with object-oriented software design—fragility. Large, complex codebases evolve to become more fragile over time. Changing one class impacts a large number of other classes.

Developments in object-oriented software design have migrated toward five very distinct and universal principles to solve problems such as rigidity and fragility. Although this is not a book on object-oriented software design, it will be helpful to first cover the basic principles of object-oriented design, and then discuss them in the context of the Provider Pattern, so that it will be easy to see how this pattern provides a necessary flexibility in SharePoint 2010.

The Provider Pattern is used throughout SharePoint 2010, primarily in the underlying architecture of the design storing page content in the SharePoint SQL Server databases, and secondarily, in very common customizations, such as writing a Membership and Role Provider for custom authentication, and writing a Navigation Provider to override and provide custom navigation in SharePoint 2010.

The other benefit to discussing these basic principles behind object-oriented design (OOD) is that when we are integrating our ASP.NET solutions into SharePoint 2010 and designing custom solutions, adhering to the tenets of good OOD is something that we want to strive for in our solution design. This will make higher-quality solutions, as well as ensure that ongoing use and additional development of your solutions will be as painless as possible.

The Open/Closed Principle

The open/closed principle (OCP) states that entities should be open for extension but closed for modification. Classes or modules should be written in a fashion that allows subsequent modifications by extension only, as opposed to continuing to modify the entity. This concept comes into play in APIs by defining a strong set of base classes that are not modified. The API can be solidified in this fashion by using the abstract word in .NET as an identifier of these classes. Abstract base classes are a staple of OCP design throughout the .NET API, as well as the SharePoint 2010 object. If you use .NET Reflector to decompile some of the class libraries in SharePoint 2010, you will see many examples of abstract base classes that are sealed for modification. Several specific techniques exist to ensure that classes remain open for extension but closed for modification, but the key principle involved is abstraction. The language construct introduced in .NET 3.0 of Generics also is an advance toward implementing abstraction of software design following the idea or pattern of the OCP.

Liskov Substitution Principle

The Liskov substitution principle (LSP) conveys the idea that derived classes must be able to be substituted for their base class. This principle preserves a baseline of modularity in designs, as it divorces a base design from its derived implementation, and preserves the transparency of inheritance. LSP ensures that the contract of an abstract base class is honored by the derived class. This principle is a basic component of ensuring that software design is modular in nature. If everywhere a derived class is used you are able to substitute a base class, this ensures that designs will not be brittle throughout the architecture implementation.

Dependency Inversion Principle

The dependency inversion principle (DIP) guides software design philosophy toward depending on abstractions, as opposed to depending on concretions. In a procedurally based architecture, the flow goes from high-level definition to low-level implementation and the definitions at the high level have to know details about the lower-level classes for the design to work correctly. This introduces a real fragility to the design, including dependencies wrapped throughout all the layers of your classes. When implementing DIP as a design philosophy, the majority of modules migrate toward pointing to abstractions, as opposed to pointing to the details of implementation.

The classes and constructs that contain implementation details are not depended upon by higher-level classes, but they themselves depend upon an abstraction or interface contract for implementation details. Thus, the normal dependency from procedural designs is inverted. The details of DIP that you can see in good object-oriented designs show that the vast majority of the design involves interfaces and abstract classes. The idea here to improve solution design is to build your code to extract dependencies into interfaces and abstract base classes.

However, one thing to keep in mind with the DIP principle, as in all design decisions, is that moderation is key. The idea behind DIP is to reduce dependencies on volatile components, as opposed to those that are relatively static and unchanging. So volatile elements are prime candidates to design into interfaces and abstract base classes.

Single Responsibility Principle

The single responsibility principle (SRP) carries the idea that there should be one primary responsibility of any class, and one primary reason to change any class. When classes start to amass many responsibilities, this increases the complexity of the interaction between classes. So a basic tenet of good software design keeps classes to one specific responsibility.

Interface Segregation Principle

The interface segregation principle (ISP) is a similar one to the SRP principle, except that it applies to interfaces. ISP conveys the basic idea that interfaces themselves should cover a simple set of abstracted elements. Rather than designing large interfaces to cover many features, a better principle would be to design many small interfaces that each contain a primary feature. This is possible in languages with single inheritance and multiple implementation features, such as C#. A couple of good examples of core C# interfaces are IEnumerable and IDisposable. Each of these interfaces is responsible for one primary action.

You will see all of these object-oriented software class design principles throughout the Microsoft product stack, as well as specifically in SharePoint 2010. Learning to recognize them and interact with them is a vital piece to being able to combine specific solutions with SharePoint 2010.

■ **Tip** You can find more information on object-oriented software design principles in the article *The Principles of OOP* at www.butunclebob.com/ArticleS.UncleBob.PrinciplesOfOod. Robert C. "Uncle Bob" Martin has been instructing software engineers on better object-oriented design for decades, and is a great resource for books and articles on that subject.

The Provider Pattern

The provider design pattern is an extension of the object-oriented techniques that we have just reviewed. It was first introduced into ASP.NET by way of the Starter Kits that were developed for the 1.1 version of ASP.NET, and were formally migrated into the ASP.NET product as of ASP.NET 2.0. The provider pattern basically provides building blocks for the functionality of an API.

The provider pattern extends the five basic principles of object-oriented design to provide a means for features to be implemented in the .NET framework, through the use of an abstract factory design pattern combined with the definition of the libraries and classes involved in the feature to be defined by way of an XML element that exists in the ASP.NET's web.config file. This pattern allows for "pluggable" elements and feature sets to be swapped out for one another, realtime, by simply changing the definition of which class and library to point to for the element.

A provider is a contract between an API and an abstracted business layer of code. It has to inherit from a provider base class. The base class performs the function of forwarding the implementation to the API to execute. Providers also have a hook into the ASP.NET framework through the <providers> XML element that is defined in an application's web.config <system.web> section. Each provider should include a default configuration.

Provider patterns are included throughout ASP.NET applications. Some of the more common patterns that you run into are ones for configuring database interaction and membership authentication and roles for web applications. SharePoint 2010 also has a number of providers implemented internally for different features to connect to the API, such as the same authentication and roles providers that a regular ASP.NET application has.

■ **Tip** You can find more information on the provider pattern and the design of it in the following MSDN articles:

Provider Model Design Pattern and Specification, Part 1

`http://msdn.microsoft.com/en-us/library/ms972319.aspx`

Provider Design Pattern, Part 2

`http://msdn.microsoft.com/en-us/library/ms972370.aspx`

The Virtual Path Provider

One of the technology-changing advances that came about through the widespread use of the provider pattern in ASP.NET 2.0 was to the whole underlying structure of how pages and content were stored, retrieved, and passed to the ASP.NET framework. The .NET framework, up to that point, was completely dependent upon reading actual files from the file system. Files with .NET extensions, including .aspx, .asmx, and .ashx, were retrieved by the nature of naming conventions, compiled, and used to serve up content in ASP.NET.

With the advance of the provider pattern, it was discovered and realized that you could actually plug a provider into ASP.NET to provide page content from another source than the physical file system. While this allowed for different vendors and developers to plug in unique solutions to store and access ASP.NET page and service content, one of the first paths that this led the SharePoint team down was to start to integrate the ability in SharePoint to store content in a database. This vastly increased the potential of SharePoint as a product, as now there was no need to completely build out physical web sites, pages, and content on the file system. Content, sites, and pages could now be replicated in database tables and still used to serve up content to web sites. Two aspects of this were large changes from a technology perspective:

- *Performance*: Barriers for performance could be broken through using the advances that SQL Server provides for the speed of processing data through a relational database.

- *Web Farm Scalability*: With web-site content now able to be served up through a centralized database, one instance of SQL Server could now serve up content to multiple web front-end (WFE) servers on a SharePoint farm.

These two aspects of the technology advance seen with virtual Path Providers now allowed SharePoint to be able to scale into an Enterprise product (in terms of flexibility and performance).

What we have in SharePoint 2010, with the integration of the virtual path provider pattern, is a combination of content that is deployed to both the file system and the content database. A large portion of the default pages, master pages, and controls for the entire SharePoint 2010 product are located in the file system, as we have seen in an earlier portion of this chapter. Many of these are application pages, used in the configuration of the product. Many others are template pages and controls, used to host content that is stored in SharePoint 2010 content databases, as we also have seen earlier in the chapter.

One of the things that brings the virtual path provider into play involves the ability that SharePoint 2010 provides to customize pages that come with the product. You can load a SharePoint 2010 site in SharePoint Designer 2010 and changed using customizations. Once a pages is customized, it no longer is loaded from the file system, but instead employs the virtual path provider to load the customized version from the web site's content database. This is one thing to keep in mind when dealing with SharePoint 2010 customizations. If there are common changes that need to be implemented across a range of site collections and sites, it is better to consolidate those changes across the board by deploying solutions to the file system, as opposed to duplicating the changes in many sites by way of changing them in each site database.

■ **Tip** SharePoint 2010 solutions are, most of the time, deployed through Features and Solution packages created by Visual Studio 2010. This type of deployment ensures that customizations are deployed to the SharePoint 2010 product file system, as opposed to being stored in a database. You can create exceptions to this in Visual Studio, through a customized module deployed as a feature, which can deploy elements of a solution to a content database.

You can find more information on the virtual path provider on MSDN at the following address:

`http://msdn.microsoft.com/en-us/library/system.web.hosting.virtualpathprovider.aspx`

Summary

Understanding some of the underlying architecture behind SharePoint 2010's construction, including elements of good object-oriented design, the provider pattern, and the virtual path provider, can provide us with a good fundamental basis for integrating customized ASP.NET solutions with SharePoint 2010.

We have looked at SharePoint 2010 from a file system perspective in this chapter, examining the different installed folders that go along with the product, as well as some of the elements in those folders. We have also looked at a high level some of the SQL Server 2008 databases that are installed along with, and utilized by, the SharePoint 2010 system. While we've learned it is not a supported path to interact directly with most of these databases, we have gained a comprehension of their content and purposes, including how to interact with them through PowerShell. And finally, we have examined some of the architectural constructs behind SharePoint 2010, in order to gain a more comprehensive understanding of the product. Now we are ready to delve into some of the basic constructs of SharePoint 2010—web parts and master pages.

CHAPTER 5

■ ■ ■

Web Parts and Master Pages

The whole is greater than the sum of its parts.

Aristotle

Now that we have a fundamental understanding of some of the parts of SharePoint 2010, including from a perspective of IIS, ASP.NET, and the .NET Framework, as well as from a file system and database point of view, it is time to get started building some things that will help us in our integration of ASP.NET solutions and SharePoint 2010.

In this chapter, we will briefly define web parts, and then get directly into code examples of building web parts. We will build both visual web parts as well as standard web parts, we will build web parts for sandboxed solutions, and we will build a Silverlight web part. In building these, we will expose both the SharePoint object model in code as well as connecting directly to external data sources with a data connection string. In doing this, we will show a couple of techniques for providing for the connection string, including using a feature receiver and using a hidden list to configure this. Our goal in code for this chapter is to become familiar with all of the different options for building web parts as well as setting them up for connecting to SharePoint internal data as well as external data sources directly.

Also in this chapter, we will present a brief overview of SharePoint master pages, which we will investigate in more detail later in conjunction with branding. These two major components will come into play later in the book with code examples as we get into specifics for integrating ASP.NET development with SharePoint 2010.

Web Parts

Web parts are some of the most versatile components in SharePoint 2010 development. They are a fundamental building block in SharePoint that allow you to reuse component. You can add components to many different pages in a SharePoint site. One of the differences in working with web parts as compared to more traditional styles of ASP.NET development is this component reuse. In ASP.NET development, typically pages are constructed to be somewhat static in that they do not depend on the user to add functional components to the page. Of course, some modular ASP.NET products such as DotNetNuke are the exception to this, but on a large scale, ASP.NET development is a "build once" type of situation.

SharePoint 2010 development is not like this. While it is possible to develop application pages and site pages, many times the framework of choice within SharePoint is the web part due to its versatility.

■ **Tip** In SharePoint 2010 development terminology, an "application page" is one that is most similar to an ASP.NET web form page. It often has a code-behind file, and compiles and runs very similar to an ASP.NET web form page. A "site page" is a page that contains artifacts on it that allow users to store custom content in SharePoint. These pages typically do not have compilable code-behind files, and are handled in a different fashion by the SharePoint 2010 framework to allow for content storage.

Web parts are typically deployed into web part zones in SharePoint 2010. There are many different kinds of web parts that come out of the box in SharePoint. Some of the standard web parts that are available to use on a SharePoint 2010 publishing site used for extranets include the following:

- Lists and Libraries—Types of web parts showing information stored in standard SharePoint lists and libraries.

- Documents—A web part listing documents used in pages on your site.

- Images—A web part listing images used in pages on your site

- Pages—Pages created on your site.

- Workflow Tasks—Listing of workflow tasks on your site.

- Content Rollup—aggregation of content in a web part.

- Content Query—A web part for showing rollups of content on subsites, lists, or specific areas of your web site. Provides easy navigation into areas.

- Relevant Documents—A web part showing a table of documents last modified by you.

- Summary Links—A web part for adding pertinent links.

- Table of Contents—A web part that contains navigational links to your site.

- Web Analytics Web Part—A web part for tying into web analytics.

- XML Viewer—A web part with which you can provide an XML file and an XSLT transform file to apply to the XML. Useful for such things as formatting syndicated content from RSS feeds.

- HTML Form Web Part—A web part for HTML form inputs for sending to other web parts

- InfoPath Form Web Part—A web part for rendering an InfoPath browser-enabled form.

- Content Editor Web Part—A web part allowing the user to edit and save rich content.

- Image Viewer—A web part for displaying a specific image.

- Media Web Part—Allows for embedding audio and video files into a page.

- Page Viewer—Renders another site page in an iFrame.

- Picture Library Slideshow Web Part—a slideshow web part that displays all the pictures in a picture library.

- Silverlight Web Part—A web part container for a Silverlight .xap file.

- Social Collaboration—Content media such as a note board, organization browser, or tag cloud.

- Site Users—Displays a list of other site users and their status.

- User Tasks—Displays tasks assigned to the current user.

The Publishing Site is a site template in SharePoint that is focused on a particular task. Web parts that are available on a Team Site intranet portal include many more categories, including:

- Business Data—External LOB systems web parts

- Excel Web Access—Exposing Excel documents to your intranet

- Filters—Aggregates or filters from multiple children web sites

- Outlook Web App—Integration with your Exchange mail servers

- Search—Content and people search

- Social Collaboration—content media such as a note board, organization browser, or tag cloud

These built-in web parts are available on certain types of sites and depending on whether or not different services are set up within SharePoint 2010. There are also tons of web parts that are available from third-party vendors, from CodePlex, and from many other sources for SharePoint 2010.

One thing of note that is different about the behavior of web parts in SharePoint 2010 is that in previous products, pages provided a web part zone for you to add your web part into. In SharePoint 2010, there still are zones, but they are rich content zones. In each of these, you can intermix free-form text with images as well as instantiating your web part. The web part itself is stored in a hidden web part zone on the page, and its place in the content is stored in a div tag that contains the GUID identifying the web part.

Building a Visual Web Part

In developing our toolchest for being able to integrate ASP.NET with SharePoint 2010 solutions, let's start with building a few basic SharePoint web parts. We will introduce programmatically the SharePoint object model and interact with the standard task list that is installed by default with the Team Site template. To take advantage of the code portions of this book, you can follow along with the steps in Visual Studio 2010, or download the example code related to the book on the Apress site.

1. To begin, open Visual Studio 2010, select File➤New➤Project, then in the pop-up window that follows, select the SharePoint 2010 Installed Templates, and the Visual Web Part template. The code for this project uploaded is under the VisualWebPartTaskList folder, but you can name the project anything you like. The New Project template window is shown in Figure 5–1.

Figure 5–1. *Visual Studio SharePoint project templates*

> 2. In the next window, select "Deploy as a farm solution" and then Finish, as shown in Figure 5–2.

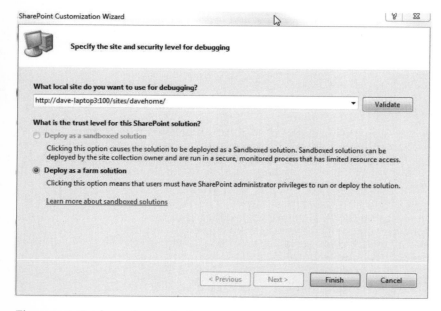

Figure 5–2. *Deploy as farm solution*

3. For this example we will deploy the solution as a farm solution to take advantage of being able to publish .dll libraries to the General Assembly Cache (GAC).

4. Next, rename the `VisualWebPart1` control to `TaskWebPart`. This is so that the web part will show up in your custom web parts section with the correct name. If you notice, this changes the name of the web part itself, but not of the underlying files beneath it. You can see the result of this in Figure 5–3.

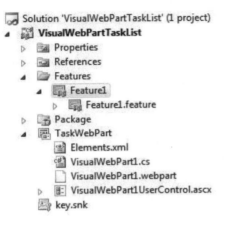

Figure 5–3. Web part rename

Next, add a Calendar control, two Labels, two TextBoxes, a Button control, and a third Label, as shown in Figure 5–4.

```
Client Objects & Events                          (No Events)
 5  <%@ Register Tagprefix="asp" Namespace="System.Web.UI" Assembly="System.Web.Extensions, Version=3.5.0.0, Culture=neu
 6  <%@ Import Namespace="Microsoft.SharePoint" %>
 7  <%@ Register Tagprefix="WebPartPages" Namespace="Microsoft.SharePoint.WebPartPages" Assembly="Microsoft.SharePoint,
 8  <%@ Control Language="C#" AutoEventWireup="true" CodeBehind="VisualWebPart1UserControl.ascx.cs" Inherits="VisualWebP
 9  <asp:Calendar ID="Calendar1" runat="server"></asp:Calendar>
10  <asp:Label ID="Label1" runat="server" Text="Task:"></asp:Label>
11  <asp:TextBox ID="TextBox1" runat="server"></asp:TextBox><br />
12  <asp:Label ID="Label2" runat="server" Text="Description:"></asp:Label>
13  <asp:TextBox ID="TextBox2" runat="server" TextMode="MultiLine"></asp:TextBox><br />
14  <asp:Button ID="Button1" runat="server" Text="Add Task" /><br />
15  <asp:Label ID="lblResults" runat="server"></asp:Label>
16
100 %
```

Figure 5–4. Web part controls

Note that you can do this by typing in the source window, or by dragging controls from the Toolbox into the window. If you examine the Visual Studio 2010 Toolbox that is available to you, you will see many of the standard .NET controls that you are used to working with in ASP.NET web forms development. Figure 5–5 shows these controls.

Figure 5–5. *Toolbox in visual web parts*

These are particularly useful in developing visual web parts. One way to think about visual web parts is that you are doing nothing more than developing an ASP.NET user control in the same fashion that you would doing ASP.NET development. You can see that actually in the files under the web part that you created in Figure 5–3, the file that you are adding the controls to in Figure 5–4 is the file named `VisualWebPart1UserControl.ascx`. The `.ascx` extension on this file is the same extension used by ASP.NET user controls in web development. This particular type of project that we are working on in the Visual Web Part is a new addition to SharePoint 2010, and one of the benefits to it is that it will be helpful to developers coming from an ASP.NET background.

In our Visual Web Part project, the designer window looks like Figure 5–6.

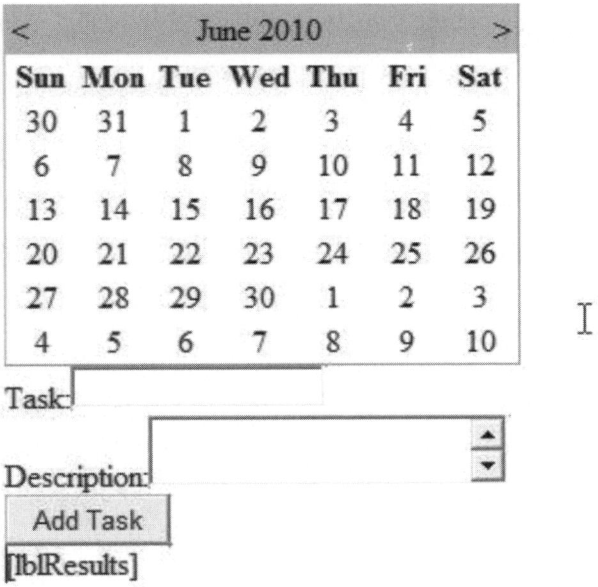

Figure 5–6. Designer window

In this project, we are not really focusing on the UI aspects of the layout, more on the mechanics of programming web parts. However, to obtain a better visual UI, one of the suggestions would be to utilize CSS. SharePoint 2010's UI interfaces have been overhauled from 2007 to clean up the CSS in a lot of areas, one of the most important being the migration from a table-based layout to a `div`-based layout with CSS driving most of the visuals. We will cover UI aspects later in the book in the chapter on Branding SharePoint 2010.

Adding Code

Next, let's add code to the code-behind file of our `VisualWebPart1UserControl.ascx` file. First, double-click the Add Task button so that an event handler is added to the `Button1_Click` event. Then, add the following code.

```
using System;
using System.Web.UI;
using System.Web.UI.WebControls;
```

```
using System.Web.UI.WebControls.WebParts;
using Microsoft.SharePoint;

namespace VisualWebPartTaskList.VisualWebPart1
{
    public partial class VisualWebPart1UserControl : UserControl
    {
        protected void Page_Load(object sender, EventArgs e)
        {
        }

        protected void Button1_Click(object sender, EventArgs e)
        {   SPListItem task =
                SPContext.Current.Web.Lists["Tasks"].Items.Add();
            task["Due Date"] = Calendar1.SelectedDate.ToShortDateString();
            task["Title"] = TextBox1.Text;
            task["Description"] = TextBox2.Text;
            task.Update();
            lblResults.Text = String.Format("Task '{0}' added",
                TextBox1.Text);
            TextBox1.Text = "";
            TextBox2.Text = "";
        }
    }
}
```

Notice that the UserControl class that we are inheriting from in our VisualWebPart1UserControl is of the type System.Web.UI.UserControl, which is the exact same base control that is used in user controls in ASP.NET development.

The next thing to point out is the interaction with the SharePoint Object Model. Because this code is in a web part that will be instantiated on a SharePoint Site page, we do not need to instantiate a new version of the SharePoint context. Instead, we can use the currently loaded context that is surrounding the web part code. If the code we were running did not run in a context that could be picked up from the surrounding environment, we would access the object model in a different fashion, such as in the following code segment.

```
using (SPSite siteColl = new SPSite("http://localhost"))
{
    using (SPWeb site = siteColl.RootWeb)
    {
        ///Custom code here
    }
}
```

One thing that will probably take a little time to get used to is the hierarchy of the SharePoint object model as we introduced in Chapter 1. SPSite represents not a SharePoint site, but a site collection. SPWeb represents not a web application, but a SharePoint site. The preceding code is the general syntax used to access a particular SharePoint site.

■ **Tip** When you are not depending on the SharePoint context that surrounds the code you are using, you always need to dispose of any SharePoint object model you instantiate, especially SPSite and SPWeb objects. These objects represent large hierarchies of underlying objects, some of which are COM objects. If these are not specifically disposed of by either implementing a using statement such as in the previous example, or specifically calling the SPSite.Dispose() method, then this can lead to memory leaks in your SharePoint farm. The best practices for SharePoint development encourage the use of surrounding context where it is available such as in our web part example code. When it is not available, dispose of objects with a using statement or by calling the Dispose() method directly. Failure to do this can cause performance issues with a SharePoint farm, although these objects will be garbage collected by the .NET Framework eventually. For more information on this very important best practices coding practice, see http://msdn.microsoft.com/en-us/library/aa973248(office.12).aspx .

Examining How SharePoint Loads User Controls

Another thing to be aware of in SharePoint 2010 development is how the SharePoint framework actually loads this user control. The code for this can be seen in the VisualWebPart1.cs file, and is shown here:

```
using System;
using System.ComponentModel;
using System.Web;
using System.Web.UI;
using System.Web.UI.WebControls;
using System.Web.UI.WebControls.WebParts;
using Microsoft.SharePoint;
using Microsoft.SharePoint.WebControls;

namespace VisualWebPartTaskList.VisualWebPart1
{
    [ToolboxItemAttribute(false)]
    public class VisualWebPart1 : WebPart
    {
        // Visual Studio might automatically update this path when you change the Visual Web
Part project item.
        private const string _ascxPath =
@"~/_CONTROLTEMPLATES/VisualWebPartTaskList/TaskWebPart/VisualWebPart1UserControl.ascx";

        protected override void CreateChildControls()
        {
            Control control = Page.LoadControl(_ascxPath);
            Controls.Add(control);
        }
    }
}
```

Note the path given to the .ascx file. This is a path that when the web part is added to a page in a SharePoint site, it references the file system path that is under the SharePoint root directory, under the TEMPLATE directory beneath this. The full path where your user control is deployed is typically:

```
C:\Program Files\Common Files\Microsoft Shared\Web Server Extensions\14\TEMPLATE\
CONTROLTEMPLATES
```

followed by your specific solution directory. You can also see this path if you look in IIS under the web site in the _controltemplates folder.

Also note that the web part, which inherits from the standard ASP.NET web part in System.Web.UI.WebParts.WebPart, has the CreateChildControls() function overridden so that the .ascx user control can be added programmatically to the web part. This is done behind the scenes so that you as an ASP.NET developer can simply use the Visual Studio 2010 Designer and a familiar interface to develop user controls, and deploy them to a SharePoint 2010 environment without the need for you to wire up the specific controls used.

Examining the Configuration Files

There are two other files of importance to look into in this Visual Web Part project. The first is the actual webpart file, which specifies to SharePoint what to name the web part and other metadata aspects. This is the VisualWebPart1.webpart file, and it appears as follows:

```
<?xml version="1.0" encoding="utf-8"?>
<webParts>
  <webPart xmlns="http://schemas.microsoft.com/WebPart/v3">
    <metaData>
      <type name="VisualWebPartTaskList.VisualWebPart1.VisualWebPart1,
$SharePoint.Project.AssemblyFullName$" />
      <importErrorMessage>$Resources:core,ImportErrorMessage;</importErrorMessage>
    </metaData>
    <data>
      <properties>
        <property name="Title" type="string">VisualWebPart1</property>
        <property name="Description" type="string">My Visual WebPart</property>
      </properties>
    </data>
  </webPart>
</webParts>
```

In the properties element, the Title and Description are what will show up on the SharePoint 2010 site when the web part is deployed. For these, let's change the Title to TaskAddWebPart, and the Description to "Add a Task to your Tasks List".

The last file to look at is the Elements.xml file, which indicates to SharePoint where the elements of the web part are to be found. It is shown in the following:

```
<?xml version="1.0" encoding="utf-8"?>
<Elements xmlns="http://schemas.microsoft.com/sharepoint/" >
  <Module Name="TaskWebPart" List="113" Url="_catalogs/wp">
    <File Path="TaskWebPart\VisualWebPart1.webpart"
Url="VisualWebPartTaskList_VisualWebPart1.webpart" Type="GhostableInLibrary" >
      <Property Name="Group" Value="Custom" />
    </File>
  </Module>
</Elements>
```

This file contains the file path to the webpart file, as well as a URL for locating the file. The Property element shows the particular group that the web part will show up when you are inserting the web part on a page. We will leave this as Custom for now.

Using Strongly Named Assemblies

One more file to be aware of in SharePoint development that works behind the scenes is the key.snk file. When you select "Deploy to farm" in the first wizard you encounter, the default location that the assembly you produce will be deployed to is the General Assembly Cache (GAC). To do this, you need to have a strongly named assembly, which is done for you automatically by the project template.

With strongly named assemblies, it is relatively easy to maintain more than one version of a SharePoint code deployment on a web site at once. To manage this, right-click the Feature1 folder, go into the Feature Designer, and look at the Properties window. There is a Version property that you can use to maintain multiple assembly versions representing different versions of the codebase. This is shown in Figure 5–7.

For this feature, let's enter a version number of 1.0.0.0 in this property.

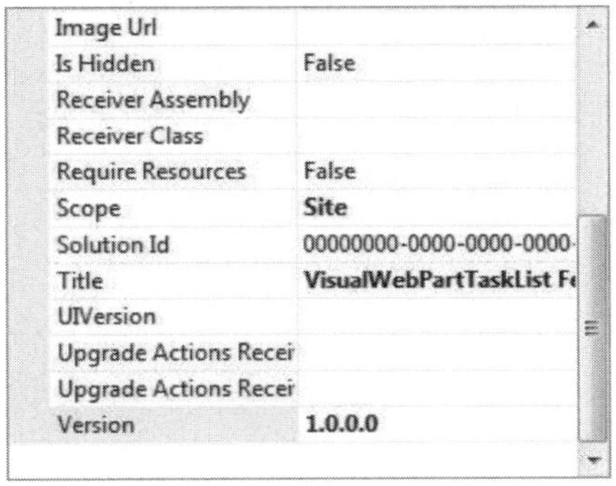

Image Url	
Is Hidden	False
Receiver Assembly	
Receiver Class	
Require Resources	False
Scope	**Site**
Solution Id	00000000-0000-0000-0000-
Title	**VisualWebPartTaskList Fe**
UIVersion	
Upgrade Actions Recei	
Upgrade Actions Recei	
Version	**1.0.0.0**

Figure 5–7. *Properties window for Feature1*

Now that we have examined all of the pertinent files in the solution for our visual web part, let's go ahead and deploy the solution to our SharePoint 2010 team site environment.

Deploying the Visual Web Part

Press F5 to compile and deploy your web part project. As we covered in the chapter on Visual Studio 2010 enhancements, a number of things occur when you use F5 to debug a program. The output window records these things, as you can see in the following, including what happens when you stop debugging.

```
------ Build started: Project: VisualWebPartTaskList, Configuration: Debug Any CPU --
  VisualWebPartTaskList ->
D:\dev\APress\Chapter5\VisualWebPartTaskList\VisualWebPartTaskList\bin\Debug\VisualWebPartTa
skList.dll
  Successfully created package at:
D:\dev\APress\Chapter5\VisualWebPartTaskList\VisualWebPartTaskList\bin\Debug\VisualWebPartTa
skList.wsp
------ Deploy started: Project: VisualWebPartTaskList, Configuration: Debug Any CPU -
Active Deployment Configuration: Default
Run Pre-Deployment Command:
  Skipping deployment step because a pre-deployment command is not specified.
Recycle IIS Application Pool:
```

```
  Skipping application pool recycle because no matching package on the server was found.
Retract Solution:
  Skipping package retraction because no matching package on the server was found.
Add Solution:
  Found 1 deployment conflict(s).  Resolving conflicts ...
  Deleted file
'http://localhost/sites/davehome/_catalogs/wp/VisualWebPartTaskList_VisualWebPart1.webpart'
from server.
  Adding solution 'VisualWebPartTaskList.wsp'...
  Deploying solution 'VisualWebPartTaskList.wsp'...
Activate Features:
  Activating feature 'Feature1' ...
Run Post-Deployment Command:
  Skipping deployment step because a post-deployment command is not specified.
========== Build: 1 succeeded or up-to-date, 0 failed, 0 skipped ==========
========== Deploy: 1 succeeded, 0 failed, 0 skipped ==========
Active Deployment Configuration: Default
Recycle IIS Application Pool:
  Recycling IIS application pool 'SharePoint - 100'...
Retract Solution:
  Deactivating feature 'VisualWebPartTaskList_Feature1' ...
  Retracting solution 'visualwebparttasklist.wsp'...
  Deleting solution 'visualwebparttasklist.wsp'...
```

You can note the different things that are occurring with the F5 key from the output perspective:

1. The build is started.

2. The .wsp package is successfully created.

3. Deployment is started—debug configuration.

4. Skips pre-deployment step—not there.

5. Recycle IIS skips—no matching package on server found.

6. Retract Solution—skips—no matching solution found.

7. Add Solution—adds our current solution.

8. Finds a file deployment conflict—deletes conflicting file.

9. Adds Solution—.wsp.

10. Deploys Solution—.wsp.

11. Activates Feature—Feature1.

12. Run Post-Deployment Command—skips.

Note that because we changed the name and version of the solution, but the components didn't change names, the solution retraction did not happen. However, because we have files named the same, Visual Studio was able to detect this and adjust for it, and still provide us with a viable F5–deployed debugging alternative.

After the debugging session stops, the last steps of deactivating the feature, retracting the solution, and deleting the solution take place. This is important to highlight to understand that F5 debugging deployment sessions do not leave multiple artifacts out on your farm, but adjust to the environment you have and retract the elements you work on. If you wish to deploy the solution, you may switch the configuration to a more permanent build and select Deploy Solution from the Build menu. Also, if you wish to stop the auto-retract feature during the debugging session, there is check box labeled "Auto-retract after debugging" on the project page under the SharePoint section that you can uncheck.

Once you deploy the web part, the debugger takes you to the home page of your team site. You need to either edit the page, or go to Site Pages to create a new page that will be a container page to host your web part. Figure 5–8 shows the page on a team site that is in edit mode with the Web Part➤Insert Web Part dialog box open.

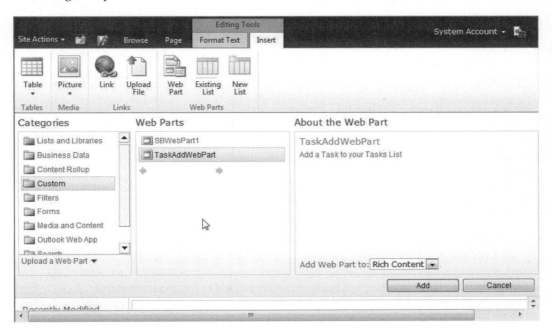

Figure 5–8. Adding a web part to a SharePoint 2010 page

Once the web part is added to the page, you can save the page out of edit mode to ensure it remains there. You can see the web part on the page in Figure 5–9.

Finally for this project, you may select a date, enter text for the task title and description, and click the Add Task button. At this point during this event handler, or during other events for which you have breakpoints set, the breakpoints will be hit, as shown in Figure 5–10.

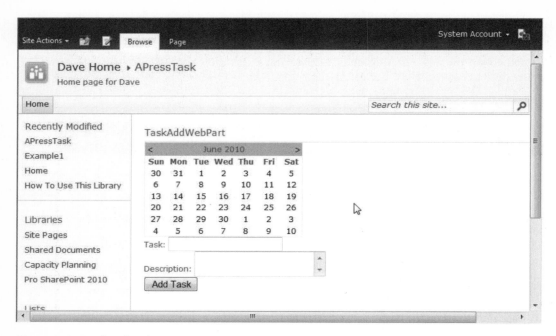

Figure 5–9. *Deployed web part*

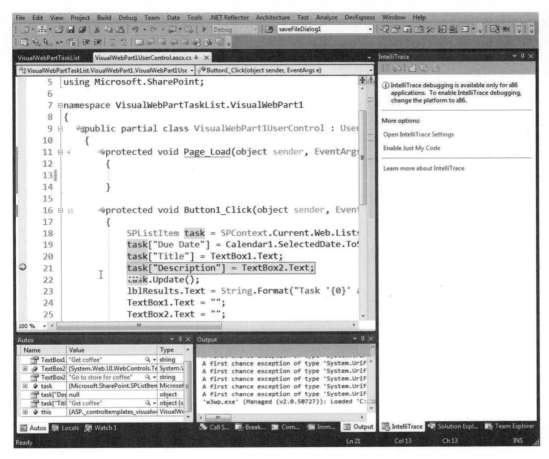

Figure 5–10. Break point in web part code execution

At this point, your standard debugging features are available.

■ **Note** As you may observe in the graphic, Intellitrace is not available for x64 systems as of this release, so by default is not available for SharePoint development. Intellitrace also is only available for certain SKUs of Visual Studio 2010, so may not be enabled in your environment.

Although Intellitrace is not available for SharePoint debugging, other standard debugger features are available, such as the Locals window, the Call Stack, and the Immediate windows. There is also a Watch window available.

Using the Developer Dashboard

Another tool that is available to assist with debugging and helping with page analysis in development is the SharePoint 2010 Developer Dashboard. You can turn the Dashboard on via a PowerShell command. Open up the SharePoint 2010 Management Shell through your menu commands under Microsoft SharePoint 2010 Products and enter the following commands:

```
SPPerformanceMonitor perfMon = SPFarm.Local.PerformanceMonitor;
perfMon.DeveloperDashboardLevel = SPPerformanceMonitoringLevel.OnDemand;
```

The OnDemand setting is what places the icon in the top right-hand corner for clicking to enable the Dashboard for a page (as shown in Figures 5–10 and 5–12). Other performance monitoring levels can include On and Off, which globally turn on performance monitoring completely, or globally turns it off. OnDemand is the most flexible to use when doing development, as the performance monitoring output may be obtained when you want it by simply clicking the icon. Figure 5–11 shows the output of the page request for our visual web part when the Developer Dashboard is turned on. Note that the normal page is rendered just as before, there is just a scrollbar on the right-hand side of the page that enables you to scroll down to see the Dashboard output.

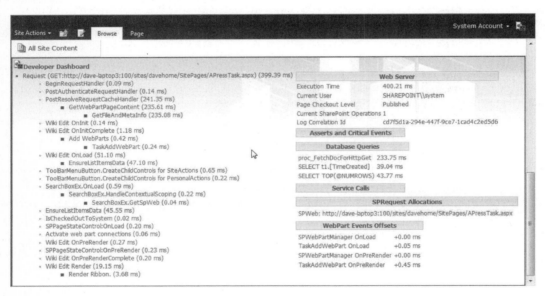

Figure 5–11. Developer Dashboard output

Notice that all of the page lifecycle events are recorded for the SharePoint environment page cycle— you can see the records of those firing as well as the runtime each takes. You can also see the request, service calls, asserts (which you can programmatically add to your SharePoint Controls to fire showing specific things), critical events, and web-part events offsets, which show the load and runtimes of your web-parts events.

■ **Tip** The value for Log Correlation ID, which is a GUID, is a key to troubleshooting issues with a particular page. You can take the Correlation ID GUID and search through the Universal Log (ULS) for this value as well as search through Windows Application event logs. This vastly helps debugging efforts. There is a tool that you can use to view the ULS Log available at `http://code.msdn.microsoft.com/ULSViewer` .

So that is our introduction to web part development, including deployment, debugging, and several tools for use within SharePoint 2010 and Visual Studio 2010. Next, we will examine building web parts in another way.

Building a Standard SharePoint Web Part

Another method used to build web parts involves building a regular web part as opposed to a visual web part. This technique is similar to the approach that you would use in ASP.NET development to build a server control as opposed to a user control. The main difference in building this type of a web part is that we will take over handling the rendering of the control directly and that we will also not have the benefit of the Visual Designer interface in Visual Studio 2010 to review our work prior to deploying it.

1. To begin, select File➤New➤Project in Visual Studio 2010. For this project instead of using a solution template, we will be using a project item template. Select the Empty SharePoint Project template, as shown in Figure 5–12 and name your project `WebPartTaskList`. There is also the finished solution for this included in the code downloads for this book under Chapter 5—the solution will also be named `WebPartTaskList`.

Figure 5–12. Empty SharePoint Project

2. For this particular project, we will also take advantage of a completely different way to deploy the project by selecting "Deploy as a sandboxed solution" then Finish, as shown in Figure 5–13.

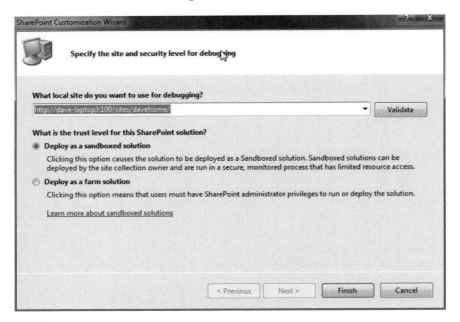

Figure 5–13. Deploy as a sandboxed solution

You can deploy a web part as either a farm solution or a sandboxed solution. This is a little different than the visual web part that we created in the first part of the chapter. You can only deploy visual web parts with standard out-of-the-box functionality from Visual Studio 2010 as a farm solution.

■ **Tip** Since the release of SharePoint and Visual Studio 2010, the project team has subsequently released Visual Studio 2010 SharePoint Power Tools. These tools are located at `http://visualstudiogallery.msdn.` `microsoft.com/en-us/8e602a8c-6714-4549-9e95-f3700344b0d9`, or you can search for them by name. These tools specifically provide for building sandboxed-compatible visual web parts as well as a feature for sandboxed compilation. The tools provide a visual designer to use to create SharePoint web parts that are compatible with sandboxed solutions.

We have mentioned sandboxed solutions previously in the book, and there are a couple of reasons to deploy code in this fashion. One of the main ones is that it will enable site administrators to deploy the code to their site, which can allow for decentralizing some of the responsibility for SharePoint in an organization. Also, sandboxed solutions allow for deployment to online versions of SharePoint. In general, sandboxed Solutions will protect an existing SharePoint 2010 farm better than deploying as a farm solution.

■ **Note** At the time of writing of this book, SharePoint had not yet been added to the standard Microsoft Business Productivity Online Standard Suite (BPOS). However, plans to do so have been announced, so it is likely that it will happen by publication time. With all the typical caveats to functionality that isn't yet existent, deploying sandboxed solutions to BPOS versions of SharePoint should be supported.

■ **Tip** For further information on sandboxed solutions, including a hands-on lab that covers this feature more fully, Channel 9 has an excellent learning section on this at `http://channel9.msdn.com/learn/courses/SharePoint2010Developer/SandboxedSolutions/`

Adding a Web Part to the Project

After initializing the empty SharePoint project, we want to add a web part to this project using a SharePoint 2010 template. To do this, select Project➤Add New Item from the Visual Studio 2010 menus. You need to have the `WebPartTaskList` highlighted in the Solution Explorer for this menu selection to be shown. Select the Web Part template, and name your web part `TaskListAdd,` as shown in Figure 5–14.

Figure 5–14. Add Web Part template

After you add the web part, you will notice that the template creates many different artifacts similar to the ones that we saw with the Visual Web Part template, including the Feature, references to Microsoft SharePoint libraries, the .webpart file, the Elements.xml file, and a TaskListAdd.cs file. This file is the only code file added, and you will notice no corresponding .ascx file referenced.

Adding Code

The initial look of the main code file TaskListAdd.cs that we will be working with is shown in Figure 5–15.

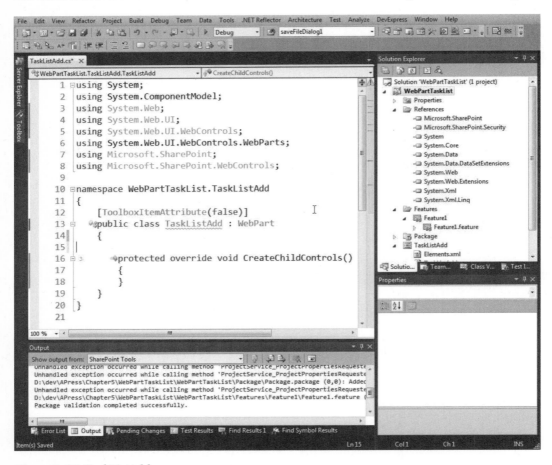

Figure 5–15. TaskListAdd.cs

Because we don't have a designer, we will need to instantiate, populate, and add all of the controls ourselves for the Web part. Add the following code to the class:

```
Calendar calendar1 = new Calendar();
Label lblTask = new Label();
Label lblDescription = new Label();
Label lblResult = new Label();
TextBox txtTask = new TextBox();
TextBox txtDescription = new TextBox();
Button btnAddTask = new Button();
```

This code can go inside the TaskListAdd class above the CreateChildControls() function.

Next, in the CreateChildControls() function, we will need to add code for initializing and displaying the controls, as well as to add the event handler for the Button control. Add the following code to the CreateChildControls() function:

```
lblTask.Text = "Task:   ";
lblDescription.Text = "Description:   ";
btnAddTask.Text = "Add Task";
Controls.Add(calendar1);
Controls.Add(new LiteralControl("<br/>"));
Controls.Add(lblTask);
Controls.Add(txtTask);
Controls.Add(new LiteralControl("<br/>"));
Controls.Add(lblDescription);
Controls.Add(txtDescription);
Controls.Add(new LiteralControl("<br/>"));
Controls.Add(btnAddTask);
Controls.Add(new LiteralControl("<br/>"));
Controls.Add(lblResult);
btnAddTask.Click += new EventHandler(btnAddTask_Click);
```

The order in which the controls are added, as well as some of the literal controls that are added to provide a line break, control the UI aspects of the web part.

Finally, add an event to handle the button click, as follows:

```
void btnAddTask_Click(object sender, EventArgs e)
{
    SPListItem task =
        SPContext.Current.Web.Lists["Tasks"].Items.Add();
    task["Due Date"] = calendar1.SelectedDate.ToShortDateString();
    task["Title"] = txtTask.Text;
    task["Description"] = txtDescription.Text;
    task.Update();
    lblResult.Text = String.Format("Task '{0}' added", txtTask.Text);
    txtTask.Text = "";
    txtDescription.Text = "";
}
```

Notice that the code to interact with the SharePoint model in the Button event handler is very similar to the code in the visual web part. Here, you can start to see the distinction. Additional code that is handled by the markup language in the .ascx file in the visual web part needs to be handled by code in the web part.

Deploying the Web Part

You are now ready to deploy and use the web part in your Team site. Use F5 to deploy the project, navigate to the site page you would like to use, and add the web part to the page. The appearance of the web part is almost identical to the appearance of the visual web part. The difference is in the coding approach only.

The choice of whether to build web parts in either the visual web part way or the standard web part way is up to the developer's discretion. There are tradeoffs to each approach, which we have covered in the previous section. Visual web parts offer the design view and a developer experience more like ASP.NET development; standard web parts offer a little cleaner interface with less code.

Building a Silverlight Web Part

The final approach that we will examine in this section on interacting with the SharePoint object model in web parts is a Silverlight web part. SharePoint 2010 has introduced support for Silverlight along with its rich UI and media integration. Here, we will take advantage of this by building our Task Adder web part in Silverlight.

1. To start, just as in the web part example, select File➤New➤Project, and select the Empty SharePoint Project. Name the project SilverlightTaskAdd. You can choose to either deploy the project as a sandboxed solution or a farm solution.

2. For now, we will leave the SharePoint part of the project alone, and go and build the Silverlight portion. Right-click the solution file, select Add➤New Project, then select the Silverlight Application template under the Silverlight section, as shown in Figure 5–16.

Figure 5–16. *Silverlight Application template*

3. Name the new project SilverlightTaskAdder. In the subsequent window, de-select the checkbox for "Host the Silverlight application in a new web site" as shown in Figure 5–17. We do not need to host the Silverlight application in a web site; instead we will be hosting it in SharePoint2010.

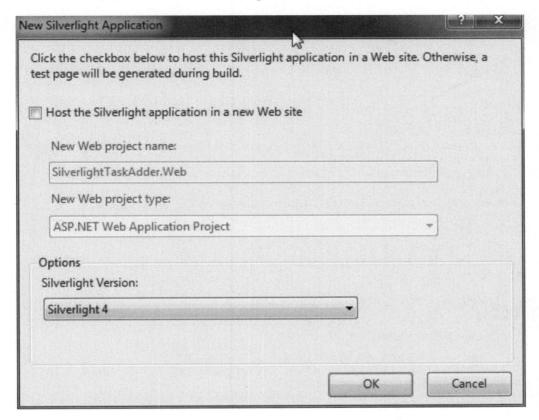

Figure 5–17. *Silverlight Application hosting dialog*

At this point, your application should look like Figure 5–18 in Solution Explorer. If at any time you get lost in following the coding examples in this chapter, you can find the completed project examples in the download section for the book at Apress.

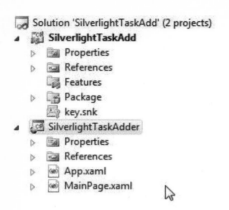

Figure 5–18. *SilverlightTaskAdd Solution*

Add a reference to `System.Windows.Controls.Data.Input`, as well as the `Microsoft.SharePoint.Client.Silverlight` and `Microsoft.SharePoint.Client.Silverlight.Runtime` libraries in the Silverlight project. You can find the two SharePoint Silverlight libraries in the following directory:

```
C:\Program Files\Common Files\Microsoft Shared\Web Server Extensions\14\TEMPLATE\LAYOUTS\
ClientBin
```

Adding Code

Add the following code to your Silverlight `MainPage.xaml` file:

```xml
<UserControl x:Class="SilverlightTaskAdder.MainPage"
    xmlns="http://schemas.microsoft.com/winfx/2006/xaml/presentation"
    xmlns:x="http://schemas.microsoft.com/winfx/2006/xaml"
    xmlns:d="http://schemas.microsoft.com/expression/blend/2008"
    xmlns:mc="http://schemas.openxmlformats.org/markup-compatibility/2006"
    mc:Ignorable="d"
    d:DesignHeight="403"
    xmlns:dataInput="clr-namespace:System.Windows.Controls;
                assembly=System.Windows.Controls.Data.Input"
    xmlns:controls="clr-namespace:System.Windows.Controls;
                assembly=System.Windows.Controls"
    Width="858">
    <Grid x:Name="LayoutRoot" Height="292" Width="325">
    <dataInput:Label Height="21" HorizontalAlignment="Left"
        Margin="25,19,0,0" Name="label1" VerticalAlignment="Top" Width="111"
        Content="Task:">
    </dataInput:Label>
        <TextBox Height="23" HorizontalAlignment="Left"
            Margin="108,17,0,0" Name="txtTask" VerticalAlignment="Top"
            Width="191" Background="{x:Null}" Foreground="Black"></TextBox>
        <controls:Calendar HorizontalAlignment="Left" Margin="46,75,0,0"
```

```
            Name="calendar1" VerticalAlignment="Top" Background="{x:Null}"
            Width="185">
        </controls:Calendar>
        <Button Content="Add Task" Height="23" HorizontalAlignment="Left"
            Margin="46,248,0,0" Name="button1" VerticalAlignment="Top"
            Width="75" Click="button1_Click" Background="Black"/>
        <dataInput:Label Height="13" HorizontalAlignment="Left"
            Margin="46,273,0,0" Name="label2" VerticalAlignment="Top"
            Width="230" FontSize="10" Background="{x:Null}" />
        <dataInput:Label Height="20" HorizontalAlignment="Left"
            Margin="26,44,0,0" Name="label3" VerticalAlignment="Top"
            Width="75" Content="Description:" />
        <TextBox Background="{x:Null}" Foreground="Black" Height="38"
            HorizontalAlignment="Left" Margin="109,45,0,0"
            Name="txtDescription" VerticalAlignment="Top" Width="191" />
        <Grid.Background>
            <LinearGradientBrush EndPoint="0.5,1" StartPoint="0.5,0">
                <GradientStop Color="#1E009100" Offset="0" />
                <GradientStop Color="#FF0023E1" Offset="0.893" />
            </LinearGradientBrush>
        </Grid.Background>
    </Grid>
</UserControl>
```

This code basically renders in Silverlight the same labels, text boxes, calendar control, and button controls that we have used in the previous web part development examples. As always, you can load the working solution from the code download section to save time.

■ **Note** Building the components of the `SilverlightTaskAdder` project first outside of the SharePoint project environment and then adding them to the project is also an effective way to develop Silverlight projects. This way, you can modify the UI elements and any animation and graphic elements you want to add, and test them in a hosting web application before migrating them over to a SharePoint project. Also, using Expression Blend as a tool to help with Silverlight UI can save time, as Expression Blend is specifically designed to do front-end UI Silverlight development. Figure 5–19 shows the Silverlight Task Adder project loaded in a host web project in Expression Blend 4.

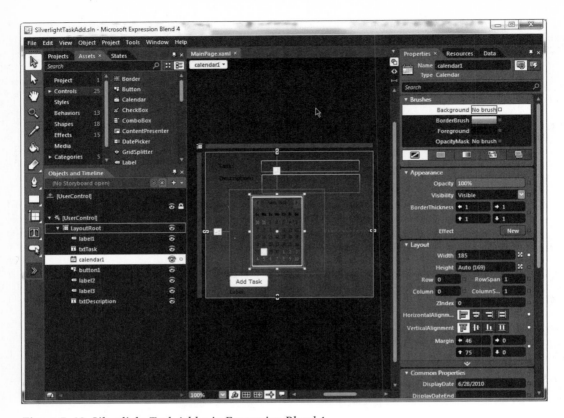

Figure 5–19. *Silverlight Task Adder in Expression Blend 4*

In the code-behind file for your `MainPage.xaml`—`MainPage.xaml.cs`, add a using `Microsoft.SharePoint.Client` statement to the top of your page, then add the following event for the button click:

```
private void button1_Click(object sender, RoutedEventArgs e)
{
    ClientContext context = new
      ClientContext(ApplicationContext.Current.Url);
    List taskList = context.Web.Lists.GetByTitle("Tasks");
    ListItemCreationInformation itemCreateInfo = new
      ListItemCreationInformation();
    ListItem newItem = taskList.AddItem(itemCreateInfo);
    newItem["Title"] = txtTask.Text;
    newItem["Description"] = txtDescription.Text;
    newItem["DueDate"] =
      calendar1.SelectedDate.Value.ToShortDateString();
    newItem.Update();
    context.ExecuteQueryAsync(ClientRequestSucceeded,
      ClientRequestFailed);
}
```

In working with Silverlight applications, there is a specific Silverlight runtime that SharePoint 2010 exposes. This runtime uses a `ClientContext` such as you can see in the preceding click event. This `ClientContext`, unlike some of the SharePoint object model contexts, does not suffer from the same `Dispose` issues the server side model does. Also, rather than directly invoking the change on the server side, with Silverlight `ExecuteQueryAsync()` is the method that sends the request to the SharePoint 2010 farm. Then there are events necessary to handle the success and failure returns from this asynchronous event. Notice that an advantage of asynchronous calling is that your Silverlight client is free to do other things while waiting for the result as opposed to being bound directly to the call.

Next, add code for the `ClientRequestSucceeded` and `ClientRequestFailed` events:

```
private void ClientRequestSucceeded(object sender,
    ClientRequestSucceededEventArgs args)
{
    Dispatcher.BeginInvoke(() =>
    {
        label2.Content = String.Format("Task '{0}' added for you!",
            txtTask.Text);
        txtTask.Text = "";
        txtDescription.Text = "";
    });
}

private void ClientRequestFailed(object sender,
    ClientRequestFailedEventArgs args)
{
    Dispatcher.BeginInvoke(() =>
    {
        MessageBox.Show("Connection failed. Error code: "
                + args.ErrorCode.ToString() + ". Message: "
                + args.Message);
    });
}
```

The `Dispatcher.BeginInvoke` statement in the previous two functions uses threading to specifically execute the delegate defined in the containing brackets referred to by the lambda expression =>.

Deploying the Silverlight Web Part

At this point, the Silverlight project is ready to be deployed to the SharePoint environment. To do this, we will add a Module to the SharePoint project. Select the SilverlightTaskAdd project in the Solution Explorer window of Visual Studio 2010. Select Project Adding Code Add New Item, and select the Module template in the SharePoint 2010 template section, as shown in Figure 5–20.

Figure 5–20. *Add Module*

The module itself adds a Feature to the SharePoint project, as well as adds a `Sample.txt` file inside it with a reference to that file in the `Elements.xml` file. This looks like Figure 5–21.

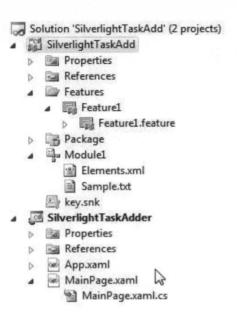

Figure 5–21. SilverlightTaskAdd Solution with Module

To deploy the Silverlight application to SharePoint, we are going to have to take a couple extra steps. SharePoint 2010 has a Silverlight Web Part available, which is basically a wrapper around the Silverlight-compiled content that is deployed in a .xap file. So we need to take the extra step of compiling the Silverlight application to a .xap file, and adding the .xap file to the Module for deployment.

    1.   Start by building the entire solution, then remove the Sample.txt file.

After this, add the Silverlight .xap file in by right-clicking on the Module element, Add➤Existing Item, then navigate to the Silverlight Task Adder's bin/debug directory and select SilverightTaskAdder.xap.

■ **Note** For Silverlight web parts, although it is a little inconvenient, when the Silverlight application changes, you will need to re-add the Silverlight .xap file back to the module, as it has copied the .xap file from the /bin directory location to the Module1 directory.

---

    2.   Next, we need to modify the Elements.xml file to reference the SilverlightTaskAdder.xap file. Part of this was done automatically when we added the .xap file to the Module. For the second part, add a URL attribute to the Module element as follows:

```
<Module Name="Module1" Url="Apps">
```

3. Now we are ready to deploy our Silverlight Web Part to our farm. Go ahead and press F5 to deploy the web part.

4. Once you deploy the web part, it is still going to take a little configuration to load it. Go to the test page on which you want to place the web part, , edit the page, select the Media and Content categories, then under this, select the Silverlight Web Part, as shown in Figure 5–22.

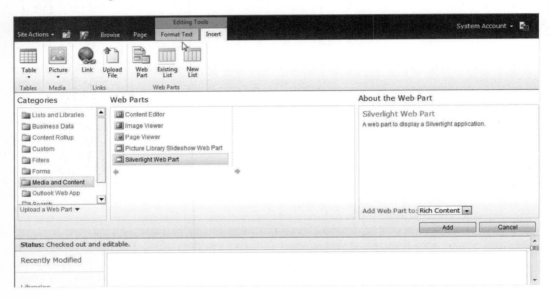

Figure 5–22. *Adding a Silverlight Web Part to a page*

5. The next screen will involve configuring access to the web part. It is shown in Figure 5–23. To configure the path to your web part, the URL starts with your site collection address—for instance, in my farm it is /sites/davehome. Taking this into account, we add the path to the .xap file-/sites/davehome/Apps/Module1/SilverlightTaskAdder.xap. Substitute the path to your environment.

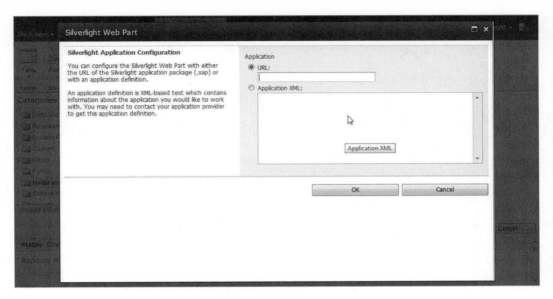

Figure 5–23. *Configure Silverlight Web Part*

6. Clicking OK finalizes the configuration, and you will see the Silverlight Web Part instantiated in edit mode on the page.

7. Save the page, and the web part will function as expected. You can see the instantiated web part in Figure 5–24.

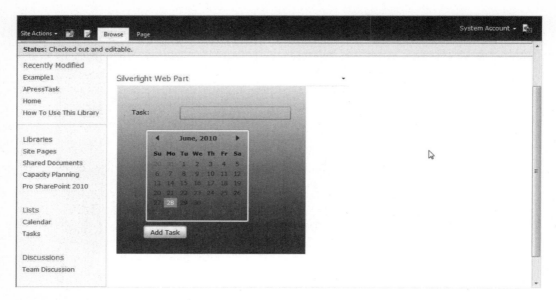

Figure 5–24. *Instantiated Silverlight Web Part*

The Silverlight Web Part functions in adding a task to the Tasks list as well as executes within its framework of seamless UI movement. There are no postbacks to the server for this web part to work.

Now that we are wrapping up the Silverlight approach to web-part development, I wanted to highlight a few more things that Silverlight can do. As a result, I included in the code samples a fun little Silverlight Snow application, which is a Silverlight Web Part that you can deploy to your SharePoint 2010 Farm in a similar fashion to the one we deployed already. There are two project directories, SilverlightSnow1, which is the Silverlight animation application and web container, and the SilverlightSnowWebPart, which is the SharePoint project for deploying the web part. Enjoy a little bit of what you can do with Silverlight animation in SharePoint 2010!

Accessing External Database Content in a Web Part

For our next effort in web-part development, we will delve into connecting a web part to an external SQL Server database using .NET. While there certainly is a built-in way to do this with the Business Connectivity Solutions (BCS) feature, it is also valuable to be able to connect to outside sources for external data as well. We will cover BCS in a later chapter.

There are many approaches to being able to access external data, and many of them do not involve databases. For example, it is possible to connect to the Twitter API directly and display data from there. It is also possible to obtain data from an external web service, either directly in .NET code, via AJAX calls, or via Silverlight. It is possible to connect to Windows Azure for cloud data.

However, one of the core concepts we are investigating in this book is the ability to blend ASP.NET and SharePoint 2010 development. This concept includes the ability to utilize existing ASP.NET applications and code and wrap SharePoint 2010 features around it. For this reason, we will look into connecting directly to a SQL Server database to obtain data directly and display it.

■ **Note** The database that is used in this example is SQL Server 2008 R2, and the specific databases are the `AdventureWorks` 2008R2 RTM databases. We will use tables from the `AdventureWorksLT2008R2` database. These sample databases are available at Codeplex at `http://msftdbprodsamples.codeplex.com/` for download and installation.

To begin this project, let's use a Visual Web Part template shown in Figure 5–25.

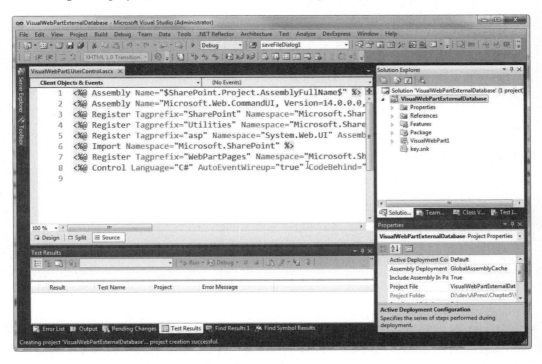

Figure 5–25. VisualWebPartExternalDatabase project

Add a DropDownList, a Label, and a GridView to the `VisualWebPart1UserControl.ascx` file from the toolbox—it should look like the following:

```
Sales Order:  <asp:DropDownList ID="ddSalesOrder"
OnSelectedIndexChanged="ddSalesOrder_SelectedIndexChanged" AutoPostBack="True" runat="server"
>
</asp:DropDownList>
<asp:GridView ID="gvSalesOrderDetail" runat="server">
</asp:GridView>
<asp:Label ID="lblErrorMessage" runat="server"></asp:Label>
```

To continue on with our example, what we will build in this project is a drop-down list that contains the Sales Order numbers from the AdventureWorksLT SalesOrderHeader table. Selecting a value from the drop-down list will populate a GridView control with the details of the Sales Order from the SalesOrderDetail table.

First, add the following code to the code-behind file VisualWebPartUserControl.ascx.cs:

```
public string connectionString;

protected void Page_Load(object sender, EventArgs e)
{
  connectionString = GetConnectionString1();
  //connectionString = GetConnectionString2();
  //connectionString = GetConnectionString3();

  if (!Page.IsPostBack)
  {

    string queryString = "SELECT SalesOrderId, SalesOrderNumber FROM
      [AdventureWorksLT2008R2].[SalesLT].[SalesOrderHeader]";

    using (SqlConnection connection = new SqlConnection(connectionString))
    {
      using (SqlDataAdapter sdaSO = new SqlDataAdapter(queryString,
          connection))
      {
        try
        {
          DataTable dtSO = new DataTable();
          sdaSO.Fill(dtSO);
          ddSalesOrder.DataSource = dtSO;
          ddSalesOrder.DataTextField = "SalesOrderNumber";
          ddSalesOrder.DataValueField = "SalesOrderId";
          ddSalesOrder.DataBind();
        }
        catch (Exception ex)
        {
          lblErrorMessage.Text = "Error retrieving data " + ex.Message;
        }
      }
    }
  }
}
```

This code obtains a connection string from a function we will write momentarily called GetConnectionString1(), and uses standard ADO.NET SqlData objects to execute the included query, return data from the database, and bind the data to the SalesOrder drop-down list that we defined in our user control. Also, we create an event handler for the SelectedIndexChanged event of the drop-down list so that we can use that to retrieve Sales Order Detail information. Most of this code will look very familiar to you if you are coming from an ASP.NET development background.

Also, before compiling, add the following using statements to the top of the file:

```
using System;
using System.Data;
using System.Web.UI;
using System.Linq;
```

```
using System.Xml.Linq;
using System.Data.SqlClient;
using Microsoft.SharePoint;
```

Next we want to add a method for ddSalesOrderSelectedIndexChanged, as follows:

```
public void ddSalesOrder_SelectedIndexChanged(object sender, EventArgs e)
{
    string queryString = "SELECT * FROM
[AdventureWorksLT2008R2].[SalesLT].[SalesOrderDetail] WHERE SalesOrderId = " +
ddSalesOrder.SelectedValue.ToString();

using (SqlConnection connection = new SqlConnection(connectionString))
{
    using (SqlDataAdapter sdaSO = new SqlDataAdapter(queryString, connection))
    {
        try
        {
            DataTable dtSO = new DataTable();
            sdaSO.Fill(dtSO);
            gvSalesOrderDetail.DataSource = dtSO;
            gvSalesOrderDetail.DataBind();
        }
        catch (Exception ex)
        {
            lblErrorMessage.Text = "Error retrieving data " + ex.Message;
        }
    }
}
}
```

This code, in a fashion similar to the Page_Load code, retrieves data from the SalesOrderDetail table in AdventureWorks and loads it into a GridView. This method will be called automatically when the selection of the drop-down list changes.

Up to this point, the code is complete as far as being able to load information onto a page through a web part. The main thing missing is that we do not have any connection string information to be able to connect to this database.

Next, we need to add an external database connection to the project. Normally in an ASP.NET project, we would simply add the connection string to the ASP.NET application's web.config file to accomplish this. While this is possible in SharePoint 2010 by modifying the web.config file found in the SharePoint Application directory, this is not a recommended approach, as changes will not remain through service pack updates and changes in Web Application deployment.

There are a few ways to accomplish storing database connection information in the project. They include:

- Using a hidden list to store configuration information.

- Adding a custom XML file to the feature that contains connection string information. This file can be modified and updated with no risk to the SharePoint environment.

- Using a class in the Microsoft.SharePoint.Administration namespace named SPWebConfigModification. This can be used to add connection strings programmatically to the SharePoint Web Application web.config file through a feature receiver.

We will show examples of doing all three of these approaches. Some of the tradeoffs that exist with each of these approaches include the fact that modifications using SPWebConfigModification have the potential to corrupt the web.config file at times when retracting a feature. Adding a custom XML file can work for relatively static database connections, and can offer the ability to redeploy for new information. However, changes to this file will need to either be re-deployed by way of a solution package, or manually changed on the production server. Using a hidden list offers the ability to add more settings later and is also a viable option. You can change settings without touching the production server.

In our first example, we will store the connection string in an XML file along with the feature. Since this approach deploys the setting of the connection string along with the feature, any changes to the connection string will have to be repackaged with the feature.

Storing the Connection String in an XML File

Next, we will code the first example method for obtaining a connection string. We need to take a few other steps to make this viable as well. Add a file to the VisualWebPart called ConnectionStrings.xml, and populate it with the following information:

```
<?xml version="1.0" encoding="utf-8" ?>
<connectionStrings>
  <add name="AdventureWorks"
      connectionString="data source=MYSERVER;Integrated Security=SSPI;Initial
Catalog=AdventureWorksLT2008R2"
      providerName="System.Data.SqlClient" />
</connectionStrings>
```

Next, we need to change one of the attributes on this ConnectionStrings.xml file, as shown in Figure 5–26.

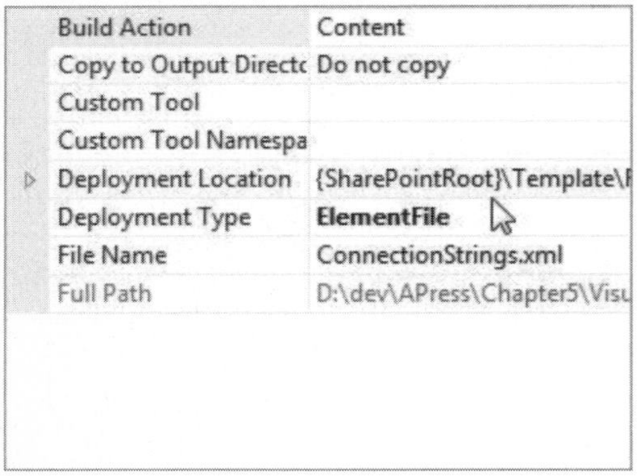

Build Action	Content
Copy to Output Directc	Do not copy
Custom Tool	
Custom Tool Namespa	
Deployment Location	{SharePointRoot}\Template\F
Deployment Type	**ElementFile**
File Name	ConnectionStrings.xml
Full Path	D:\dev\APress\Chapter5\Visu

Figure 5–26. Deployment Type attribute

We need to change the Deployment Type attribute on the ConnectionStrings.xml file from "No Deployment" to "ElementFile". You will notice that changing this value automatically changes the Deployment Location of the file as well. What this will do is cause this XML file to be deployed to the Feature root of the feature we are deploying. This is located at:

```
C:\Program Files\Common Files\Microsoft Shared\Web Server Extensions\14\TEMPLATE\
FEATURES\VisualWebPartExternalDatabase_Feature1
```

Next, we will add code to the GetConnectionString1() function to retrieve the connection string value from the ConnectionStrings.xml file:

```
private static string GetConnectionString1()
{
    string featureDir = @"C:\Program Files\Common Files\Microsoft Shared\Web
        Server Extensions\14\TEMPLATE\FEATURES\
        VisualWebPartExternalDatabase_Feature1\VisualWebPart1\";

    XElement xEl = XElement.Load(featureDir + "ConnectionStrings.xml");
    XElement xElConnection = (from x in xEl.Elements("add")
                    where (string)x.Attribute("name") == "AdventureWorks"
                    select x).First();
    return xElConnection.Attribute("connectionString").Value;
}
```

This function is relatively simple, and uses LINQ to XML to load the ConnectionStrings.xml file from the feature directory it is deployed to, extracts the connection string information, and returns it.

■ **Note** The connection strings stored in ConnectionStrings.xml are exactly in the same format that they would be found in a web.config file of an ASP.NET application. This makes it convenient to copy and paste connection strings from your .NET application into your SharePoint 2010 web part.

At this point, you can go ahead and deploy this web part and confirm that it works.

Storing the Connection String in a Hidden List

The next option we will cover for database connectivity is another simple one. We will store the connection string in a hidden list that the majority of the users who have access to the SharePoint 2010 site will not be able to see. This is a good option for storing artifacts for working with within SharePoint simply because a SharePoint list can be updated realtime with no interaction with deploying code.

1. First, we'll create the list for Connection Strings—navigate to Site Settings ➤ Lists to get to your list management page, as shown in Figure 5–27.

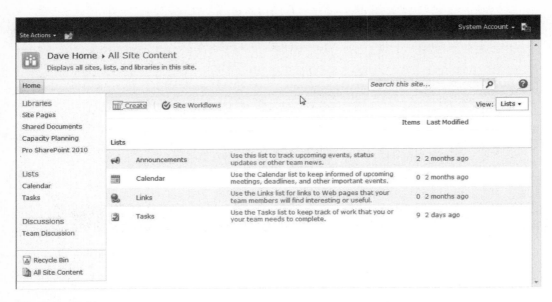

Figure 5–27. *Lists*

2. From here, create a list, and select the Custom List template. Name the list "Connection Strings" and select the option to not display the list on the Quick Launch, as shown in Figure 5–28.

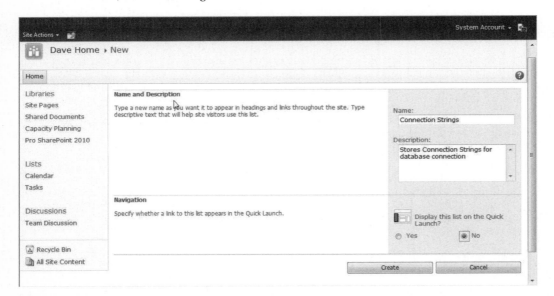

Figure 5–28. *Create a custom list*

3. The Custom List template instantiates a list that has only one column on it, named "Title" that is visible. There are two others—Created By and Modified By—that don't show up on the standard view. This is fine, but we also need to add another column to the list, named "ConnectionString". We can add a column by selecting List Settings on the far right of the navigation Ribbon. This brings you to the standard Edit page for lists. You can add a column here under the Columns section: select Create Column, select the radio button for Single line of text as the type of information, leave the maximum number of characters at 255, and select adding it to the default view.

4. Now we have a custom list for storing connection strings. Go ahead and add a new item to the list, with a title of "AdventureWorks", and a ConnectionString of the value you need to use. You should end up with an entry and list that looks like Figure 5–29.

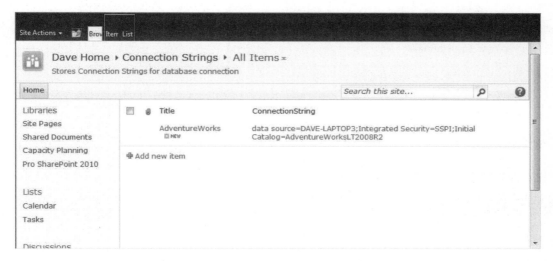

***Figure 5–29.** Connection string stored in the Connection Strings list*

Now that we have the connection string stored in our SharePoint site, we can go back and add code for the GetConnectionString2() function to access it.

Add the following function to your VisualWebPart1UserControl.ascx.cs file:

```
private string GetConnectionString2()
{
    SPList csList = SPContext.Current.Web.Lists["Connection Strings"];
    SPQuery query = new SPQuery();
    query.Query = "<Where><Eq><FieldRef Name='Title'/>
     <Value Type='Text'>AdventureWorks</Value></Eq></Where>";
    SPListItemCollection csItems = csList.GetItems(query);
    if (csItems.Count == 1)
       return csItems[0]["ConnectionString"].ToString();
    else
       return string.Empty;
}
```

In this function, we are using the SharePoint Object Model on the server side to obtain a reference to the Connection Strings list that we created to store the database connection string. Then, we are building a CAML query to access the list, and returning the value.

This portion of accessing data through a data connection is now ready to be deployed and tested.

CAML

CAML is an underlying XML language that is used in SharePoint throughout the product. You can query a list either directly through CAML as we have done in the previous example, or by using LINQ to SharePoint, which is a new feature in SharePoint 2010. We will cover a LINQ to SharePoint example later in the book. For more information about CAML, here are some other resources—the first two links had not at the time of the book writing been updated for Office 12 but are still accurate for Office 12/SharePoint 2010:

- http://msdn.microsoft.com/en-us/library/dd588106(office.11).aspx— How To Use CAML

- http://msdn.microsoft.com/en-us/library/dd588092(office.11).aspx— Introduction—What Is CAML

- http://msdn.microsoft.com/en-us/library/ms467521.aspx—Query Schema

Storing the Connection String in the web.config File

In our final example of how to connect directly to external data from within SharePoint 2010, the actual code itself will be almost identical to the way that we access connection strings from within an ASP.NET application. However, the main difference will be that we need to be able to get a connection string added to the SharePoint Web Application's web.config file.

Before we continue down this path, it is important for you to know that since SharePoint 2010 is really nothing more than an ASP.NET application with features added in, it certainly is possible to modify the web.config file in your virtual directory and add a connectionStrings element to it directly. This file is found at:

C:\inetpub\wwwroot\wss\VirtualDirectories\80

Or, instead of 80, use whatever port you set it to be when you initialed the Web Application at runtime.

The web.config file there is no different in how it interacts with the .NET Framework and IIS than any other web.config file, as we've seen in a previous chapter. In fact, if you examine the directory, you will see that SharePoint internally makes a backup of this file during different events, such as installing a farm feature. Figure 5–30 shows this.

Name	Date modified
_app_bin	4/27/2010 5:32
_vti_pvt	4/27/2010 5:32
App_Browsers	4/27/2010 5:32
App_GlobalResources	4/27/2010 5:32
aspnet_client	4/27/2010 5:32
bin	4/27/2010 5:32
wpresources	4/27/2010 5:32
clientaccesspolicy	5/6/2010 11:40
crossdomain	5/6/2010 11:31
global	4/27/2010 5:32
web.bak	5/6/2010 3:51 F
web	6/29/2010 11:4
web_2010_06_26_23_47_43.bak	6/26/2010 9:37
web_2010_06_27_01_54_43.bak	6/26/2010 11:4
web_2010_06_27_01_55_48.bak	6/27/2010 1:54
web_2010_06_27_01_56_07.bak	6/27/2010 1:55

Figure 5–30. *WSS Virtual Directory with web.config file and backups*

Now as a best practice, Microsoft does not recommended you edit the web.config file for a SharePoint installation directly, and the bulk of most knowledgeable IT professionals that are adept at maintaining a SharePoint farm will also discourage this practice. For the most part, I agree with these best practices. However, we will introduce a scenario later in the book in High Touch Point Solutions that can be an exception to this.

For the purposes of this book, instead of just stating "it's not a best practice" and moving on, I am going to highlight the reasons why it is not a best practice. The main reason for this has to do with Microsoft's released service pack updates and future products. If you have made changes directly to a SharePoint site web.config file, and install a SP1 or SP2, there exists the distinct possibility that the product update will contain new elements to add to these web.config files, and will overwrite your custom changes with a new file. The other risk that exists with modifying the files directly is simply how integral web.config is to the operation of any ASP.NET application, which includes a SharePoint Farm.

Now why am I taking the time to spell all of this out, you might ask? The reason is that the method I am going to show you next involves the more highly recommended way of interacting with SharePoint 2010's web.config file, and that is to utilize the SharePoint Administrative class SPWebConfigModification. This class will automate your changes to web.config, and if written properly to deploy in a feature, will better automate the changes to your web.config file.

While this approach is more highly recommended, and stated as a best practice, there is variance in mileage that people have experienced with it. As with anything else, this decision is a tradeoff between preserving a farm and automating changes and the amount of effort it takes to do it in this fashion. There are some anecdotes that exist in the SharePoint community of people corrupting their web.config files by programmatically accessing them instead of directly editing them.

You may very well find that in a particular circumstance, rather than having developers code feature event receivers like we will that update web.config, you would rather centralize that initiative all in one place, and have your primary SharePoint 2010 server administrators handle this piece.

■ **Note** Feature event receivers are classes that provide hooks into your SharePoint 2010 farm on events that are associated with the administration of features. Available events include feature activation, deactivation, installation, uninstallation, and upgrade. These hooks are valuable to manage aspects of your feature that have to do with its impact on your SharePoint farm.

If they are not developers, it may be more efficient to have them handle providing connection strings and other modifications in web.config directly by editing them. Source control for change management of these files is always an option so that service pack applications and individual edits may be merged together. Just be aware that if you decide to take this approach, take the time to back things up, use proper source control, and do it in a fashion that allows for SharePoint environment or server downtime in case you make a mistake.

With either approach that you take, it is always a good thing to understand the elements of the web.config file in your SharePoint applications. This is of course why we took a chapter to highlight some of that earlier in the book. The risk in either case is something to manage just as any other risk in your organization, and there is no foolproof way of doing this that does not require attention to detail and change control practices.

Now, on to the feature event receiver. Right-click the Feature1 node in your Visual Studio 2010 Solution Explorer and select Add Event Receiver. This adds two files, one of which is the Feature1.EventReceiver.cs file.

In the Feature1.EventReceiver.cs file, add the following function:

```
public override void FeatureInstalled(SPFeatureReceiverProperties properties)
{
    SPWebApplication webApp = new
        SPSite("http://dave-laptop3:100/sites/davehome").WebApplication;
    SPWebConfigModification mod = new
        SPWebConfigModification("connectionStrings", "configuration");
    mod.Owner = "VWPAdventureWorks";
    mod.Sequence = 0;
    mod.Type = SPWebConfigModification.SPWebConfigModificationType.EnsureSection;

    webApp.WebConfigModifications.Add(mod);
    SPWebConfigModification mod1 = new
      SPWebConfigModification("add", "configuration/connectionStrings");
    mod1.Owner = "VWPAdventureWorks";
    mod1.Sequence = 0;
    mod1.Type = SPWebConfigModification.SPWebConfigModificationType.EnsureChildNode;
mod1.Value = "<add name=\"AdventureWorks\" connectionString=\"data source=DAVE-
LAPTOP3;Integrated Security=SSPI;Initial Catalog=AdventureWorksLT2008R2\"
providerName=\"System.Data.SqlClient\" />";

    webApp.WebConfigModifications.Add(mod1);
    webApp.Farm.Services.GetValue<SPWebService>().ApplyWebConfigModifications();
        webApp.Update();
}
```

This code implements the changes necessary to the web.config file on this web application. A few things to notice here include that we are using a specific owner to this particular feature, so we can identify these changes upon feature uninstall and roll them back. Also, the other thing to be aware of is that the standard out-of-the-box SharePoint 2010 installation does not include the connectionStrings element of the web.config file. As a result of this, rather than being able to accomplish this minimally in one step, we need two steps for the process. The first step involves actually adding the connectionStrings section to the web.config file. Second, we must add the specific AdventureWorks connection string that we've used in previous projects here.

The last step is to ensure that upon feature deactivation, these changes will be rolled back.

Add the following code to instantiate the Feature_Uninstalling event:

```
public override void FeatureUninstalling(SPFeatureReceiverProperties properties)
{
    SPWebApplication webApp = new
      SPSite("http://dave-laptop3/sites/davehome").WebApplication;
    Collection<SPWebConfigModification> collection =
        webApp.WebConfigModifications;

    int iStartCount = collection.Count;

    for (int c = iStartCount - 1; c >= 0; c--)
    {
        SPWebConfigModification configMod = collection[c];

        if (configMod.Owner == "VWPAdventureWorks")
            collection.Remove(configMod);
    }

    if (iStartCount > collection.Count)
    {
                webApp.Farm.Services.GetValue<SPWebService>().ApplyWebConfigModifications();
        webApp.Update();
    }

}
```

The code in the uninstall activation hook attempts to use the Owner ID of what was deployed previously and remove the modifications, then update.

■ **Note** The code that is included in the FeatureUninstalling example here is very heavily based upon a blog post by Vincent Rothwell. You can see the original code and approach in his blog post on the SharePoint 2007 product at http://blog.thekid.me.uk/archive/2007/03/20/removing-web-config-entries-from-sharepoint-using-spwebconfigmodification.aspx. The features in SharePoint 2010 have not changed with respect to the SPWebConfigurationModification codebase.

This code will execute not when the web part itself executes, but will execute upon the installation and de-installation of this feature.

Finally, for the third option, we need to write the code for GetConnectionString3(), which is a one-line statement of code as follows:

```
private string GetConnectionString3()
{
    return ConfigurationManager.ConnectionStrings["AdventureWorks"].ConnectionString;
}
```

As is readily apparent, the code to access the connection string here is virtually identical to code that will do this in an ASP.NET application. The only difference is the programmatic approach to adding the connection string to the web application's `web.config` file.

Web Parts Summary

The topic of web parts is a very large topic, encompassing such a great breadth of technology and applications that it would be virtually impossible to give complete coverage to each and every different kind of web part. In this approach, as this book is related to blending ASP.NET and SharePoint 2010, we presented three different options from a code perspective of being able to access external data outside the SharePoint 2010 farm from within web parts. By no means does this exhaust the possibilities of how to access data outside of SharePoint. The rapid growth of connected systems are starting to become more and more prevalent and SharePoint 2010 can consume data from a wide variety of resources, including not only SQL Server, but other databases, web services, and cloud services such as Azure.

Also within this section, we endeavored to expose you to a number of different key coding practices that will come up within SharePoint development, and familiarize you with interacting with the SharePoint Object Model as well as other best practices.

Speaking personally with my journey in SharePoint, I would have really appreciated some examples like this early on for clear direction on how to connect SharePoint with external systems. To me, there has been plenty of coverage of Business Connectivity Services (BCS), or in previous versions of SharePoint BDC as the primary way to connect SharePoint with external Line of Business (LOB) systems, but BCS has some limits as well, which we will cover in our chapter on BCS. There is far less material available on topics like this, connecting a web part, an application page, or another SharePoint construct to external data.

Master Pages

In this chapter, we will also introduce the topic of master pages as related to SharePoint 2010 and blended solutions. This section of the chapter will serve as a simple introduction as opposed to a more thorough development of coding concepts like the web parts section represents. Then, in later chapters on branding and our blended-solution–focused chapters, master pages will come into focus again and we will focus on specific aspects of them in more detail.

Master pages in SharePoint 2010 are actually the same as the master pages in ASP.NET as far as the base page architecture and functionality. SharePoint master pages allow you to create a consistent surrounding layout for your sites by consolidating common elements all in one place. These elements normally include UI elements that provide the look and feel of a web site as well as some of the major navigation elements on a web site. The primary place that you will run into SharePoint 2010 master pages in developing solutions for SharePoint and ASP.NET blended solutions will be in branding SharePoint sites for a specific appearance and layout. We will cover this in detail later on in the branding chapter of our book and include tools for working with master page layouts, testing and deploying them, as well as example code for deploying a branding solution as a feature.

Master pages are defined by the extension .master, and can include static text, HTML elements, server controls, and JavaScript. They interact with .aspx .NET Web Form pages or application pages in SharePoint by exposing ContentPlaceHolder controls that are declared inline in the master page. The .aspx content pages fill the ContentPlaceHolder controls with page-level content.

Understanding Where Master Pages are Used

Master pages are used in every page in SharePoint 2010 in one fashion or another. You can find the master pages that are deployed with SharePoint 2010 in the `C:\Program Files\Common Files\Microsoft Shared\Web Server Extensions\14\TEMPLATE\LAYOUTS` directory directly. They are installed to the SharePoint root there. Figure 5–31 shows the 13 master pages deployed with SharePoint 2010.

Name	Date modified	Type
GetSpotlight	3/16/2010 3:20 AM	ASP.NET Generic Handler
ScriptResx	11/3/2009 9:20 PM	ASP.NET Generic Handler
WsaUpload	11/3/2009 9:20 PM	ASP.NET Generic Handler
application	11/3/2009 9:18 PM	ASP.NET Master Page
applicationv4	3/26/2010 9:25 PM	ASP.NET Master Page
default	3/26/2010 9:26 PM	ASP.NET Master Page
dialog	3/26/2010 9:25 PM	ASP.NET Master Page
layouts	11/3/2009 9:18 PM	ASP.NET Master Page
layoutsv3	11/3/2009 9:21 PM	ASP.NET Master Page
minimal	3/26/2010 9:26 PM	ASP.NET Master Page
pickerdialog	11/3/2009 9:18 PM	ASP.NET Master Page
RteDialog	11/3/2009 9:18 PM	ASP.NET Master Page
simple	11/3/2009 9:18 PM	ASP.NET Master Page
simplev4	3/26/2010 9:25 PM	ASP.NET Master Page
sspadmin	3/12/2010 9:55 PM	ASP.NET Master Page
v4	3/26/2010 9:26 PM	ASP.NET Master Page
AccessDenied	11/3/2009 9:18 PM	ASP.NET Server Page

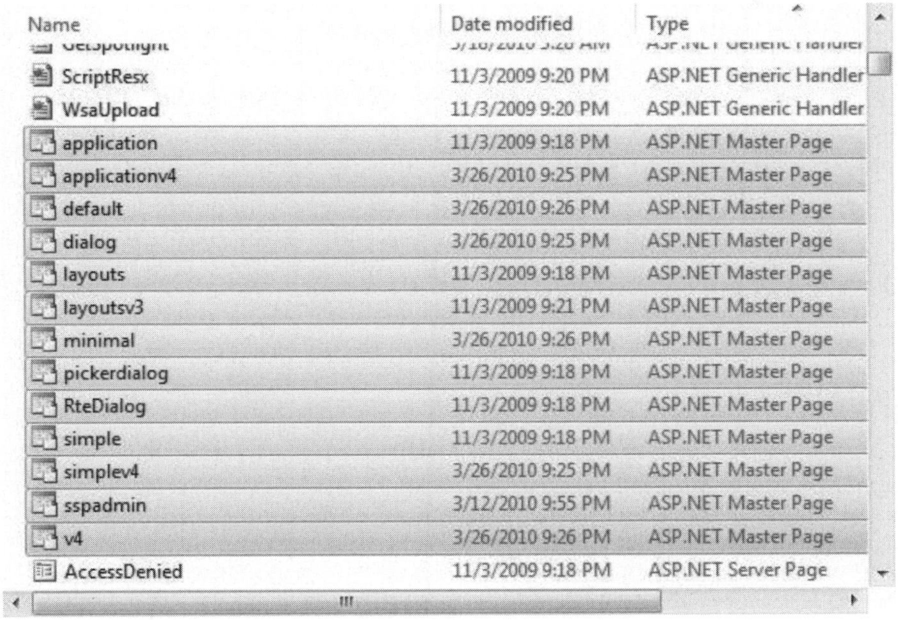

***Figure 5–31.** SharePoint 2010 master pages*

Of all of these master pages, two of them are utilized in many more locations than others. `V4.master` is the standard master page that is used in a SharePoint 2010 default installation. It has all of the UI elements in a version 4 level page that includes the new ribbon in SharePoint 2010 as well as support for the modal dialogue interface. `default.master` is the v3-compatible master page that is used for SharePoint 2007 upgrades to SharePoint 2010. If the installation type you are working with is an upgrade, then the `default.master` page is the one that is activated.

One of the changes that is new with SharePoint 2010 with respect to master pages is that in SharePoint 2007, all of the application pages and content pages could be modified by branding using a newly developed master page, but all of the administrative pages and layouts directory pages would use the stock `application.master` page. In SharePoint 2010, there is a setting that you can modify in Central Administration per Web Application to allow the applications page to use the standard SharePoint 2010 master pages along with the rest of your web application. To modify this setting:

1. Go to Central Administration and select Application Management➤Manage web applications.

2. Then select the web application you wish to change the setting on this for, and click the General Settings button on the ribbon. This page is shown in Figure 5–32.

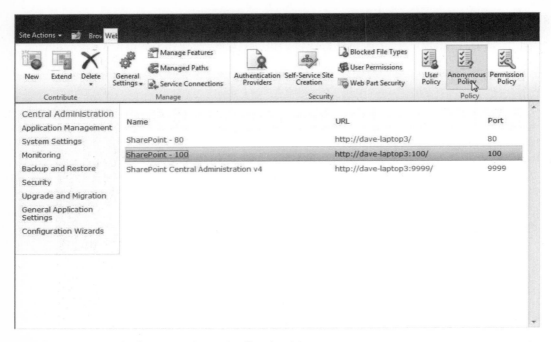

Figure 5–32. *Central Administration ➤ Application Management*

3. Click the General Settings menu selection on the General Settings ribbon control. This brings up a modal dialog box that includes setting items for the web site, such as Default Time Zone, Quota, Online Status for members, and others.

■ **Tip** There is a warning that pops up annoyingly for SharePoint public-facing sites that you can get rid of in these General Settings as well. The pop-up states "This website wants to run the following add-on: 'Name ActiveX Control' from Microsoft Corporation. If you trust the website and the add-on and want to allow it to run, click here…" This little pop-up is known in SharePoint circles as the "Name.dll ActiveX control", and sometimes referred to as a *nemesis*. This feature is used in conjunction with Online Status for people at sites to indicate their presence online. While it can be helpful in a corporate intranet environment using User Profile settings and My Sites, it usually doesn't really add anything to an online site other than annoyance. You can ensure this pop-up warning does not occur by modifying the Person Name Actions and Presence Settings setting here in this modal dialog and set it to No for the feature Enable additional actions and Online Status for members.

You can see the setting we are looking for related to master pages in Figure 5–33.

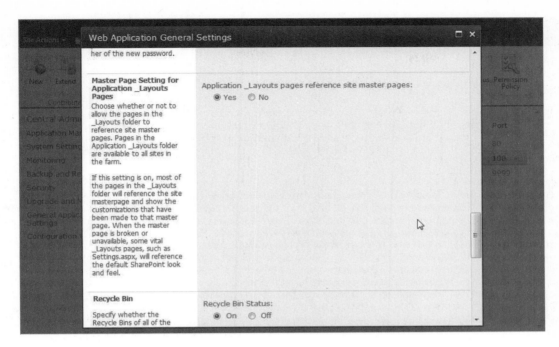

Figure 5–33. *Master page setting*

This setting is set to Yes by default, meaning that all application pages and _layouts directory pages (pages found in the `C:\Program Files\Common Files\Microsoft Shared\Web Server Extensions\14\TEMPLATE\LAYOUTS` directory) will use the `v4.master` page. If you do not want them to use this, select No. If set to no, the pages will use the applicationv4.master page instead.

V4.master

The `v4.master` page is an important one in SharePoint 2010 because not only is it new, but it supports several elements that represent new features in SharePoint 2010. One of these features is the new ribbon interface, which is the Microsoft Office 2010-looking ribbon that displays user actions in a more visual sense that you notice in SharePoint 2010. The other feature is that this new master page includes the ability to work with the new modal dialog framework, which shows dialog windows in the fashion seen in Figure 5–33. This modal dialog is still using `v4.master`, but using a *no chrome* feature included in `v4.master`. The standard display of `v4.master` shows *full chrome*.

■ **Tip** If you are not used to the term *chrome* when referring to SharePoint, it is kind of a product jargon term used to indicate all of the UI elements that surround the content of the page. So the chrome would be the ribbon, navigation, and all of the slick UI features that you see in SharePoint 2010. If you are coming from an ASP.NET development background, you may not be familiar with this term.

The minimal.master page is one that ships with the product that includes no chrome. Some people start off their branding and development of custom master pages with this. We will highlight more of these options in our chapter on Branding.

Master Page Content

The master page content in SharePoint 2010 includes specific directives, imports, and register tags to include core pieces of SharePoint 2010. As follows, we will examine the main v4.master page, which is the standard installation default master page used by the majority of the pages on a SharePoint site.

Let's take a look at the markup included in v4.master to get a feel for the elements in a SharePoint 2010 master page.

```
<%@Master language="C#"%>
<%@ Register Tagprefix="SharePoint" Namespace="Microsoft.SharePoint.WebControls"
Assembly="Microsoft.SharePoint, Version=14.0.0.0, Culture=neutral,
PublicKeyToken=71e9bce111e9429c" %> <%@ Register Tagprefix="Utilities"
Namespace="Microsoft.SharePoint.Utilities" Assembly="Microsoft.SharePoint, Version=14.0.0.0,
Culture=neutral, PublicKeyToken=71e9bce111e9429c" %> <%@ Import
Namespace="Microsoft.SharePoint" %> <%@ Assembly Name="Microsoft.Web.CommandUI,
Version=14.0.0.0, Culture=neutral, PublicKeyToken=71e9bce111e9429c" %>
<%@ Import Namespace="Microsoft.SharePoint.ApplicationPages" %>
<%@ Register Tagprefix="WebPartPages" Namespace="Microsoft.SharePoint.WebPartPages"
Assembly="Microsoft.SharePoint, Version=14.0.0.0, Culture=neutral,
PublicKeyToken=71e9bce111e9429c" %>
<%@ Register TagPrefix="wssuc" TagName="Welcome" src="~/_controltemplates/Welcome.ascx" %>
<%@ Register TagPrefix="wssuc" TagName="MUISelector"
src="~/_controltemplates/MUISelector.ascx" %>
<%@ Register TagPrefix="wssuc" TagName="DesignModeConsole"
src="~/_controltemplates/DesignModeConsole.ascx" %>
```

SharePoint 2010 master pages are deployed in the C# language, as is evident on the first line of the master page. The next Register tag includes the standard SharePoint assemblies Microsoft.SharePoint, Microsoft.SharePoint.Utilities, and Microsoft.Web.CommandUI so that they will be accessible for all SharePoint pages.

The next two lines import the Microsoft.SharePoint.ApplicationPages namespace for handling SharePoint application pages, and register a tag for WebPartPages for pages that allow inserting web parts.

The following three lines with the TagPrefix wssuc include User Controls that are found in the _controltemplates directory at C:\Program Files\Common Files\Microsoft Shared\Web Server Extensions\14\TEMPLATE\CONTROLTEMPLATES. These User controls handle the Welcome message, the MultiLanguage User Interface selector control for the MUI language feature, and a Design Mode Console for dealing with page design.

These lines comprise the .NET include portions of the master page.

Below these, the html and head sections of the page are found, as seen here:

```
<html lang="<%$Resources:wss,language_value%>"
dir="<%$Resources:wss,multipages_direction_dir_value%>" runat="server" xmlns:o="urn:schemas-
microsoft-com:office:office">
<head runat="server">
        <meta http-equiv="X-UA-Compatible" content="IE=8"/>
        <meta name="GENERATOR" content="Microsoft SharePoint"/>
        <meta name="progid" content="SharePoint.WebPartPage.Document"/>
        <meta http-equiv="Content-Type" content="text/html; charset=utf-8"/>
        <meta http-equiv="Expires" content="0"/>
```

```
        <SharePoint:RobotsMetaTag runat="server"/>
        <title id="onetidTitle"><asp:ContentPlaceHolder id="PlaceHolderPageTitle"
runat="server"/></title>
        <SharePoint:CssLink runat="server" Version="4"/>
        <SharePoint:Theme runat="server"/>
        <SharePoint:ULSClientConfig runat="server"/>
        <script type="text/javascript">
        var _fV4UI = true;
        </script>
        <SharePoint:ScriptLink language="javascript" name="core.js" OnDemand="true"
runat="server" />
        <SharePoint:CustomJSUrl runat="server" />
        <SharePoint:SoapDiscoveryLink runat="server" />
        <asp:ContentPlaceHolder id="PlaceHolderAdditionalPageHead" runat="server"/>
        <SharePoint:DelegateControl runat="server" ControlId="AdditionalPageHead"
AllowMultipleControls="true"/>
        <SharePoint:SPShortcutIcon runat="server" IconUrl="/_layouts/images/favicon.ico" />
        <asp:ContentPlaceHolder id="PlaceHolderBodyAreaClass" runat="server"/>
        <asp:ContentPlaceHolder id="PlaceHolderTitleAreaClass" runat="server"/>
        <SharePoint:SPPageManager runat="server" />
        <SharePoint:SPHelpPageComponent Visible="false" runat="server" />
</head>
```

As you can see in the components shown here, there are many links here for ContentPlaceHolders, meta tags for crawlers and robots, language elements that are loaded from an external resources file, and placeholders for CSS and JavaScript. Key components also exist for defining this as a "version 4" master page that supports all of the new and cool UI features in SharePoint 2010.

■ **Note** One other element that is quite interesting to show can be highlighted in a section of the body of v4.master as follows—it is interesting to highlight the increased CSS and HTML standards and best practices design compliance built into SharePoint 2010:

```
<div id="TurnOffAccessibility" style="display:none" class="s4-notdlg noindex">
        <a id="linkTurnOffAcc" href="#" class="ms-TurnOffAcc"
onclick="SetIsAccessibilityFeatureEnabled(false);UpdateAccessibilityUI();document.getElementBy
Id('linkTurnOnAcc').focus();return false;"><SharePoint:EncodedLiteral runat="server"
text="<%$Resources:wss,master_turnoffaccessibility%>" EncodeMethod="HtmlEncode"/></a>
</div>
<div class="s4-notdlg s4-skipribbonshortcut noindex">
        <a href="javascript:;" onclick="javascript:this.href='#startNavigation';" class="ms-
SkiptoNavigation" accesskey="<%$Resources:wss,skipribbon_accesskey%>"
runat="server"><SharePoint:EncodedLiteral runat="server"
text="<%$Resources:wss,skipRibbonCommandsLink%>" EncodeMethod="HtmlEncode"/></a>
</div>
<div class="s4-notdlg noindex">
        <a href="javascript:;" onclick="javascript:this.href='#mainContent';" class="ms-
SkiptoMainContent" accesskey="<%$Resources:wss,maincontent_accesskey%>"
runat="server"><SharePoint:EncodedLiteral runat="server"
text="<%$Resources:wss,mainContentLink%>" EncodeMethod="HtmlEncode"/></a>
</div>
```

```
<a id="HiddenAnchor" href="javascript:;" style="display:none;"></a>
<SharePoint:DelegateControl runat="server" ControlId="GlobalNavigation" />
<div id="s4-ribbonrow" class="s4-pr s4-ribbonrowhidetitle">
        <div id="s4-ribboncont">
                <SharePoint:SPRibbon
                        runat="server"
                        PlaceholderElementId="RibbonContainer"
                        CssFile="">
```

■ **Note** While all of these features are relatively complex, one of the things to note about the overall construction of this master page is all of the `div` tags. SharePoint 2010 is notable in reworking all of the version 4 master pages to be based upon a CSS and `div` structure layout, as opposed to the table layouts that were present in SharePoint 2007.

The rest of the `v4.master` page is relatively long and complex and we will discuss elements of it in future chapters.

Summary

In this chapter, we have moved from the conceptual level of knowledge of SharePoint 2010 well into the application-specific knowledge that we will need to be able to successfully integrate ASP.NET elements and SharePoint 2010 elements into a blended solution. We have covered detailed and extensive examples of web parts, including building them in three separate ways that are available in standard SharePoint application development. Then we have also built in three examples of how to connect to external database sources directly without using BCS. Note that if you have not yet found it, there is downloadable code for all of the examples in this chapter that is available at the Apress site. These examples should prove helpful in starting to work on connecting your own ASP.NET applications to SharePoint through web parts and master pages.

CHAPTER 6

■ ■ ■

The Client Object Model

It doesn't matter where you are coming from. All that matters is where you are going.

Brian Tracy

In the previous chapter, we built our functional technical knowledge in SharePoint 2010 development by showing how we can connect to external systems directly from within SharePoint. This technique will become helpful in our blended solution chapters later in the book.

In this chapter, we will examine connectivity from the other perspective: connecting to SharePoint 2010 data from outside the SharePoint application. The SharePoint 2010 methods that enable this are known as the client object model.

Introducing the Client Object Model

The client object model consists primarily of two separate technologies:

- A model for connecting technologies that are able to fully understand .NET Framework objects

- An ECMA/JavaScript connecting library that is exposed primarily over JSON objects

.NET-Managed and Silverlight-Based Clients

The first part of the client object model will be utilized by external applications that include external .NET web sites and web applications, WPF applications, Windows forms applications, and Silverlight applications. This model is basically for other types of .NET solutions and applications to be able to talk to SharePoint 2010 and retrieve information about their objects.

ECMAScript/JavaScript Clients

The second part of the client object model will be utilized both from within SharePoint 2010 as well as from outside of SharePoint 2010 by ANY technology that supports ECMA/JavaScript and the JSON object model. This would include a wide variety of applications such as PHP web sites, straight HTML web sites, external .NET web sites that prefer to connect with jQuery, and virtually any other programming language application that supports initiating a JavaScript call and supports returning JSON objects.

Taking Advantage of the Client Object Model

The main advances in both of these approaches over the previous versions of SharePoint is that SharePoint 2007 only exposed SharePoint data over an .asmx web service call. This limited the types of applications that could connect to SharePoint data to .NET applications of some kind, or building a custom layer in .NET to expose SharePoint data. With the new approach, SharePoint 2010 can make data available as a SOA tier with its built-in functionality. This opens up what you can do with respect to integrating SharePoint 2010 with other applications.

For our purposes in building blended ASP.NET and SharePoint 2010 solutions, the client object model will come into play during one major strategic approach to blended solutions that we will cover later in the book—the medium touch-point Strategy. The client object model lays the foundation for interacting with SharePoint 2010 by utilizing services to expose the SharePoint object model.

Through the course of this chapter, we will introduce the client object model by code examples, showing how to utilize it from both the .NET perspective as well as the ECMA/JavaScript perspective.

Client Object Model Components

The components of the client object model consist of a WCF web service and several primary .dll libraries. When you are doing development against the client object model, if your development environment does not have SharePoint 2010 installed, you will need to copy the .dlls found in the following locations to your development environment.

.NET Components

The WCF web service and the .dlls are located physically on your server under the SharePoint root at

`C:\Program Files\Common Files\Microsoft Shared\Web Server Extensions\14\ISAPI`

In your runtime environment, the web service is exposed through each of your SharePoint web applications, under the _vti_bin directory, and is named `Client.svc`. The .dlls are the following two, named:

- `Microsoft.SharePoint.Client.dll`

- `Microsoft.SharePoint.Client.Runtime.dll`

These .dlls are installed in the GAC on the server running SharePoint 2010. The `Client.dll` mainly contains classes that you will interact with directly through code, either by way of .NET languages, or JavaScript. The `Runtime.dll` primarily consists of classes responsible for proxy function in interacting with the `Client.svc` WCF Web service. There actually is a third .dll that is part of the client object model codebase, named `Microsoft.SharePoint.Client.Runtime.Resources.dll`, but this just consists of localized error messages compiled as a resource and is not consequential to our purposes.

Silverlight Components

SharePoint 2010 and the client object model provide two separate .dlls to use with Silverlight development. They are

- `Microsoft.SharePoint.Client.Silverlight.dll`

- `Microsoft.SharePoint.Client.Silverlight.Runtime.dll`

These libraries are located in a different place than the previous ones, at

```
C:\Program Files\Common Files\Microsoft Shared\Web Server
Extensions\14\TEMPLATE\LAYOUTS\ClientBin
```

The reason for these .dlls being installed in a different location is due to how Silverlight works—these .dlls are deployed to the same folder that some of the Silverlight building blocks are located in, which makes it easier to access them from Silverlight.

Client Object Model API Support

One of the first things to investigate is to find out the boundaries of the API that is exposed. The client object model exposes a subset of the API that the server object model does, mainly focused on the Site-Collection level and lower. By limiting the API to interacting with the most commonly accessed objects in SharePoint 2010, the size of the libraries is kept down for better performance. Also of note is that the design of the client object model is to batch interaction with SharePoint to minimize the number of round trips that it takes to interact with SharePoint services for common actions.

The client object model for .NET managed and Silverlight is broken down into four major namespaces, as shown in Table 6–1.

Table 6–1. .NET and Managed Silverlight API

.NET Managed and Silverlight Namespace	Description
Microsoft.SharePoint.Client	A subset of members and types in the Microsoft.SharePoint namespace for working with a top-level site and its lists or child web sites
Microsoft.SharePoint.Client.Utilities	A namespace for encoding strings, working with security principals, and other utilities.
Microsoft.SharePoint.Client.WebParts	A subset of Microsoft.SharePoint that enables working with web parts
Microsoft.SharePoint.Client.Workflow	An entry point into SharePoint Foundation Workflow; members map the server object model

The client object model for ECMAScript/JavaScript is broken down into the namespaces shown in Table 6–2.

Table 6–2. Namespaces of ECMAScript/JavaScript Client Object Model

ECMAScript / JavaScript Namespace	Description
SP	A subset of members and types in the Microsoft.SharePoint namespace for working with a top-level site and its lists or child web sites
SP.Ribbon	Provides types and members for working with the server ribbon
SP.Ribbon.PageState	Provides types and members for working with page state on the ribbon
SP.UI	Provides types and members for working with UI in SharePoint Foundation; includes status messages, notifications, and dialogs
SP.Utilities	A namespace for encoding strings, working with security principals. and other utilities
SP.WebParts	Provides types and members to work with web parts
SP.Workflow	Provides types and members to work with workflows.

One of the things that is potentially more difficult to keep track of is that the naming of many of these different objects changes a little bit depending on which model you are using, whether it is the SharePoint 2010 server object model, the .NET managed and Silverlight client object model, or the ECMAScript/Javascript Client Object model. Table 6–3 shows the major elements of SharePoint across all three of these scenarios.

Table 6–3. Object Model Equivalents

Server Object Model	.NET Managed & Silverlight	ECMAScript / JavaScript
Microsoft.SharePoint.SPContext	Microsoft.SharePoint.Client.ClientContext	SP.ClientContext
Microsoft.SharePoint.SPSite	Microsoft.SharePoint.Client.Site	SP.Site
Microsoft.SharePoint.SPWeb	Microsoft.SharePoint.Client.Web	SP.Web
Microsoft.SharePoint.SPList	Microsoft.SharePoint.Client.List	SP.List
Microsoft.SharePoint.SPListItem	Microsoft.SharePoint.Client.ListItem	SP.ListItem
Microsoft.SharePoint.SPField	Microsoft.SharePoint.Client.Field	SP.Field

Data Retrieval and Interaction

One vital concept to investigate with respect to the client object model programming paradigm is to look at specifics regarding data retrieval and interaction including create, read, update, and delete functionality that is exposed.

LoadQuery and Load

One primary method for retrieving information from SharePoint 2010 via the client object model is through the LoadQuery methods. LoadQuery exposes LINQ to interact with, in both the query syntax and the method syntax.

■ **Note** The LINQ that you utilize with the client object model is not the same LINQ as you would use in the server model. The server model uses LINQ to SharePoint with the SPMetal tool being necessary. SPMetal is a command-line tool that generates the classes and artifacts for you to be able to use LINQ-to-SQL in your projects. You can include it with your pre-build scripts to ensure your LINQ entity models are up-to-date with your database before coding against it. The client object model exposes LINQ to objects, which does not require running SPMetal.

Query Syntax Example—LoadQuery

Following is a code segment that uses the LINQ query syntax to retrieve data from a site collection.

```
ClientContext context = new ClientContext("http://portal/sites/sitecollection");

var query = from list
    in context.Web.Lists
    where list.Title != null
    select list;

var result = context.LoadQuery(query);
context.ExecuteQuery();
```

This code segment will retrieve all of the default elements of the lists in the site collection specified in the context. Note that to retrieve specific properties that are not in the default properties, you must refer to them by name, such as in the following code segment.

```
context.Load(oList,
    list => list.Title,
    list => list.Created,
    list => list.OnQuickLaunch);
```

This code segment will load specific elements, such as the Title and Created properties, which are default properties, and the OnQuickLaunch property, which is not.

■ **Tip** You can ONLY use the LINQ query syntax in the LoadQuery method. This syntax is the one without lambda expressions.

Method Syntax Example—Load

Following is a code segment that uses the LINQ method syntax to retrieve data from a site collection.

```
ClientContext context = new ClientContext("http://portal/sites/sitecollection");

context.Load(context.Web,
    website => website.Lists.Include(
        list => list.Title).Where(
            list => list.Title != null));

context.ExecuteQuery();
context.Dispose();
```

Here, lambda expressions are used in the parameters of the Load method to retrieve data.

■ **Tip** You can use the LINQ method syntax in BOTH the Load and LoadQuery methods with the client object model.

Next, we will examine methods to update data through the client object model.

Updating Items Through the Client Object Model

In the following code, we will update an item through the client object model:

```
ClientContext context = new ClientContext("http://portal/sites/sitecollection");
Web web = context.Web;
ListCollection collList = web.Lists;

List list = collList.GetByTitle("Custom List");
ListItem item = list.GetItemById(5);
item["Title"] = "Hello World";
item.Update();

context.ExecuteQuery();
context.Dispose();
```

Notice in the code that to update the item, we call the Update method, and then call the context.ExecuteQuery() method to run it.

■ **Tip** The client object model batches data back to the server for performance reasons. You can take advantage of this by calling `context.ExecuteQuery()` in strategic places after you have performed more than one operation.

Creating Items Through the Client Object Model

The following code segment shows how to create an item through the client object model.

```
ClientContext context = new ClientContext("http://portal/sites/sitecollection");
Web web = context.Web;
ListCollection collList = web.Lists;
List list = collList.GetByTitle("Tasks");
CamlQuery query = new CamlQuery();
ListItemCollection collListItem = list.GetItems(query);


context.Load(list,
        itms => itms.ListItemCollectionPosition,
        itms => itms.Include(
            item => itm["Title"],
            item => itm["Body"],
            item => itm["DueDate"]));

context.ExecuteQuery();
ListItemCreationInformation newTask = new ListItemCreationInformation();
ListItem newTaskItem = list.AddItem(newTask);

newTaskItem["Title"] = "New Task";
newTaskItem["Body"] = "This is a brand new task";
newTaskItem["DueDate"] = DateTime.Now;
newTaskItem.Update();

context.ExecuteQuery();
context.Dispose();
```

Note in this code the use of `ListItemCreationInformation` to hold the information about the item that is to be created. As with all other client object model examples, the actual creation of the object happens upon the execution of the `ExecutyQuery()` call.

Deleting Items Through the Client Object Model

The following code segment shows how to delete an item through the client object model.

```
ClientContext context = new ClientContext("http://portal/sites/sitecollection");
Web web = context.Web;
ListCollection collList = web.Lists;
List list = web.Lists.GetByTitle("Announcements");
list.DeleteObject();
context.ExecuteQuery();
context.Dispose();
```

Note that the `DeleteObject()` method is the one that will perform deletion of the element you are calling it on. But this will not happen until the `ExecuteQuery()` call.

Client Object Model—The Big Three

Throughout the rest of the chapter, we will examine the client object model through direct code samples, which will illustrate the use of some of the previous code segments and concepts. The aim of the rest of the chapter is to get working code into your hands quickly so that you can incorporate it into your development lifecycles in building out blended ASP.NET and SharePoint 2010 projects. In these examples, we will connect to the client object model with examples of the Big Three—Silverlight and ECMAScript/JavaScript, as well as straight .NET managed objects.

Client Object Model Reading List Data via ASP.NET

For this first example, we will show an example of using the .NET Framework portion of the client object model to access SharePoint 2010 data residing in lists from an ASP.NET application. This example will provide the backbone for one of the core approaches to blended ASP.NET and SharePoint 2010 applications that we will see in medium touch-point solutions.

■ **Note** You can find the sample code for this project as well as all of the other projects in this chapter in the code downloads for this book.

---

1. Start a new ASP.NET application project by opening Visual Studio 2010, selecting File ➤ New, and selecting the ASP.NET Application project template. The initial files will look similar to the ones in Figure 6–1.

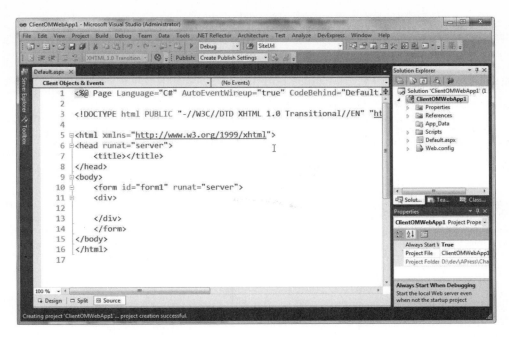

Figure 6–1. Client object model ASP.NET application

    2.   Next, add the client object model .dll references to your project. Right-click the References folder, select Add Reference, and then utilize the new SharePoint tab that is in Visual Studio 2010 for SharePoint references, as shown in Figure 6–2.

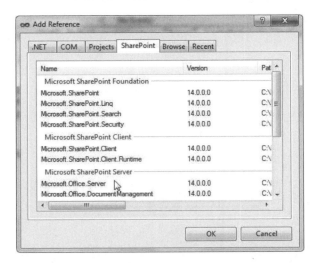

Figure 6–2. *SharePoint References window*

3. Select the Microsoft.SharePoint.Client and the
   Microsoft.SharePoint.Client.Runtime libraries and add them to your project.

4. Next, add two labels, a TextBox and a Button control, as shown in Figure 6–3.
   The TextBox will be used to type in the URL of the SharePoint 2010 site
   collection that we will be reading the task list from. The second label will be
   used to hold the descriptions of the tasks retrieved through the client object
   model.

```
Client Objects & Events                              ▼   (No Events)                                              ▼
 1   <%@ Page Language="C#" AutoEventWireup="true" CodeBehind="Default.aspx.cs" Inherits="ClientOMWeb/‡
 2   <!DOCTYPE html PUBLIC "-//W3C//DTD XHTML 1.0 Transitional//EN" "http://www.w3.org/TR/xhtml1/DTD/‡
 3   <html xmlns="http://www.w3.org/1999/xhtml">
 4   <head runat="server">
 5       <title>Get Tasks Through Client Object Model</title>
 6   </head>                                         ***
 7   <body>
 8       <form id="form1" runat="server">
 9       <div>
10       <asp:Label ID="Label1" runat="server" Text="SharePoint Site Collection:  "/>
11       <asp:TextBox ID="txtSiteCollection" runat="server" Width="150"></asp:TextBox>
12       <br />
13       <asp:Button ID="btnGetTasks" runat="server" Text="Get Tasks" onclick="btnGetTasks_Click" />
14       <br />                                  I
15       <asp:Label ID="lblTasks" runat="server" />
16       </div>
17       </form>
18   </body>
19   </html>
20
100 %  ▼  ◄                          III                                              ►
```

Figure 6–3. *Default page ASP.NET form*

5. Next, we will add the following using statements to the head of our
   Default.aspx.cs file:

```
using System;
using System.Collections.Generic;
using System.Linq;
using System.Web;
using System.Web.UI;
using System.Web.UI.WebControls;
using Microsoft.SharePoint.Client;
using CLOM = Microsoft.SharePoint.Client;
```

■ **Note** We will use the tag CLOM in our references so that it will be clear when we are utilizing elements of the
client object model and when we are utilizing other .NET elements that could be named similarly.

6. We will want to set the lblTasks Label to have no content on page load so that
   values left over between post-backs of the Button click will not remain. Add the
   following code to the Page load event:

```
protected void Page_Load(object sender, EventArgs e)
{
    lblTasks.Text = "";
}
```

7. And lastly, let's populate the Button click event with the following code:

```
protected void btnGetTasks_Click(object sender, EventArgs e)
{
    string SiteCollectionURL = txtSiteCollection.Text;

    CLOM.ClientContext context = new CLOM.ClientContext(SiteCollectionURL);
    CLOM.Web site = context.Web;
    CLOM.ListCollection lists = site.Lists;
    var taskList = context.Web.Lists.GetByTitle("Tasks");

    CLOM.CamlQuery query = new CamlQuery();
    CLOM.ListItemCollection myTaskList = taskList.GetItems(query);
    context.Load(myTaskList);
    context.ExecuteQuery();

    foreach (CLOM.ListItem tmpTaskItem in myTaskList)
    {
        lblTasks.Text += tmpTaskItem.FieldValues.Values.ElementAt(1).ToString() +"<br/>";
    }
        context.Dispose();
}
```

First, we will collect the URL from the text box and create a collection that can be looped over with a foreach statement to hold our task list we will retrieve from the SharePoint 2010 site collection.

In the next block of code, we set up the variables necessary to interact with the ClientContext. Note that we are utilizing the Load() method to load the data in place in the same object, as opposed to the LoadQuery() method that loads data to a new object.

When you run the application, you get an output window that looks similar to Figure 6–4.

Note that while this example is in ASP.NET, it is just as simple to access the .NET Framework version of the client object model through other .NET technologies such as Windows forms and WPF applications.

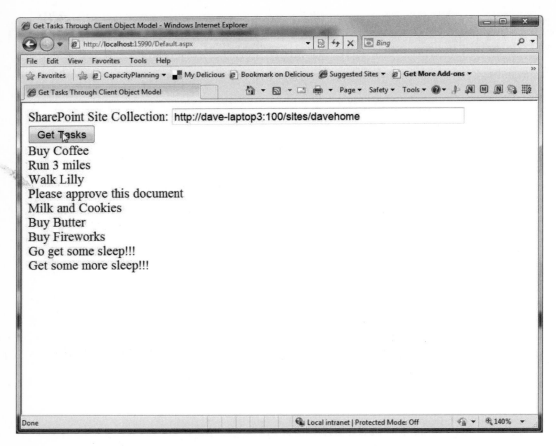

Figure 6–4. Finished ASP.NET application using client object model

Client Object Model Writing List Data via ASP.NET

To continue on with our example of interacting with the .NET Framework portion of the client object model, we will build our second example in this chapter also using an ASP.NET application to interact with SharePoint 2010 list data, but this time we will write data to our tasks list.

1.   Create a new ASP.NET application project, and name it ClientOMWebApp2. We will utilize the same references as in the last project, and we can keep the label and the textbox from that project as well. Your project should look like Figure 6–5 when you get finished copying those items over.

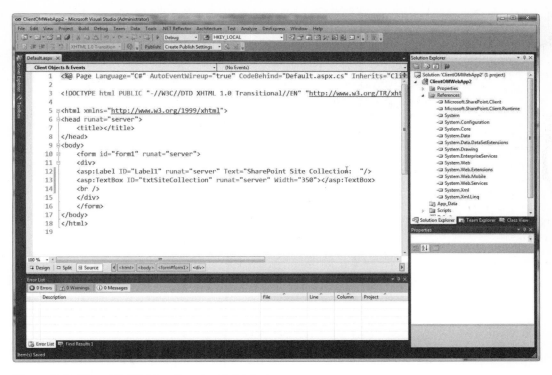

Figure 6–5. ClientOMWebApp2 project initial view

2.   Next, we will add controls that will support adding a title, a description, and a
     due date to the task list. Go ahead and add three Labels, two TextBoxes, and a
     Calendar control to your project. When you are through with this portion, your
     Default.aspx form should look similar to Figure 6–6. We are not taking time to
     make the layout of the controls pretty at this point, but just focusing on the bare
     minimum to delve into the functionality of the client object model.

Client Objects & Events	(No Events)

```
8    </head>
9  ⊟<body>
10 ⊟    <form id="form1" runat="server">
11 ⊟    <div>
12         <asp:Label ID="Label1" runat="server" Text="SharePoint Site Collection:  "/>
13         <asp:TextBox ID="txtSiteCollection" runat="server" Width="350"></asp:TextBox>
14         <br />
15         <asp:Label ID="Label2" runat="server" Text="Title:  "/>
16         <asp:TextBox ID="txtTitle" runat="server" Width="250"></asp:TextBox>
17         <br />
18         <asp:Label ID="Label3" runat="server" Text="Description:  "/>
19         <asp:TextBox ID="txtDesc" runat="server" Width="350"></asp:TextBox>
20         <br />
21         <asp:Label ID="Label4" runat="server" Text="Due Date:  "/>
22         <asp:Calendar ID="Calendar1" runat="server"></asp:Calendar>
23         <br />
24         <asp:Button ID="btnAddTask" runat="server" Text="Add Task" />
25         <br />
26         <asp:Label ID="lblResult" runat="server" Text=""/>
27     </div>
28     </form>
```

Figure 6–6. Finished default.aspx form

3. Next, add the following code to the Button click event:

```
protected void btnAddTask_Click(object sender, EventArgs e)
{
    string SiteCollectionURL = txtSiteCollection.Text;

    CLOM.ClientContext context = new CLOM.ClientContext(SiteCollectionURL);
    CLOM.List taskList = context.Web.Lists.GetByTitle("Tasks");
    CLOM.CamlQuery query = new CamlQuery();
    CLOM.ListItemCollection myTaskList = taskList.GetItems(query);

    context.Load(myTaskList,
        itms => itms.ListItemCollectionPosition,
        itms => itms.Include(
            itm => itm["Title"],
            itm => itm["Body"],
            itm => itm["DueDate"]));

    context.ExecuteQuery();

    ListItemCreationInformation newTask = new ListItemCreationInformation();
    CLOM.ListItem newTaskItem = taskList.AddItem(newTask);

    newTaskItem["Title"] = txtTitle.Text;
    newTaskItem["Body"] = txtDesc.Text;
    newTaskItem["DueDate"] = Calendar1.SelectedDate;
    newTaskItem.Update();

    context.ExecuteQuery();
```

```
    lblResult.Text = "Added Task " + txtTitle.Text;
    context.Dispose();
}
```

Some things to note about the client object model in this code segment are the SPContext.Load commands. By default, the client object model only loads a few primary fields such as Id and Title from lists when you load a list with the default parameter specified. In order to gain access to other columns in the list, they must specifically be loaded. This is what the Load command here is doing. The second parameter is a LINQ expression instructing the CLOM to load those particular fields along with the default ones.

Another gotcha to note in the preceding code is the column "Body." This column is the "Description" column in the task list. However, that is not the internal name of the column. This information cannot be seen in any of the administrative screens for interacting with or managing the data. Where you need to obtain this is by actually going to the task list itself, selecting Add New to bring up the modal view box, and then right-clicking the Add screen and selecting View Source. As you search down through the form, you will see commented HTML such as that shown in the following:

```
<nobr>Description</nobr>
        </h3></td>
                <td valign="top" class="ms-formbody">
                <!-- FieldName="Description"
                        FieldInternalName="Body"
                        FieldType="SPFieldNote"
                -->
```

Most of the time, the FieldName, which is what shows up in the column definitions, is the same as the FieldInternalName. However, here it is dramatically different (and this pattern carries through for the description field in other lists, as well). If you try to reference the field by its FieldName, you will have an error thrown by the application indicating that the column does not exist. So if that error occurs, remember to check the View Source of the Add or Edit view on the list. Always access a column in a list by its FieldInternalName. That will save you hours of frustration. This also is a similar process, but with quite different naming conventions, as to what you would do in SharePoint 2007 versions.

After you run this project, the output will look similar to Figure 6–7.

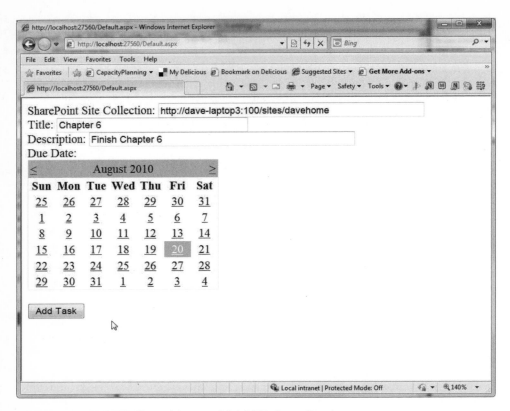

Figure 6–7. ASP.NET client object model Add Task application

Now we have built a basic understanding of working with the managed client object model through the .NET Framework. Next, we will move on to Silverlight applications.

Client Object Model Reading List Data via Silverlight—From a Web Part

In this example, we will utilize the second part of the *Big Three* – Silverlight. Interacting with the Silverlight portion of the client object model will require using different .dlls than the managed client object model. Working with Silverlight in a SharePoint development context in this fashion is a two-part process. In the first part, we will build the Silverlight application in a stand-alone Silverlight application. Then, we will build a Visual Studio SharePoint project to deploy the Silverlight application to a SharePoint 2010 installation.

There are several ways to deploy Silverlight applications to a SharePoint 2010 environment. This simplest of these would be to take the output from a Silverlight application (the Silverlight .xap file), and upload it to a SharePoint 2010 document library. Then this file can be referenced from within a Silverlight web part. In these examples, we are going to go a few steps further, and package up the Silverlight that we will code into a web part, and deploy it along with a new site page to the SharePoint 2010 site collection by way of a .wsp solution file. While this will make the SharePoint project a little bit more complicated, it will be of more value as this will be the fashion that will be mostly used in best practices in business application development with Silverlight and SharePoint 2010.

We will also be coding the Silverlight application in a very simple implementation of the common practice of using Model View ViewModel (MVVM) just so our example is encapsulated in a best-practices format.

1. First, open Visual Studio 2010 and select File ➤ New ➤ Project. Select the .NET Framework 4 as the filter for templates, and then select the Silverlight tab. This template will provide a basic framework without the necessity of all of the elements present in the Silverlight Business Application including the authorization there. Name your application SilverlightTasks and click OK (see Figure 6–8).

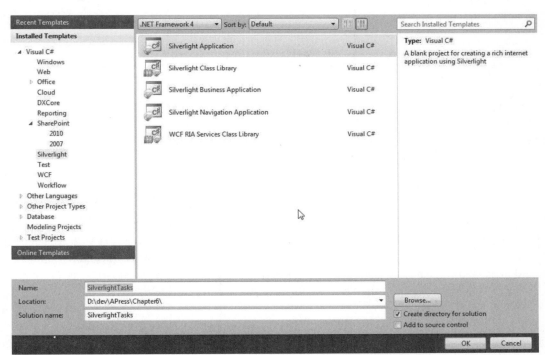

Figure 6–8. *Silverlight Application template*

2. In the next window that appears, deselect the Host the Silverlight application in a new Web site check box and select Silverlight 4 in the Silverlight version drop-down, as shown in Figure 6–9.

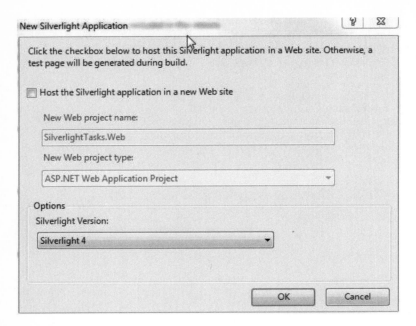

Figure 6–9. *New Silverlight application window*

■ **Note** You may wonder why we are able to utilize .NET 4.0 Framework versions of Silverlight in SharePoint 2010, when the SharePoint product is only compatible with .NET 3.5 code. The answer to this is that Silverlight applications are very well packaged within themselves and do not have a great deal of crossover in libraries with managed .NET code. So the .xap file that is produced in the Silverlight application can be wrapped in the Silverlight web part in SharePoint 2010, which is a .NET 3.5 compiled control.

---

3. Next, we will add references that will be necessary in the project. Add the
    `System.Windows.Data` reference, and add the SharePoint client object model
    Silverlight references (`Microsoft.SharePoint.Client.Silverlight.dll` and
    `Microsoft.SharePoint.Client.Silverlight.Runtime.dll`), found in the
    following directory

```
C:\Program Files\Common Files\Microsoft Shared\Web Server
Extensions\14\TEMPLATE\LAYOUTS\ClientBin
```

4. Next, add a DataGrid and a Label control, as seen in the following code. I added
    a LinearGradientBrush just so it's easy to tell a Silverlight web control from
    another type. The colors there are, well, colorful!

```xml
<UserControl
    xmlns:sdk="clr-
namespace:System.Windows.Controls;assembly=System.Windows.Controls.Data.Input"
    xmlns:my="clr-namespace:System.Windows.Controls;assembly=System.Windows.Controls.Data"
    x:Class="SilverlightTasks.MainPage"
    xmlns="http://schemas.microsoft.com/winfx/2006/xaml/presentation"
    xmlns:x="http://schemas.microsoft.com/winfx/2006/xaml"
    xmlns:d="http://schemas.microsoft.com/expression/blend/2008"
    xmlns:mc="http://schemas.openxmlformats.org/markup-compatibility/2006"
    mc:Ignorable="d"
    d:DesignHeight="400" d:DesignWidth="500">
    <Grid x:Name="LayoutRoot" Loaded="LayoutRoot_Loaded">
        <sdk:Label Height="25" HorizontalAlignment="Left" Margin="12,0,0,25" Name="lblStatus"
VerticalAlignment="Bottom" Width="450" />
        <my:DataGrid Name="dgTasks" HorizontalAlignment="Left" Margin="20,20,0,0"
VerticalAlignment="Top" Height="325" Width="460" ItemsSource="{Binding Tasks}"  />
        <Grid.Background>
            <LinearGradientBrush EndPoint="0.5,1" StartPoint="0.5,0">
                <GradientStop Color="#1E009100" Offset="0" />
                <GradientStop Color="#FFE1FF00" Offset="0.893" />
            </LinearGradientBrush>
        </Grid.Background>
    </Grid>
</UserControl>
```

5. Next, let's add a folder for Entities, and a class to hold data from the SharePoint task list, as follows—add a new file Task.cs that contains:

```csharp
using System;

namespace SilverlightTasks
{
    public class Task
    {
        public string Title { get; set; }
        public string Description { get; set; }
        public DateTime DueDate { get; set; }

    }
}
```

We will implement the Silverlight application as a MVVM application. This pattern helps to separate out the loading concerns of the data context into layers. In fact, the MVVM model is similar to the ASP.NET MVC pattern that has become popular, with a few exceptions.

We will take advantage of MVVM by instantiating an Entities folder that contains our simple Task class, and a ViewModel folder that contains our TaskViewModel. The project looks like Figure 6–10 when completed.

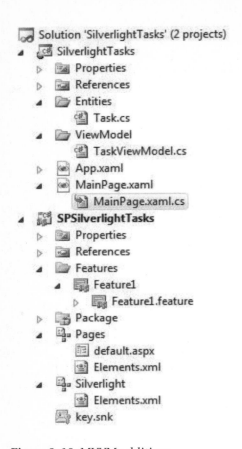

Figure 6–10. *MVVM additions*

The Task class is a simple class, as you can see next.

6. The TaskViewModel.cs class is where we will abstract away the loading of all the data. This way the front end MainPage will not have to have the concerns for data loading mixed up in what it will accomplish. It simply uses a DataContext that is set to the ViewModel, and the elements load themselves on the page. Add code to the TaskViewModel class as follows:

```
using System;
using System.Net;
using System.Collections.Generic;
using System.Collections.ObjectModel;
using System.ComponentModel;
using System.Linq;
using System.Windows;
using CLOM = Microsoft.SharePoint.Client;
using SilverlightTasks.Entities;
using SilverlightTasks;
```

```
namespace SilverlightTasks.ViewModel
{
    public class TaskViewModel : INotifyPropertyChanged, IDisposable
    {
        CLOM.ClientContext context;
        CLOM.ListItemCollection taskListItems;

        public ObservableCollection<Task> Tasks { get; private set; }


        public TaskViewModel()
        {
            context = new CLOM.ClientContext(CLOM.ApplicationContext.Current.Url);
            Tasks = new ObservableCollection<Task>();
        }

        public void GetTasks()
        {
            Tasks.Clear();
            CLOM.List taskList = context.Web.Lists.GetByTitle("Tasks");
            CLOM.CamlQuery query = new CLOM.CamlQuery();
            taskListItems = taskList.GetItems(query);
            context.Load(taskListItems);
            context.ExecuteQueryAsync(onQuerySucceeded, onQueryFailed);
        }

        private void onQuerySucceeded(object sender, CLOM.ClientRequestSucceededEventArgs
args)
        {
            Deployment.Current.Dispatcher.BeginInvoke(() =>
            {
                foreach (var item in taskListItems)
                {
                    Task task = new Task();
                    task.Title = item["Title"].ToString();
                    task.Description = item["Body"].ToString();
                    task.DueDate = DateTime.Parse(item["DueDate"].ToString());
                    Tasks.Add(task);
                }
            });
        }

        private void onQueryFailed(object sender, CLOM.ClientRequestFailedEventArgs args)
        {
            Deployment.Current.Dispatcher.BeginInvoke(() => MessageBox.Show("Execution
Failed:" + args.Exception.InnerException.Message));
        }


        public event global::System.ComponentModel.PropertyChangedEventHandler
PropertyChanged;
        protected virtual void OnPropertyChanged(string property)
        {
```

```
            if ((this.PropertyChanged != null))
            {
                this.PropertyChanged(this, new
global::System.ComponentModel.PropertyChangedEventArgs(property));
            }
        }

        protected virtual void Dispose(bool disposing)
        {
            if (disposing)
            {
                context.Dispose();
            }
        }

        public void Dispose()
        {
            Dispose(true);
            GC.SuppressFinalize(this);

        }
    }
}
```

7. For the MainPage.xaml.cs file, let's load the View Model in to the initialization, as follows; this initializes the View Model, and sets the Main Page DataContext to the View Model:

```
SilverlightTasks.ViewModel.TaskViewModel viewModel;

public MainPage()
{
    InitializeComponent();
    viewModel = new ViewModel.TaskViewModel();
    this.DataContext = viewModel;
}
```

8. Next, let's add the event for loading tasks data to the LayoutRoot_Loaded event in the MainPage.xaml.cs file:

```
private void LayoutRoot_Loaded(object sender, RoutedEventArgs e)
{
    lblStatus.Content = "Starting data retrieval...";
    viewModel.GetTasks();
    lblStatus.Content = "Data retrieval complete...";

}
```

This pretty much completes the SilverlightTasks project.

■ **Tip** The MVVM pattern may involve a little more code than going after data directly in a code-behind file, but once you get used to the principle it uses—the separation of concerns—it really makes Silverlight development more modular and easier to keep track of. The more you have going on in a Silverlight project, the more it will help you out.

Next, we will add and configure the SharePoint project to deploy our `SilverlightTasks` project.

1. Right-click on the solution and select Add ➤ New Project. Then select the SharePoint templates and add an Empty SharePoint project. Name it `SPSilverlightTasks`, as shown in Figure 6–11.

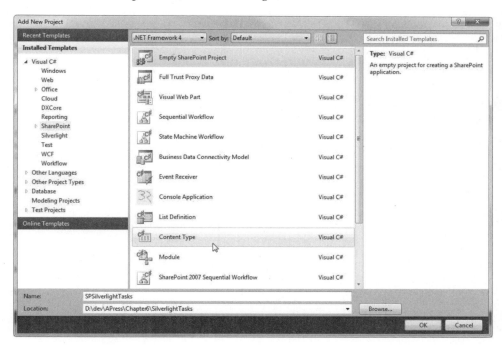

Figure 6–11. Add SharePoint project

2. Select Deploy as a farm solution from the next window.

3. Next, we will add two modules to the empty SharePoint project—one named `Silverlight` and one named `Pages`. The `Silverlight` module will be used to deploy our `SilverlightTasks` application, and the `Pages` module will be used to initiate a page and a Silverlight web part to place the `SilverlightTasks` application on.

4. After adding the modules, delete the `Sample.txt` files from each of the `Module` directories. In the `Silverlight` module, select the main node so that the Properties window for the module is shown, as in Figure 6–12.

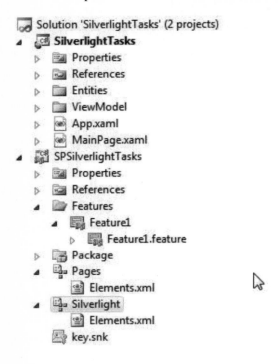

Figure 6–12. SPSilverlight Tasks project

5. In the Properties window, select the Collection ellipsis at the right-hand side of the window for the Project Output References. Select Add, then change the Deployment Type drop-down from No Action to Element File, and switch the Project Name to the SilverlightTasks project. You will end up with the window looking like Figure 6–13.

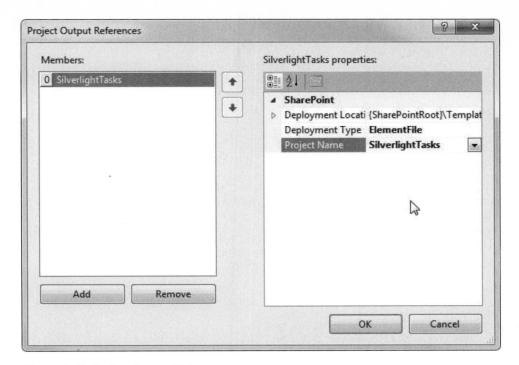

Figure 6–13. Project Output References

6. Select the `Elements.xml` file of the `Silverlight` module, and modify it so it appears as in the following XML fragment:

```xml
<?xml version="1.0" encoding="utf-8"?>
<Elements xmlns="http://schemas.microsoft.com/sharepoint/">
  <Module Name="Silverlight" Url="Apps">
  <File Path="Silverlight\SilverlightTasks.xap" Url="Silverlight/SilverlightTasks.xap" />
</Module>
</Elements>
```

■ **Note** We added a URL to the `Module` name so that the Silverlight web part can find the output .xap file.

7. Next, in the Pages module, right-click the Pages node, click Add, and click Existing Item. Then browse to the SharePoint root `14\TEMPLATE\SiteTemplates\sts` and select the default.aspx page. This will add a copy of the default.aspx file to the Pages node. After this is complete, open the `Elements.xml` file and change it to look like the following (add the `Url` of SitePages and change the `File Url` to SilverlightTest.aspx:

```xml
<?xml version="1.0" encoding="utf-8"?>
<Elements xmlns="http://schemas.microsoft.com/sharepoint/">
  <Module Name="Pages" Url="SitePages">
  <File Path="Pages\default.aspx" Url="SilverlightTest.aspx" />
</Module>
</Elements>
```

8. Next, change the File node to have a closing XML tag `</File>`. Then add the following to the internal segment of the File node:

```xml
<AllUsersWebPart WebPartOrder="1"
                 WebPartZoneID="Left"
                 ID="SilverlightExternalService">
    <![CDATA[
    <webParts>
      <webPart xmlns="http://schemas.microsoft.com/WebPart/v3">
        <metaData>
          <type name="Microsoft.SharePoint.WebPartPages.SilverlightWebPart,
                      Microsoft.SharePoint, Version=14.0.0.0,
                      Culture=neutral, PublicKeyToken=71e9bce111e9429c" />
          <importErrorMessage>Cannot import this WebPart.
          </importErrorMessage>
        </metaData>
        <data>
          <properties>
            <property name="HelpUrl" type="string" />
            <property name="AllowClose" type="bool">True</property>
            <property name="ExportMode" type="exportmode">All</property>
            <property name="Hidden" type="bool">False</property>
            <property name="AllowEdit" type="bool">True</property>
            <property name="Direction" type="direction">NotSet</property>
            <property name="TitleIconImageUrl" type="string" />
            <property name="AllowConnect" type="bool">True</property>
            <property name="HelpMode" type="helpmode">Modal</property>
            <property name="CustomProperties" type="string" null="true" />
            <property name="AllowHide" type="bool">True</property>
            <property name="Description" type="string">A web part to display
                         Silverlight Tasks.</property>
            <property name="CatalogIconImageUrl" type="string" />
            <property name="MinRuntimeVersion" type="string" null="true" />
            <property name="ApplicationXml" type="string" />
            <property name="AllowMinimize" type="bool">True</property>
            <property name="AllowZoneChange" type="bool">True</property>
            <property name="CustomInitParameters" type="string" null="true"/>
            <property name="Height" type="unit">550px</property>
            <property name="ChromeType" type="chrometype">Default</property>
            <property name="Width" type="unit">700px</property>
            <property name="Title" type="string">Silverlight Task List</property>
            <property name="ChromeState" type="chromestate">Normal</property>
            <property name="TitleUrl" type="string" />
            <property name="Url" type="string">
                    ~site/Apps/Silverlight/SilverlightTasks.xap</property>
            <property name="WindowlessMode" type="bool">True</property>
          </properties>
```

```
        </data>
      </webPart>
    </webParts> ]]>
  </AllUsersWebPart>
```

9. Next, right-click the SPSilverlightTasks project and select Properties. Under the SharePoint tab, check the box for Enable Silverlight debugging (instead of Script debugging).

10. Lastly, set the SPSilverlightTasks project as the Startup project and press F5 to run. You will see the home page for your team site, but select the Site Pages selection from the left navigation element, and you will notice a new SilverLightTest page for you to check your work on.

After you complete those steps, you can press F5 to deploy your project and debug it. Your finished product will look something like Figure 6–14.

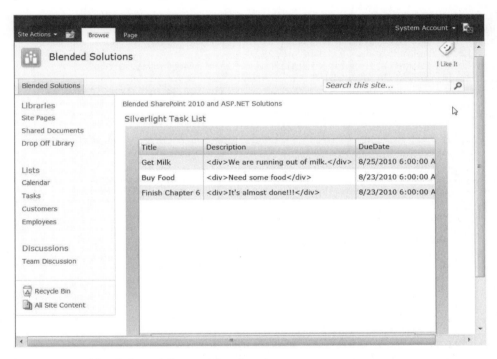

Figure 6–14. *Silverlight task list completed project*

Client Object Model Writing List Data via Silverlight

In our next example, we are going to write items to the tasks list through Silverlight and the client object model.

1. Start a new Visual Studio project, just like in the last project, and select File ➤ New ➤ Project.

2. Then select Silverlight again, and add a new Silverlight application just as in the previous example.

3. Then add the client object model Silverlight .dlls just like in the previous example. Also add System.Windows.Controls in to the References.

4. After this, add the following markup (XAML) to the MainPage.xaml file; this provides the XAML interface for the Silverlight web part. You can see the state of the project after adding this XAML can be seen in Figures 6–15 and 6–16.

```
<UserControl x:Class="SilverlightTaskAdder.MainPage"
    xmlns="http://schemas.microsoft.com/winfx/2006/xaml/presentation"
    xmlns:x="http://schemas.microsoft.com/winfx/2006/xaml"
    xmlns:d="http://schemas.microsoft.com/expression/blend/2008"
    xmlns:mc="http://schemas.openxmlformats.org/markup-compatibility/2006"
    mc:Ignorable="d"
    d:DesignHeight="294" d:DesignWidth="325"
    xmlns:dataInput="clr-
namespace:System.Windows.Controls;assembly=System.Windows.Controls.Data.Input"
    xmlns:controls="clr-namespace:System.Windows.Controls;assembly=System.Windows.Controls">
    <Grid x:Name="LayoutRoot" Height="292" Width="325">
        <dataInput:Label Height="21" HorizontalAlignment="Left" Margin="46,15,0,0"
Name="label1" VerticalAlignment="Top" Width="111" Content="Task Description:" />
        <TextBox Height="23" HorizontalAlignment="Left" Margin="46,34,0,0" Name="textBox1"
VerticalAlignment="Top" Width="230" Background="{x:Null}" Foreground="Black"></TextBox>
        <controls:Calendar HorizontalAlignment="Left" Margin="46,75,0,0" Name="calendar1"
VerticalAlignment="Top" Background="{x:Null}"></controls:Calendar>
        <Button Content="Add Task" Height="23" HorizontalAlignment="Left" Margin="46,250,0,0"
Name="button1" VerticalAlignment="Top" Width="75" Click="button1_Click"
Background="Black"></Button>
        <dataInput:Label Height="13" HorizontalAlignment="Left" Margin="46,273,0,0"
Name="label2" VerticalAlignment="Top" Width="230" FontSize="10" Background="{x:Null}" />
        <Grid.Background>
            <LinearGradientBrush EndPoint="0.5,1" StartPoint="0.5,0">
                <GradientStop Color="#1E009100" Offset="0" />
                <GradientStop Color="#FFE1FF00" Offset="0.893" />
            </LinearGradientBrush>
        </Grid.Background>
    </Grid>
</UserControl>
```

■ **Tip** If you want to debug the Silverlight portion of this, all you need to do is double-click the button to ensure the method stub is created on the back end. Then you can run the solution in either Visual Studio 2010, or in Expression Blend to make XAML adjustments.

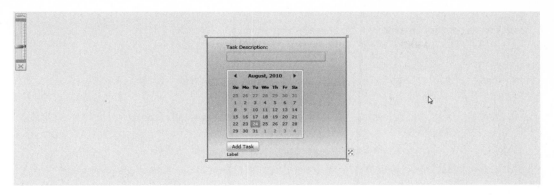

Figure 6–15. Silverlight Task Adder

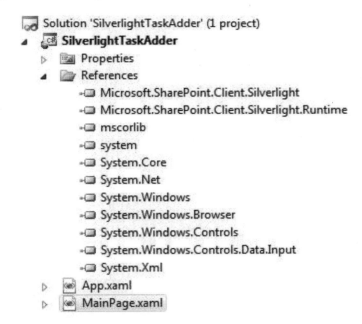

Figure 6–16. Silverlight Task Adder project.

5.   handle the Silverlight client object model Async call, return, and error
     representations. First is the code for the Button click event, as follows:

```
private void button1_Click(object sender, RoutedEventArgs e)
{
    CLOM.ClientContext context = new
        CLOM.ClientContext(CLOM.ApplicationContext.Current.Url);

    CLOM.List taskList = context.Web.Lists.GetByTitle("Tasks");
```

```
CLOM.ListItemCreationInformation itemCreateInfo = new
    CLOM.ListItemCreationInformation();
CLOM.ListItem newItem = taskList.AddItem(itemCreateInfo);
newItem["Title"] = textBox1.Text;
newItem["DueDate"] = calendar1.SelectedDate.Value.ToShortDateString();
newItem.Update();

context.ExecuteQueryAsync(ClientRequestSucceeded, ClientRequestFailed);
}
```

6. Next, add the following two functions to your MainPage.xaml.cs file:

```
private void ClientRequestSucceeded(object sender, CLOM.ClientRequestSucceededEventArgs args)
{
    this.Dispatcher.BeginInvoke(() =>
    {
        label2.Content = "Task '" + textBox1.Text + "' added for you!";
        textBox1.Text = "";
    });
}

private void ClientRequestFailed(object sender, CLOM.ClientRequestFailedEventArgs args)
{
    this.Dispatcher.BeginInvoke(() =>
    {
        MessageBox.Show("Connection failed. Error code: "
                + args.ErrorCode.ToString() + ". Message: " + args.Message);
    });
}
```

Note that in both of the async ClientRequestSucceeded and ClientRequestFailed methods that instead of using the standard notation with the Dispatcher.BeginInvoke calling another delegate, we are just using the in-line version of that syntax to keep the code contained in the function.

At this point, your Silverlight project is complete (although in this state, it will not compile and run because we have introduced code that depends on the SharePoint 2010 environment).

Next, just as in the last project, we will add a SharePoint project so that we can package up and deploy our Silverlight to the SharePoint environment, wrap it in a web part, and create a page on which to install it.

We won't show all of the steps here explicitly for this; however, if you return to Figure 6–11, the steps starting there and adding the SharePoint project all the way through deploying the project to your SharePoint environment are exactly the same.

■ **Tip** Everyone has their own naming conventions with code and projects, but I tend to use the naming convention for SharePoint projects constructed to deploy things as just adding an SP on to the prefix of my solution—so in this instance, my SharePoint deployment project would be named SPSilverlightTaskAdder. You can use this convention or one you like better. It is beneficial to develop a consistent pattern to do things of this nature.

After you complete those steps, you can press F5 to deploy your project and debug it. Your finished product should appear as in Figure 6–17.

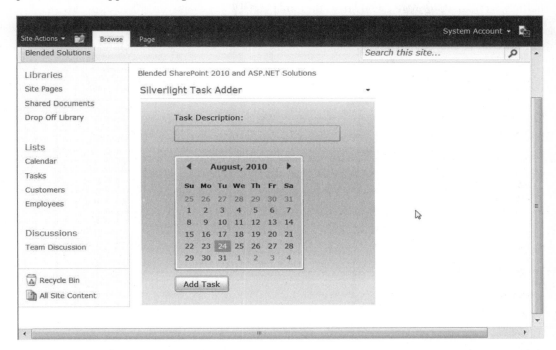

Figure 6–17. Finished SilverlightTaskAdder project

■ **Tip** Sometimes my enviornments have not expanded the `~site` tag as they should, and I have received a cryptic message "Could not download Silverlight application" when browsing to my test page. In this case, when I opened the tool pane and checked the configuration, the expanded location appeared as `sites/mysite`. To correct the error, all I needed to do was to place a forward slash in front of the *sites* word so it appears `/sites/mysite` as opposed to `sites/mysite`. The rest of the path is fine.

■ **Note** SharePoint 2010 itself, in addition to the Silverlight web part, has a Silverlight Media web part that is a great way to show rich media in your applications. Look for ways to use Silverlight to increase your user interaction.

Debugging Silverlight in SharePoint 2010

To configure your SharePoint 2010 deployment to enable you to debug your Silverlight application, right-click on the SharePoint project SPSilverlightTaskAdder, select Properties, and go to the SharePoint node. Check the check box Enable Silverlight debugging (instead of Script debugging), as shown in Figure 6–18. Then you can set breakpoints in your Silverlight web part to help you debug it.

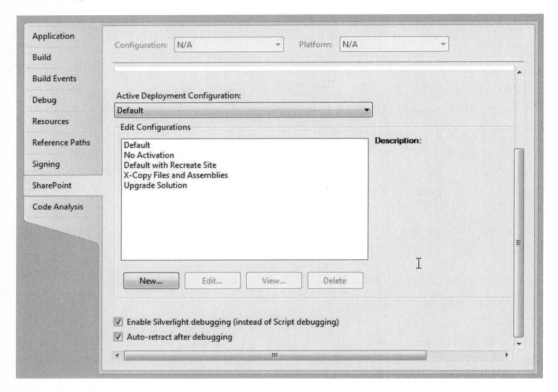

Figure 6–18. *Enable Silverlight debugging*

This rounds off our examples of Silverlight and the client object model. As you can see, there is a lot available with blending Silverlight and SharePoint 2010.

Client Object Model—Reading List Data via ECMAScript/JavaScript

The last example we will walk through in this chapter and the final one in the Big Three is interacting with the client object model via ECMAScript/JavaScript. As we saw earlier in the chapter, the client object model has similar properties and methods that are exposed to ECMAScript and JavaScript that are exposed to the managed client object model and the Silverlight client object model. For our example interacting with SharePoint 2010 in this instance, we will use yet another approach.

We will integrate JavaScript, jQuery, and the ECMAScript/JavaScript client object model in an application page deployment that leverages these technologies and interacts with SharePoint.

In ECMAScript/JavaScript, the actual references to the client object model are not found in.dlls) as are the managed client object model or Silverlight object model. The full API for ECMAScript/JavaScript is found in several JavaScript libraries that reside in the following directory:

```
C:\Program Files\Common Files\Microsoft Shared\Web Server Extensions\14\TEMPLATE\LAYOUTS
```

The main libraries involved are the SP.js library (and the SP.debug.js library). However, many more JavaScript libraries exist in that directory and are available for use in SharePoint 2010 development (see Figure 6–19).

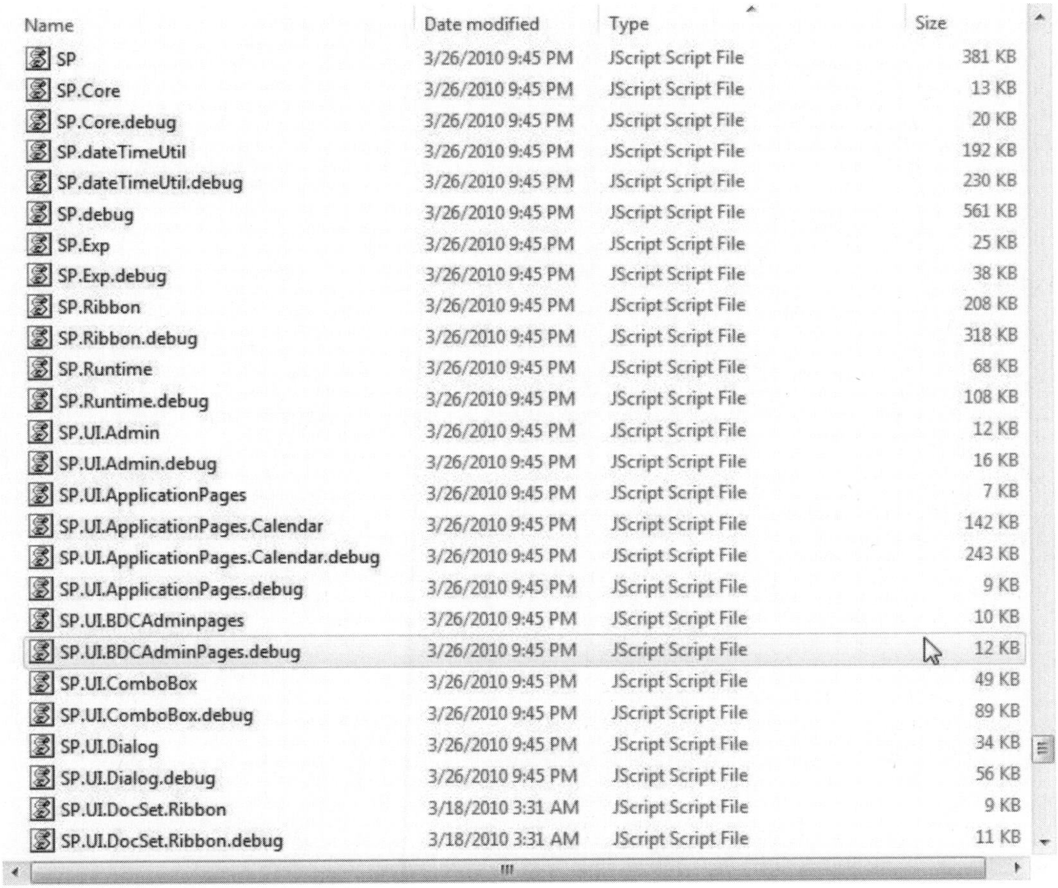

Name	Date modified	Type	Size
SP	3/26/2010 9:45 PM	JScript Script File	381 KB
SP.Core	3/26/2010 9:45 PM	JScript Script File	13 KB
SP.Core.debug	3/26/2010 9:45 PM	JScript Script File	20 KB
SP.dateTimeUtil	3/26/2010 9:45 PM	JScript Script File	192 KB
SP.dateTimeUtil.debug	3/26/2010 9:45 PM	JScript Script File	230 KB
SP.debug	3/26/2010 9:45 PM	JScript Script File	561 KB
SP.Exp	3/26/2010 9:45 PM	JScript Script File	25 KB
SP.Exp.debug	3/26/2010 9:45 PM	JScript Script File	38 KB
SP.Ribbon	3/26/2010 9:45 PM	JScript Script File	208 KB
SP.Ribbon.debug	3/26/2010 9:45 PM	JScript Script File	318 KB
SP.Runtime	3/26/2010 9:45 PM	JScript Script File	68 KB
SP.Runtime.debug	3/26/2010 9:45 PM	JScript Script File	108 KB
SP.UI.Admin	3/26/2010 9:45 PM	JScript Script File	12 KB
SP.UI.Admin.debug	3/26/2010 9:45 PM	JScript Script File	16 KB
SP.UI.ApplicationPages	3/26/2010 9:45 PM	JScript Script File	7 KB
SP.UI.ApplicationPages.Calendar	3/26/2010 9:45 PM	JScript Script File	142 KB
SP.UI.ApplicationPages.Calendar.debug	3/26/2010 9:45 PM	JScript Script File	243 KB
SP.UI.ApplicationPages.debug	3/26/2010 9:45 PM	JScript Script File	9 KB
SP.UI.BDCAdminpages	3/26/2010 9:45 PM	JScript Script File	10 KB
SP.UI.BDCAdminPages.debug	3/26/2010 9:45 PM	JScript Script File	12 KB
SP.UI.ComboBox	3/26/2010 9:45 PM	JScript Script File	49 KB
SP.UI.ComboBox.debug	3/26/2010 9:45 PM	JScript Script File	89 KB
SP.UI.Dialog	3/26/2010 9:45 PM	JScript Script File	34 KB
SP.UI.Dialog.debug	3/26/2010 9:45 PM	JScript Script File	56 KB
SP.UI.DocSet.Ribbon	3/18/2010 3:31 AM	JScript Script File	9 KB
SP.UI.DocSet.Ribbon.debug	3/18/2010 3:31 AM	JScript Script File	11 KB

Figure 6–19. Client Side Object Model Javascript Libraries

Let's get started.

1. First, start off the Visual Studio Project with File ➤ New ➤ Project. Then select an empty SharePoint project as your solution. Name it SPClientObjectModelECMA.

2. After it is instantiated, right-click the project and add an application page named ClientOMECMA.aspx. Then add the following two lines to the PageHead Content placeholder:

```
<SharePoint:ScriptLink ID="ScriptLink1" Name="sp.js" runat="server" LoadAfterUI="true"
Localizable="false" ></SharePoint:ScriptLink>
<script type="text/javascript" src="http://ajax.microsoft.com/ajax/jquery/jquery-1.3.2.min.js"
/>
```

3. Next, include the following JavaScript in the same placeholder:

```
<script type="text/javascript">
var context = null;
var web = null;
ExecuteOrDelayUntilScriptLoaded(Initialize, "sp.js");
function Initialize()
{
context = new SP.ClientContext.get_current();
web = context.get_web();
var list = web.get_lists().getByTitle("Site Pages");
var camlQuery = new SP.CamlQuery();
var q = '<View><RowLimit>5</RowLimit></View>';
camlQuery.set_viewXml(q);
this.listItems = list.getItems(camlQuery);
context.load(listItems, 'Include(DisplayName,Id)');
context.executeQueryAsync(Function.createDelegate(this, this.on  ListItemsLoadSuccess),
Function.createDelegate(this, this.onQueryFailed));
}
function onListItemsLoadSuccess(sender, args) {
var listEnumerator = this.listItems.getEnumerator();
while (listEnumerator.moveNext()) {
    var item = listEnumerator.get_current();
        var title = item.get_displayName();
        var id = item.get_id();
    alert("List title : " + title + "; List ID : "+ id);
}
}

function onQueryFailed(sender, args) {
        alert('request failed ' + args.get_message() + '\n' + args.get_stackTrace());
}
</script>
```

■ **Note** The code in this example uses an asynchronous query just as the Silverlight access code does.

From here, you may press F5 and deploy the project. To see your application page, browse to the _layouts/ SPClientObjectModelECMA/ClientOMECMA.aspx page.

The application will appear as in Figure 6–20.

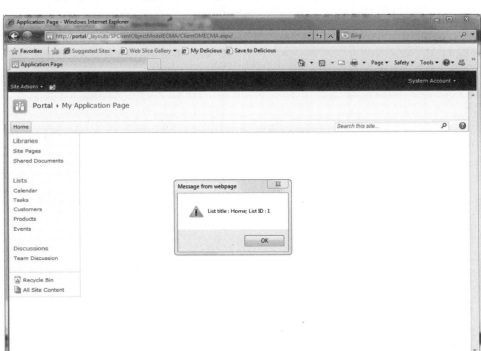

Figure 6–20. ECMAScript application

This application will iterate through the site pages in our portal and display the title and ID of each site page in an alert box. This illustrates talking to the site pages list in SharePoint through the JavaScript client object model.

Many things are available to do with ECMAScript/JavaScript. If that is the method you choose to use to interact with SharePoint 2010 by way of the client object model, then the ECMAScript version will offer many opportunities to interact, including with the ribbon control, modal dialog boxes, and user interaction. We will cover another example of interesting things to do with JavaScript in Chapter 9 on medium touch-point solutions. For more resources, refer to the SharePoint 2010 SDK client object model section. Search for SharePoint 2010 SDK and you will find both a downloadable and an MSDN online version.

Summary

In this chapter, we have introduced the client object model as a key paradigm in interacting with SharePoint 2010. We have shown examples of connecting to the client object model through the managed interface, the Silverlight interface, and the ECMAScript interface. These will prove to be valuable assets in interacting with SharePoint 2010 as we construct our approach to blended ASP.NET and SharePoint 2010 solutions.

CHAPTER 7

■ ■ ■

Business Connectivity Services

"Weak ties" – are always more important than strong ties.

Malcolm Gladwell

In building blended SharePoint 2010 and ASP.NET solutions, the next area to investigate is a built-in feature set in SharePoint 2010 known as Business Connectivity Services. While it is possible to build connected solutions without using built-in feature sets through methods such as we have investigated in previous chapters, if there are areas from which we can leverage features in the SharePoint 2010 product, it would be remiss not to investigate these. In this chapter, we will investigate the use of Business Connectivity Services and show how to use them from within SharePoint 2010 to complement ASP.NET solutions to expose external LOB systems.

What are Business Connectivity Services?

Business Connectivity Services (BCS) started out as a feature in the SharePoint 2007 product, known at that time as the Business Data Catalog (BDC). The purpose of the BDC was to enable users to read data from external systems. This provided basic connectivity between SharePoint and external databases and allowed for incorporating data from external line of business (LOB) systems and SharePoint. In the SharePoint 2007 product, BDC features were limited to the Enterprise version of the product.

BCS enables users in a similar fashion to read and write data from external systems. This can be accomplished by direct interaction with databases, through web services, and through customized connectors built as special Microsoft .NET Framework assemblies. SharePoint 2010 and Office 2010 applications have certain features that will enable them to use external data directly from online as well as offline stores. Developers can build BCS solutions in both SharePoint Designer 2010 as well as Visual Studio 2010 and gain access to rich feature sets for exposing external LOB systems to SharePoint. In the SharePoint 2010 product, aspects of BCS exist in every version of SharePoint, including SharePoint Foundation, Standard, and Enterprise SKUs. Microsoft opening up this rich feature set to the entire product line is a very helpful advance in providing connectivity to all SharePoint users.

■ **Note** SharePoint Designer 2010 is a desktop application that interacts with SharePoint 2010 through web services that expose the SharePoint object model. We examined some of the built-in web services offered by SharePoint 2010 in our previous chapter on the Client Object Model.

The main problem that BCS endeavors to solve is that in the modern information worker's environment, vital information necessary to accomplish daily tasks many times is stored in numerous different sources for data. Sources can include corporate-wide ERP systems, CRM systems, manufacturing systems, sales systems, as well as individual databases. Also a vital source for information is communication in the modern environment, including e-mail communications, blog posts, webinars, and other media offerings. Many times the challenge in the modern office is not whether or not data is available to support tasks, but the time and effort that it takes to access data in various systems. Data can be classified in many of these different systems as structured and unstructured data. Data that exists in relational databases would be an example of structured data, while e-mail communications stored in users' inboxes or public folders would be considered unstructured data. Data that exists in several places increases the complexity of amalgamating the data. Forcing the information worker to switch between several application interfaces to collect data and act upon it introduces productivity losses, data-entry errors, time loss, and potentially outdated or non synchronized data.

One other challenge is that typically applications that contain data are designed around user interfaces for that data that is specifically tailored to that data alone, as opposed to a more generic interface that can produce a portal or mashup of multiple data sources.

In SharePoint 2010, BCS allows for exposing data from a myriad of different sources under the same user interface paradigm that other SharePoint content types and lists are exposed under. This helps to solve the problem with multiple systems and different user interfaces.

Figure 7–1 is a high-level image depicting SharePoint 2010 BCS (this image is taken from the SharePoint 2010 SDK documentation).

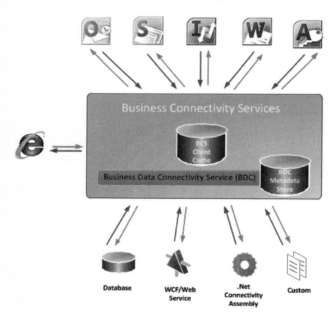

Figure 7–1. BCS high-level overview

Note the integration with the complete Microsoft Office Suite, including Outlook, SharePoint Workspace, InfoPath forms solutions, Microsoft Word, and Access databases. Internally in SharePoint 2010, BCS is represented by a Metadata Store, a BCS Client Cache, a Service, and a proxy that connect

SharePoint to BCS. The web browser is depicted as the interface into BCS through standard SharePoint 2010 items, and the bottom layer shows the methods that are available from which to interact with BCS—directly through a database, through web services, through a .NET connectivity assembly, and through a completely custom interface.

■ **Note** BCS is available in all versions of SharePoint 2010, but there are different elements and features that are available in each version. Table 7–1 has a representation of which features are available for each edition of SharePoint 2010.

Table 7–1. BCS Features in SharePoint 2010

BCS Feature	SharePoint Foundation 2010	SharePoint Server 2010 Standard Edition	SharePoint Server 2010 Enterprise Edition
External List	X	X	X
External Data Column	X	X	X
Business Data Connectivity (BDC) Service	X	X	X
Connector Framework	X	X	X
Secure Store Service		X	X
External Data Search		X	X
Profile Pages		X	X
Business Data Web Parts			X
Rich Client Integration			X

BCS has several core components that are important to understand before building a solution centered on BCS. The first of these components is external content types.

External Content Types

External content types are a core component of BCS, and are reusable metadata representations of both connectivity and external data-source information. They also expose an interface for behaviors that you want to define along with your external data representation in SharePoint 2010.

External Lists

External lists are a new component in SharePoint Foundation 2010. This feature allows users to access data from external systems in the exact same fashion that they do regular SharePoint lists. External lists use external content types behind the scenes to populate the data in the list from the configured BCS external connection. New features in SharePoint 2010 regarding BCS mean that lists can have complete interaction with back-end systems if the external content types and BCS connections are configured to allow it.

There are some built-in restrictions in External Lists when compared to regular SharePoint 2010 lists. External Lists depend completely upon the definitions set up for the list by the External Content Type, and as such, the user cannot add or modify columns in the list. Also, some list features are not available for External Lists that are available on regular SharePoint 2010 lists, such as workflow, multiple content types, versioning, and checking in and out. External lists are meant to provide a simple CRUD interface and view into an external system, as opposed to some of the built-in lists and document features present in SharePoint.

■ **Note** Whenever a feature is specified as a "SharePoint Foundation 2010 feature," this means that the feature is available in all of the SharePoint 2010 SKUs or product editions.

External Data Columns

External data columns were first introduced in the SharePoint 2007 product, and are also available to all SharePoint 2010 lists (except for External Lists). This column allows users to add a column from an External Content Type to any regular SharePoint 2010 list.

Setting Up BCS

You can set up SharePoint 2010 in two primary ways:

- Using SharePoint 2010 Central Administration
- Using PowerShell

Either way can work, but in general, Central Administration is a little more limited as far as working with your SharePoint 2010 farms and installs. PowerShell has over 200 cmdlets added to help manage your SharePoint 2010 environment, and resources, published scripts, books, and blogs are detailing out expertise in the PowerShell arena. The rule of thumb that I use is that for very quick and dirty installations, I may use the built-in wizards and Central Administration, but if I am standing up a SharePoint 2010 environment for any end-user functionality at all, I tend toward PowerShell-scripted installs. Actually, the job that I am in currently is a products lead for a company that sells a product completely based around PowerShell-scripted installs for configuring your SharePoint farms.

To set up BCS through Central Administration:

1. Navigate to Manage Services on Server, and ensure that the Business Data Connectivity Service is started. This shows up as in Figure 7–2.

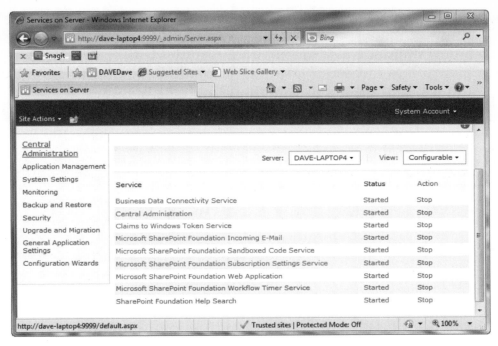

Figure 7–2. Manage services on server Page

2. After this, navigate to Application Management, and then Manage Service Applications.

3. You will need to start up a new Service Application called Business Connectivity Services, as shown in Figure 7–3.

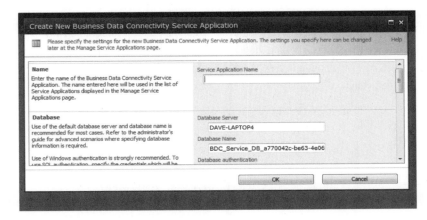

Figure 7–3. New BDC Service Application

This will set up the service application name, and create a database to store the BDC metadata in for connecting to external systems.

Alternatively, you can set up and provision BCS with PowerShell. To do this, you can execute the script entitled BCS.ps1 that is included in the downloads for the book (shown here):

```
Add-PSSnapin Microsoft.SharePoint.Powershell

$bdcName = "Business Data Connectivity Service"
$bdcDBName = "BDC_Services_DB"

$creds = Get-Credential

$managedAccount = Get-ManagedAccount $creds $true
$pool = New-SPServiceApplicationPool -Name "BDC Service App Pool" -Account $managedAccount

Write-Host "Creating $bdcName Service Application and Proxy..."
$bdc = New-SPBusinessDataCatalogServiceApplication -Name $bdcName -ApplicationPool $pool -
DatabaseName $bdcDBName

Write-Host "Starting the $bdcName Instance..."
Get-SPServiceInstance | where-object {$_.TypeName -eq $bdcName} | Start-SPServiceInstance

Write-Host "Completed Successfully!!"
```

BCS Solutions with SharePoint Designer

The first and simplest example that we will examine in setting up BCS for connections to external solutions will be done with SharePoint Designer (SPD) 2010. We will set up an example to connect up the external LOB sample system that Microsoft provides as SQL Server database samples to a SharePoint 2010 External Content Type, External List, and examine External Data Columns. We will connect our LOB system using built-in features in our SharePoint 2010 site.

■ **Tip** SharePoint Designer 2010 is an application that, as a SharePoint 2010 and Blended Solutions Architect and Developer, you will want to become familiar with. There are many tasks that SPD will perform more efficiently than interacting with SharePoint 2010 through Visual Studio 2010 and deployed solutions alone. There are tasks such as Branding SharePoint 2010 that we will cover in coming chapters that will require both SPD for initial configuration actions and VS2010 for deployment.

Open SharePoint 2010 Site

To begin:

1. Open up Microsoft SharePoint Designer 2010 and select Open Site, as shown in Figure 7–4.

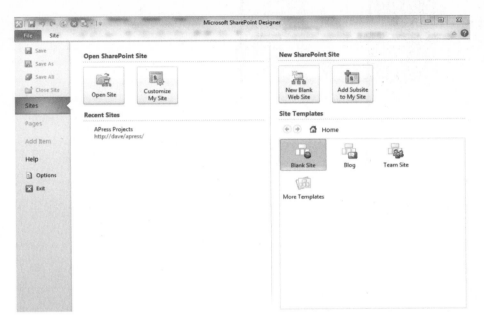

Figure 7–4. SharePoint Designer Open Site

2. Next, type in the URL of your SharePoint 2010 Site Collection, as shown in Figure 7–5.

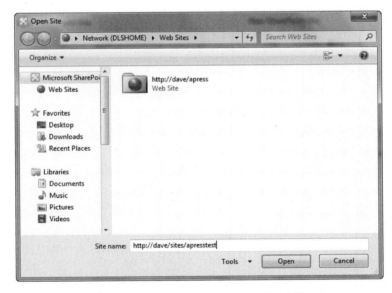

Figure 7–5. SharePoint Designer 2010—Open Site Collection

3. You will need to provide your SharePoint credentials to connect, as shown in Figure 7–6.

Figure 7–6. SharePoint Designer 2010 Credentials window

4. After opening your site in SharePoint Designer 2010, check out the main interaction window that appears (as shown in Figure 7–7):

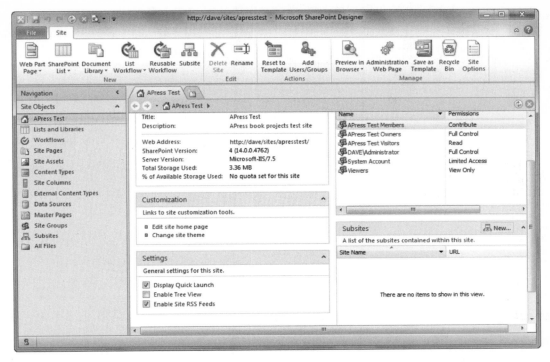

Figure 7–7. Microsoft SharePoint Designer 2010 Main Site Collection

Notice all of the items that are available to use to interact with your SharePoint Site in the left-hand navigation window. This includes interacting with all of your Lists and Libraries, Workflows, Site Pages, Site Assets such as graphics and other artifacts, Content Types, Site Columns, Master Pages, Site Groups, and Subsites. There is also another folder labeled All Files, which will expose every single file in the Site Collection.

In the middle of the left-hand navigation are items that we will use to define a BCS application. They are the External Content Types selection and the Data Sources selection. We will use these to define quickly a BCS connector, external content type, and External List for interacting with an external LOB system through our SharePoint 2010 interface.

Define New External Content Type

Let's start by defining the external content type. Select the External Content Types left navigation item and then select the New External Content Type in the top navigation section seen in Figure 7–8.

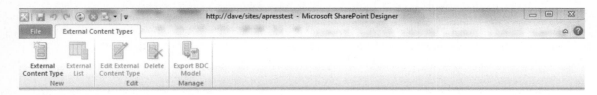

Figure 7–8. *External content type top navigation ribbon*

This will bring up the SharePoint Designer New external content type window as shown in Figure 7–9.

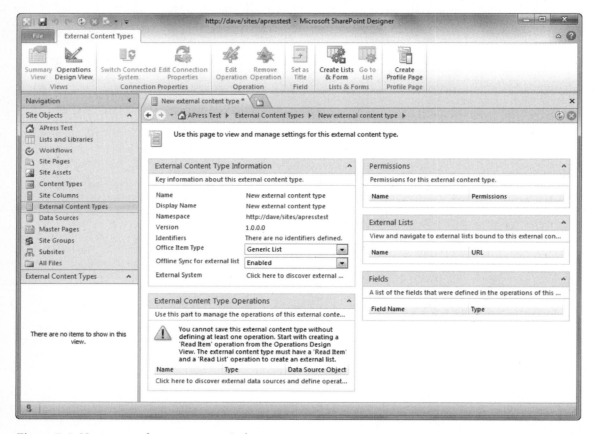

Figure 7–9. *New external content type window*

Discover Data Sources

From this window, we will access the window to discover external data sources and define the operations we will use against the data source.

1. To access the window, click the bottom link in Figure 7–9 that reads "Click here to discover external data sources and define operations". This will open up the window seen in Figure 7–10.

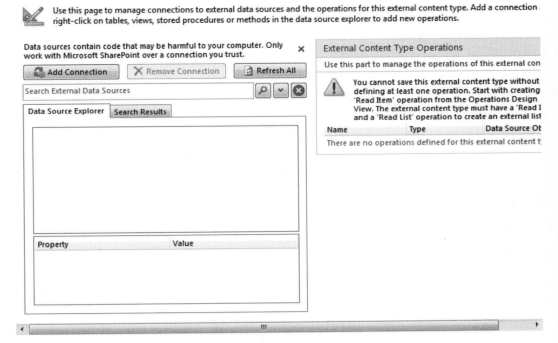

Figure 7–10. External Data Sources and Content Type Operation window

2. Click the Add Connection button, which brings up the External Data Source Connection Type window.

3. There are three types of connection types to choose between—.NET Type, SQL Server, and WCF Service. These are the three types of connectors that are available to work with in BCS. We will use SQL Server, as shown in Figure 7–11.

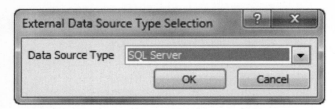

Figure 7–11. External Data Source Type Selection window

Data Source Credentials and Identity

Next, we will provide the SQL Server Connection credentials to connect to the external database that contains the LOB information, as shown in Figure 7–12.

Figure 7–12. *SQL Server Connection window*

Fill out the information for the database server, database name, and select credentials to connect to the database with. For a "least privileges" set up where you do not provide access to accounts unless it is needed, you would choose to connect with the user's identity and then define the proper credentials for the users in the external database.

Other options include impersonating a Windows identity that has permissions to access the database. This option is simpler to administer, but does not provide the same audit trail for database changes. You can also impersonate a custom identity.

■ **Tip** If you are using SharePoint Foundation 2010, there is a difference in how permissions work. In the SQL Server Connection window in Figure 7–12, there are three available choices to make with how to connect to SQL Server. Two of these choices, Connect with Impersonated Windows Identity and Connect with Impersonated Custom Identity, depend upon the Secure Store Service to store credentials to pass between SharePoint 2010 and the back-end SQL Server database systems. However, the Secure Store Service is only available in the SharePoint Server 2010 products, both the Standard and the Enterprise products. You will need to use the Connect With User's Identity option in SharePoint Foundation 2010 to connect to external lists and content types. This means that you will need to manage permissions to the SQL Server database on the back end to include logins for all of your SharePoint Users. This is somewhat higher administrative overhead on the SQL Server end for this feature, but the tradeoff is that it is free. In the SharePoint 2007 versions, no BDC features were included in the free WSS 3.0 product.

After adding the database connection, it will show up in your New external content type window as we saw in Figure 7–10. The added connection will provide interfaces into Tables, Views, and Procedures, as shown in Figure 7–13.

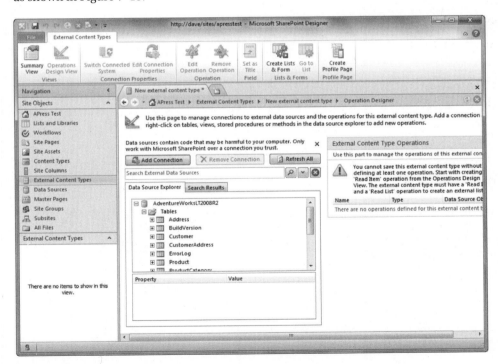

Figure 7–13. Added AdventureWorksLT2008R2 connection

Create Operations

For this exercise, we will select the Customer table to provide an interface for.

1. Right-click the Customer table and select Create All Operations. This will provide all of the basic CRUD interface for interacting with the Customer database.

■ **Note** If you do not want to provide the ability to change database values in the external system, you can specify creating the Read operation only, which will show up in the External Content Type and External List with view-only values. This is one way to protect external data. There are other ways as well, including options for setting up non-essential interaction through a replicated database table.

---

2. This brings up the Operations Parameters window. Click Next on this window, and you will see the window for defining data parameters shown in Figure 7–14.

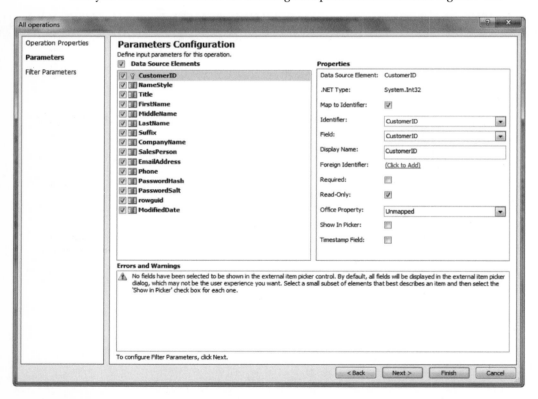

Figure 7–14. Paramaters Configuration window.

3. In this window, you can highlight and select the fields that you would like to show in the External Picker, such as LastName and FirstName. Before you do this, ensure that your CRUD operations will support adding a default value for new rows in the database.

4. The last window before finalizing is adding a filter parameter. This is shown in Figure 7–15. For this operation, we added a Limit type filter parameter limiting the rows retrieved from the Customer table to 100 at a time. This will help control performance constraints.

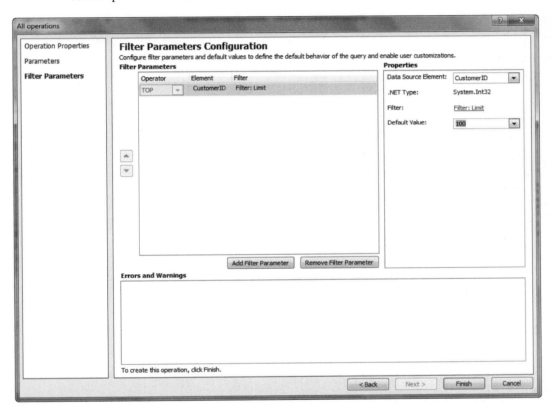

Figure 7–15. Adding a Filter Parameter

5. Next, click the Finish button and this will finish creating your External Content Type. You will see something similar to Figure 7–16 in the right-hand window in your SharePoint Designer 2010 application.

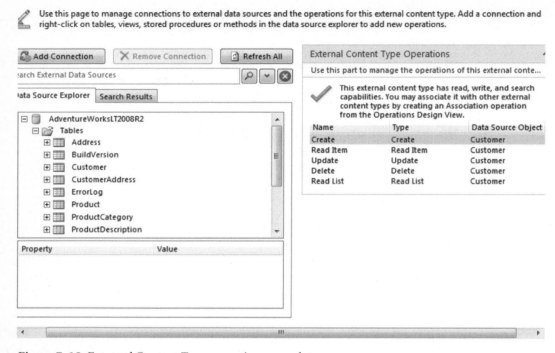

Use this page to manage connections to external data sources and the operations for this external content type. Add a connection and right-click on tables, views, stored procedures or methods in the data source explorer to add new operations.

Figure 7–16. External Content Type operations complete

Notice the check mark in the right-hand window, and the message that your external content type has read, write, and search capabilities.

Create External Lists and Forms

The last step in creating an External List and Forms that we can add to our SharePoint 2010 site is to select Create Lists and Forms from the ribbon, as seen in Figure 7–17.

Figure 7–17. Create Lists and Forms from External Content Types Designer window

For the External List, you can create a name and Description, as in Figure 7–18.

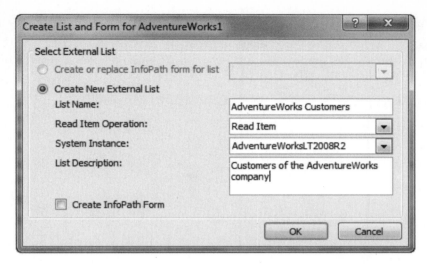

Figure 7–18. Create List and Form window

This will finalize creating the External List and you will see it on the Left Nav area of the QuickLaunch. The final external list will appear as shown in Figure 7–19.

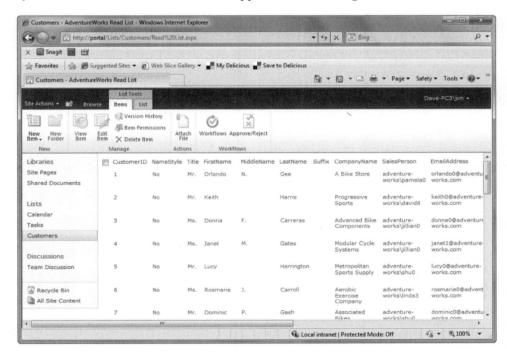

Figure 7–19. External List in SharePoint Site

Export BDC Model for Visual Studio 2010

The last thing we will do with this is to export the BDC Model so that it can be imported into Visual Studio and utilized in different SharePoint 2010 farms. Select the Export BDC Model option from the SharePoint Designer ribbon, as shown in Figure 7–20.

Figure 7–20. *Export BDC Model selection*

You can name the Model and select Default for the settings to use with Visual Studio 2010, as in Figure 7–21.

Figure 7–21. *Export BDC Model settings*

In the subsequent window, the name of the file is shown and the file is saved with a .bdcm extension. You can import this file into Visual Studio for use in other environments.

One other thing to note is that if any of these settings that you choose in configuring your connections or permissions to the back-end SQL Server database are ones that you would like to change later, you can export the BDC Model to a .bdcm file and use Central Administration to import the file. An example of a .bdcm file is shown as follows and is included in the Chapter 7 downloadable code content—named AdventureWorks.bdcm. The first part of the file including connection information is shown, then representative information from the rest of the file to save space.

```
<?xml version="1.0" encoding="utf-16" standalone="yes"?>
<Model xmlns:xsi="http://www.w3.org/2001/XMLSchema-instance"
xsi:schemaLocation="http://schemas.microsoft.com/windows/2007/BusinessDataCatalog
BDCMetadata.xsd" Name="AdventureWorks"
xmlns="http://schemas.microsoft.com/windows/2007/BusinessDataCatalog">
  <LobSystems>
    <LobSystem Type="Database" Name="AdventureWorksLT2008">
      <Properties>
        <Property Name="WildcardCharacter" Type="System.String">%</Property>
      </Properties>
      <Proxy />
      <LobSystemInstances>
        <LobSystemInstance Name="AdventureWorksLT2008">
          <Properties>
            <Property Name="AuthenticationMode" Type="System.String">PassThrough</Property>
```

```xml
                <Property Name="DatabaseAccessProvider" Type="System.String">SqlServer</Property>
                <Property Name="RdbConnection Data Source" Type="System.String">DAVE-
PC3</Property>
                <Property Name="RdbConnection Initial Catalog"
Type="System.String">AdventureWorksLT2008</Property>
                <Property Name="RdbConnection Integrated Security"
Type="System.String">SSPI</Property>
                <Property Name="RdbConnection Pooling" Type="System.String">True</Property>
                <Property Name="SsoProviderImplementation"
Type="System.String">Microsoft.Office.SecureStoreService.Server.SecureStoreProvider,
Microsoft.Office.SecureStoreService, Version=14.0.0.0, Culture=neutral,
PublicKeyToken=71e9bce111e9429c</Property>
                <Property Name="SsoApplicationId" Type="System.String">AdventureWorks</Property>
                <Property Name="ShowInSearchUI" Type="System.String"></Property>
            </Properties>
          </LobSystemInstance>
        </LobSystemInstances>
        <Entities>
          <Entity Namespace="http://portal" Version="1.0.0.0" EstimatedInstanceCount="10000"
Name="AdventureWorks" DefaultDisplayName="AdventureWorks">
            <Identifiers>
              <Identifier TypeName="System.Int32" Name="CustomerID" />
            </Identifiers>
            <Methods>
              <Method Name="Create" DefaultDisplayName="AdventureWorks Create">
                <Properties>
                  <Property Name="RdbCommandType" Type="System.Data.CommandType, System.Data,
Version=2.0.0.0, Culture=neutral, PublicKeyToken=b77a5c561934e089">Text</Property>
                  <Property Name="RdbCommandText" Type="System.String">INSERT INTO
[SalesLT].[Customer]([NameStyle] , [Title] , [FirstName] , [MiddleName] , [LastName] ,
[Suffix] , [CompanyName] , [SalesPerson] , [EmailAddress] , [Phone] , [PasswordHash] ,
[PasswordSalt] , [rowguid] , [ModifiedDate]) VALUES(@NameStyle , @Title , @FirstName ,
@MiddleName , @LastName , @Suffix , @CompanyName , @SalesPerson , @EmailAddress , @Phone ,
@PasswordHash , @PasswordSalt , @rowguid , @ModifiedDate) SELECT [CustomerID] FROM
[SalesLT].[Customer] WHERE [CustomerID] = SCOPE_IDENTITY()</Property>
                  <Property Name="BackEndObjectType"
Type="System.String">SqlServerTable</Property>
                  <Property Name="BackEndObject" Type="System.String">Customer</Property>
                  <Property Name="Schema" Type="System.String">SalesLT</Property>
                </Properties>
                <Parameters>
                  <Parameter Direction="In" Name="@NameStyle">
                    <TypeDescriptor TypeName="System.Boolean" CreatorField="true"
Name="NameStyle" />
                  </Parameter>

… omitted to end of file  …
```

Import BDC Model with Central Administration

You can import the .bdcm file from Central Administration through the Manage Service Applications window, as seen in Figure 7–22.

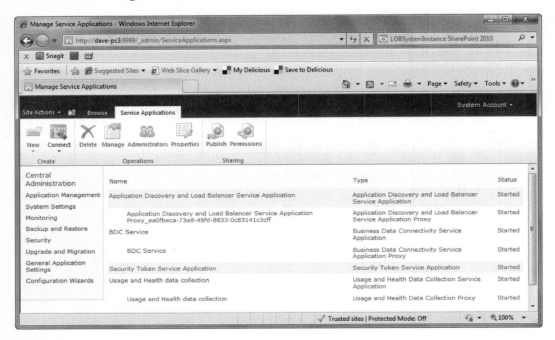

Figure 7–22. Manage Service Applications

Select the BDC Service link from the main screen, and you will be taken to the External Content Types management screen and can select Import BDC Model from the top ribbon, as seen in Figure 7–23

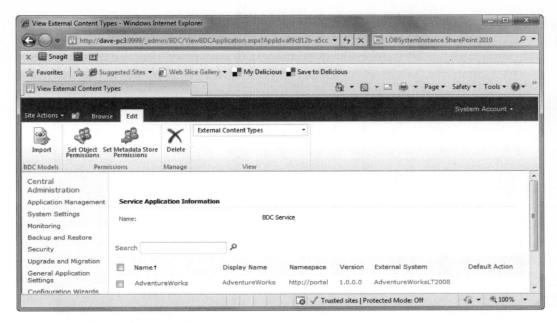

Figure 7–23. External Content Types management

You can easily import .bdcm files through this interface and use them from there. To create an External List once the BDC Model, External Content Type, and External Systems are imported and set up, you may use SharePoint Designer 2010. Select your External Content Type from the External Content Types menu on the left hand side, and create a list with the External List button at the top.

BCS Solutions with Visual Studio 2010

The next project we will be coding is to configure a .NET Assembly type BDC Model using Visual Studio 2010. This model will interact with a very simple SQL Server database named Events, which has an Events table contained in it. You can find the code for the finished Visual Studio project in the download section of the book under Chapter 7, and is entitled BDCModelEvents.

Create Events Database and Table

First, create a database named Events in your SQL Server instance, and use the following script to create the SQL table:

```
CREATE TABLE [dbo].[Events] (
    [EventID]          INT            NULL,
    [EventName]        NVARCHAR (50)  NULL,
    [EventDescription] NVARCHAR (500) NULL,
    [EventVenue]       NVARCHAR (100) NULL,
    [EventDate]        DATE           NULL
);
```

New SharePoint BDC Model Project

Next, open Visual Studio 2010 and start a New Project of type as shown in Figure 7–24. Call it
BdcModelEvents.

Figure 7–24. *New Business Data Connectivity Model project*

Choose Deploy as a farm solution in the next dialog box, and ensure that your local SharePoint
environment appears as well. The next step in creating a BDC Model is working with a couple of new
features in Visual Studio 2010, the BDC Model Editor, the BDC Explorer, and the BDC Method Details
window. You can see all of these windows in Figure 7–25.

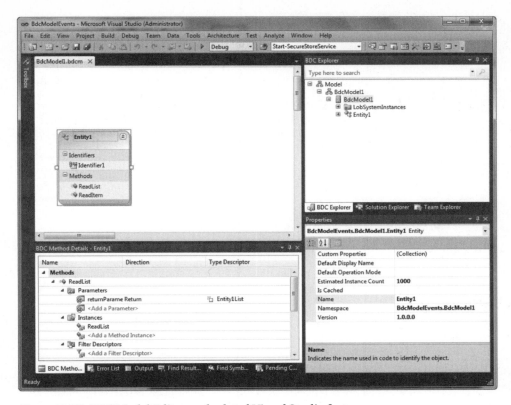

Figure 7–25. BDC Model Editor and related Visual Studio features

Create Events Code and EventsService Code

From this point, we need to code the class object that corresponds to our events that will show up in our SharePoint list. Create a class called Events.cs, and add the following code:

```
using System;
using System.Collections.Generic;
using System.Linq;
using System.Text;

namespace BdcModelEvents.BdcModel1
{
    /// <summary>
    /// Event class
    /// </summary>
    public partial class Event
    {
        public Int32 EventID { get; set; }
        public string EventName { get; set; }
        public string EventDescription { get; set; }
```

```
        public string EventVenue { get; set; }
        public DateTime EventDate { get; set; }
    }
}
```

This is a simple class used as the entity passed back and forth between the business object and the back-end system.

Next, we need to provide the code for specific operations within the BDC Model. These are ReadList, ReadItem, Create, Update, and Delete. Create a file called EventService.cs and code these methods. The following code is partial to show an example of how to interact with ReadItem; the full code is available in the downloads.

```
namespace BdcModelEvents.BdcModel1
{
    /// <summary>
    /// All the methods for retrieving, updating and deleting data are implemented in this
class file.
    /// The samples below show the finder and specific finder method for BdcModel1.
    /// </summary>
    public class EventService
    {

        static SqlConnection getSqlConnection()
        {
            SqlConnection sqlConn = new SqlConnection("Integrated Security=SSPI; Persist
Security Info=false; Data Source=DAVE-PC3; Initial Catalog=Events");
            return (sqlConn);
        }
        /// <summary>
        /// This is a sample specific finder method for BdcModel1.
        /// If you want to delete or rename the method think about changing the xml in the BDC
model file as well.
        /// </summary>
        /// <param name="id"></param>
        /// <returns>Entity1</returns>
        public static Event ReadItem(int id)
        {
            Event event1 = new Event();
            using (SqlConnection conn = getSqlConnection())
            {
                string sqlCmd = "SELECT * FROM Events WHERE EventID = " + id.ToString();
                using (SqlCommand com = conn.CreateCommand())
                {
                    com.CommandText = sqlCmd;
                    SqlDataReader rdr = com.ExecuteReader(CommandBehavior.CloseConnection);
                    if (rdr.Read())
                    {
                        event1.EventID = Int32.Parse(rdr["EventID"].ToString());
                        event1.EventName = rdr["EventName"].ToString();
                        event1.EventDescription = rdr["EventDescription"].ToString();
                        event1.EventVenue = rdr["EventVenue"].ToString();
                        event1.EventDate = DateTime.Parse(rdr["EventDate"].ToString());

                    }
```

```
        else
        {
            event1.EventID = -1;
            event1.EventName = "Event not found";
            event1.EventDescription = "";
        }
    }
}
    return event1;

}
```

Note that the method signatures are the important thing to notice for .NET Assembly BDC Models. The actual code to interact with SQL Server you probably would not implement, as that task is done more easily with the SharePoint Designer 2010 method—but this is a simple example to show how to accomplish the task. To get the BDCModelEvents project to work in your environment, you would need to replace your SiteUrl for the one in the project as well as your connection string information.

Finish BDC Model and Deploy to SharePoint

The next step is to wire up the EventService class methods to the BDC Model. Use the BDC Model Editor windows to perform this step, and the final step will look like the one in the sample code.

After you complete this step, you are ready to deploy your BDCModelEvents solution to your SharePoint environment.

DEPLOYING TO SHAREPOINT FOUNDATION 2010

If you are trying to deploy a BDC Model solution to a SharePoint Foundation 2010 environment, there are three DLLs from SharePoint Server 2010 that you will need to manually install in the GAC that are used by Visual Studio deployment packages. They are as follows:

- Microsoft.Office.SharePoint.ClientExtensions.dll
- Microsoft.Office.SharePoint.ClientExtensions.Intl.dll
- Microsoft.Office.Server.dll

The Microsoft.Office.SharePoint.ClientExtensions.Intl.dll must be extracted from the GAC on a SharePoint Server 2010 machine; you can find it here:

```
C:\Windows\assembly\GAC_MSIL\microsoft.office.sharepoint.clientextensions.intl\14.0.0.0_
_71e9bce111e9429c\
```

You can find the other two DLLs in the SharePoint Root ISAPI folder at:

```
C:\Program Files\Common Files\Microsoft Shared\Web Server Extensions\14\ISAPI
```

Install those two DLLs to the GAC—C:\Windows\Assembly. You can do this with the Visual Studio 2010 Tools command prompt using a command similar to the following (include the path to your DLL):

```
Gacutil /I Microsoft.Office.Server.dll
```

After this is completed, you can reopen Visual Studio 2010 and deploy your BDC Model solution to a SharePoint Foundation 2010 site collection.

After deployment, you will need to set permissions for your users on the BDC Objects, as seen in Figure 7–26.

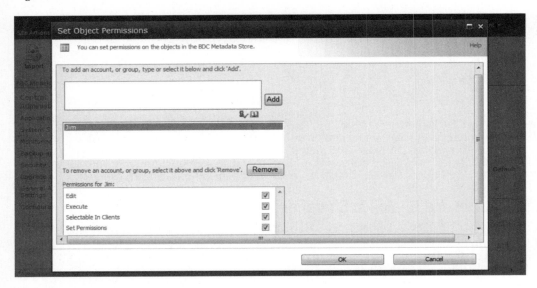

Figure 7–26. *Set object permissions*

Then, with objects deployed through Visual Studio 2010, you can use this external content type to create an External List in your Site area. Do this by going to the Lists administration page and selecting Create. You can see the screen in Figure 7–27.

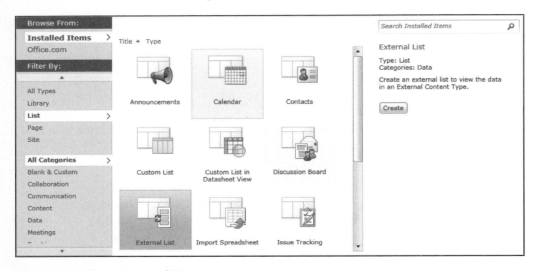

Figure 7–27. *Create External List*

Here you should be able to name your external list and access the picker to select the external content type, as shown in Figure 7–28.

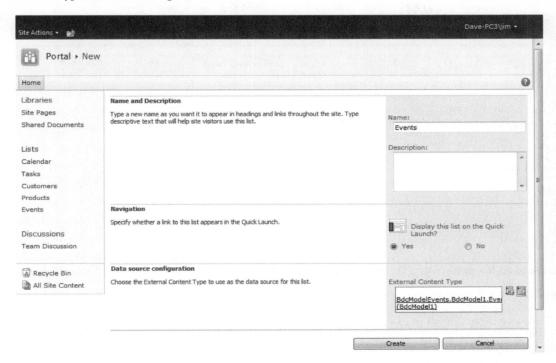

Figure 7–28. External Content Type selection

Your event list should appear, as shown in Figure 7–29.

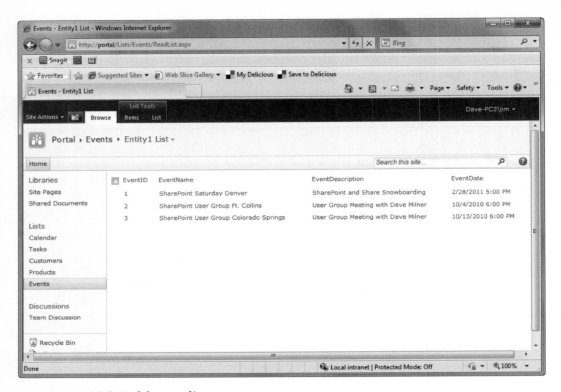

Figure 7–29. BDC Model events list

This completes the walkthrough section on creating BCS solutions with Visual Studio 2010 and examples.

BCS Architecture

After digging into the hands-on examples of producing BCS Connectors, External Content Types, and External Lists using SharePoint Designer 2010 and Visual Studio 2010, let's take a look at how the underlying architecture of BCS works. Figure 7–30 shows the common components of BCS.

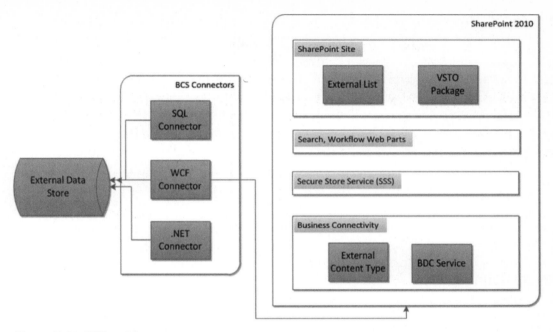

Figure 7–30. BCS architecture

External Data Store

The external data store in BCS represents any information store in your LOB applications. This could range from a serialized .xml file to a relational database, to a non-relational database, to a cloud service such as Azure or Amazon S3. If there is a connector to the external store, it can be used in SharePoint BCS 2010.

BCS Connectors

Connectors are the glue that binds external data stores and your SharePoint 2010 system together. There are built-in connectors and tools available to set them up, as we saw in SharePoint Designer 2010. SharePoint Designer can wire up direct SQL Server data connections as well as WCF Service endpoints.

■ **Tip** It is possible to use SharePoint Designer 2010 to design a SQL Server BCS Connector, then to modify the connector to work with other relational databases such as Oracle. To do this, you would export your .bdcm model from SharePoint Designer 2010 and modify some of the values for the database connectivity, and re-import it into SharePoint 2010. You can find an article describing this process in more depth at `http://msdn.microsoft.com/en-us/library/ff464424(office.14).aspx` —*How to: Connect to an Oracle Database Using Business Connectivity Services.* You could use the same process to work with other types of databases.

You can also build custom connectors using the .NET Assembly type of connector. Connectors also are a market where SharePoint third-party vendors are active, so if you are looking in this area, be sure to research this market sector to see if there is a connector available for purchase to connect to your back-end external data store.

Business Connectivity

This layer of the architecture represents the Central Administration and/or PowerShell layers for interacting with BCS, including the SQL Server databases for the BDC_Service database that stores all of the BCS metadata, as well as the BDC Service that runs on the SharePoint 2010 server.

Secure Store Service

The Secure Store Service is a shared service that provides the ability to store and map credentials of users such as account names and passwords. It is used with BCS to provide credentials required to connect to external systems and associate those credentials to a specific identity or group of identities. Multiple users can access external systems using a single set of credentials.

In order to store credentials to connect to external systems, you must create a new Target Application in the SSS Application.

1. Select Manage Service Applications from Central Administration, then select the Secure Store Service.

2. From there, select the ribbon command for New Target Application, and the form shown in Figure 7–31 appears.

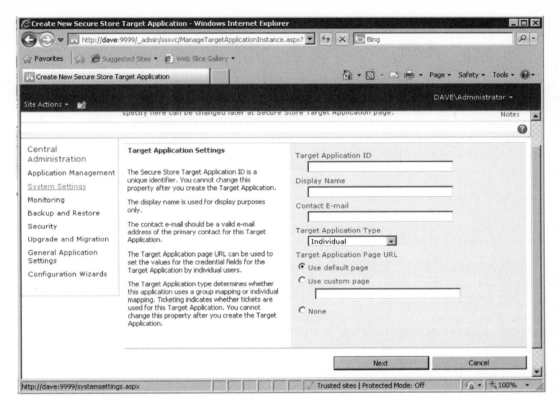

Figure 7–31. Create New Target Application in Secure Store Service

3. In this window, define a target application ID that will be tied to an external system later. The Target Application Type can be individual, but can also be used to map a Group to a single set of credentials to connect to an external system.

4. After this, select Next and enter the Windows Credentials, as shown in Figure 7–32. This window is used to define which fields are stored along with the Target Application. Here, we will use a Windows User Name and Password, but it is also available to store other credentials.

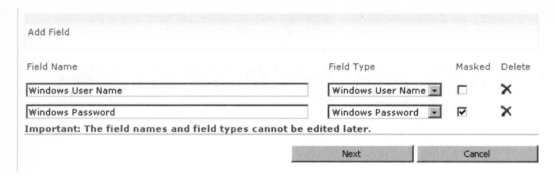

Figure 7–32. Add Credentials in New Target Application—SSS

5. Next, we will define the administrators and groups with whom the credentials will be associated, as shown in Figure 7–33.

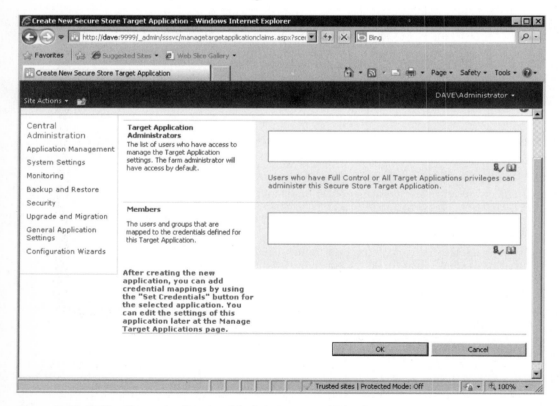

Figure 7–33. Define Target Application Administrators and Members

6. Next, after clicking OK and finalizing the definition of the Target Application, you can define specific credentials for the application. Select the Target Application and then Set Credentials, as shown in Figures 7–34 and 7–35.

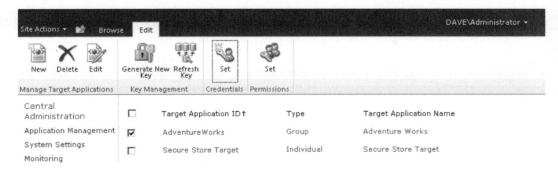

Figure 7–34. Set credentials for Secure Store Target Application

Set Credentials for Secure Store Target Application (Group)

Set values for the credential fields that are defined for this Secure Store Target Application.   Help

Warning: this page is not encrypted for secure communication. User names, passwords, and any other information will be sent in clear text. For more information, contact your administrator.

Target Application Name: Adventure Works
Target Application ID: AdventureWorks

Credential Owners: All Authenticated Users

Credential owners

Name	Value
Windows User Name	
Windows Password	
Confirm Windows Password	

Note: Once the credentials are set, they cannot be retrieved by the administrator. Any existing credentials for this credential owner will be overwritten.

OK   Cancel

Figure 7–35. Set credentials for Secure Store Target Application 2

Once these credentials are in place, they can be used when defining External Content Types to connect to external systems.

> ■ **Note** Secure Store Service is not available in SharePoint Foundation 2010, so the credentials used must be of type Pass-Through.

The Secure Store Service is a piece that is often used together with BCS to access external systems. Storing credentials to use for the external systems helps to reduce the overhead on administering access to the systems for groups of users. Just as you can define and start up the BCS Service itself through Central Administration and PowerShell, you can do so for SSS in a similar fashion.

Summary

In this chapter, we have highlighted an important built-in feature of SharePoint 2010 that is used to connect to external systems and databases. We've highlighted what Business Connectivity Services (BCS) are, talked about the SharePoint components associated with them, and how to set them up. We have provided a detailed example of how to set up BCS from SharePoint Designer, showed how to code BCS solutions with Visual Studio 2010, and highlighted the overall architecture of BCS including security. Business Connectivity Services are an important part of building blended ASP.NET and SharePoint 2010 solutions and in providing a common integration point.

■ ■ ■

CHAPTER 8

Touch Points–Integrating SharePoint 2010 and ASP.NET

"Ignorance is like a delicate fruit; touch it and the bloom is gone."

Oscar Wilde

In this section of the book (Chapters 8, 9, and 10), we will delve into strategies and approaches for integrating ASP.NET applications and SharePoint 2010 solutions. In our previous chapters, we have built some of the core fundamentals of understanding for the SharePoint 2010 product from a development standpoint. We will build upon these concepts and fundamentals in the final three chapters to put together a solid fundamental approach to using SharePoint 2010 as a development platform and planning out and executing on approaches to SharePoint 2010 living and functioning in a full suite of ASP.NET-focused web sites and products.

As we have seen in previous chapters, SharePoint 2010 is a relatively complex product. We have barely scratched the surface with what we have covered in the feature set and makeup of SharePoint 2010. We have seen that SharePoint is an ASP.NET-based product in itself, and makes use of many of the advances in the ASP.NET platform over the years in its makeup and construct. In this chapter, we will explain the thinking behind *touch points* and their help in organizing your approach to blended SharePoint 2010 and ASP.NET development. We will define integration factors behind these, present example business scenarios, and talk about impact upon your organization depending upon the touch-point approach that you select. Then we will cover low touch-point solutions, which include concepts of branding and customization of SharePoint 2010 and ASP.NET sites, talk about Publishing Layouts in SharePoint 2010, and discuss modifications to navigation in blended solutions.

Integration Factors

When we start to get into the process of integrating ASP.NET and SharePoint 2010, there are many factors to consider, and some of the top factors among them are really not software-related, but more related to the company doing the integrating and the makeup of the individuals, departments, and interactions among those companies. This may sound like a radical concept at this point in the book after spending so much time building up the technical aspects of the SharePoint 2010 product, but it is a good time to come up for air, get in our mental hot-air balloons, and take a ride back up to the 10,000-foot level where we can take a look at the countryside.

From a sheer business effectiveness standpoint, technical solutions are really of no more value than the value they provide end users to do their jobs. IT in general is a service industry. What this means is that in designing software, architecting solutions, and putting together plans for ongoing solutions, this concept must be in the forefront of our minds. How does my solution help the particular end user of my product? How does my solution help the business perspective of my end users' corporations? If we have a clear answer, then this is great. However, if the answer remains somewhat murky, then it is time to go back and examine what we are trying to accomplish with our solution.

The timeframe in which we are doing our architecture planning is absolutely the appropriate time to do this. Once we have decided upon an approach, set up servers and operating systems, installed SharePoint 2010, set up our development and test environments, and have our teams working on our projects appropriately blended, we have too large of a vested interest in traveling back to this level and re-examining things. And if our approach is flawed, then that flaw will typically carry through all the way to the end of the solution being delivered. Teams and organizations, once they set upon a path typically have a high level of difficulty backing up and going at a problem from a different approach. The best time to set the approach is right at the beginning. This is the time during which the approach and the methods we are most vital to the outcome of the solution and project. This is the time during which the top-level architects, strategists, and corporate sponsors should be involved. A lot of the beginning of this message is addressed to these individuals in an organization.

So, because I am taking the time to address this group of people, let me try to endeavor to help you clarify your business needs and approach to blended SharePoint 2010 and ASP.NET solutions. What is a good reason for doing this? What types of problems can I solve? How can I help my end users? Perhaps you already have a good idea about this, perhaps not.

With some of my work in developing this book, I have presented these concepts at a number of different .NET user groups, SharePoint user groups, and SharePoint conferences. I have carried out numerous discussions with members of the SharePoint community and the .NET development community, have talked over aspects of this with top-level individuals in both of these areas, including SharePoint product team members, Microsoft field consultants, MVPs, and MCMs in SharePoint and ASP.NET. Also, in giving presentations on this topic, I have been involved in numerous discussions with concerned IT professionals talking over their specific business environments and what they are hoping to accomplish with their approach and solutions. I have also coached teams of people working on these types of projects.

What I will present emerging from all of this and these sessions are some examples of business scenarios where both ASP.NET and SharePoint present a clear business solution that provides good end-user value. After that, I will discuss some aspects of IT organizations and cultures and how approaches may differ depending on these factors and variables.

The end goal we are trying to get to with this approach is a little bit like a popular advertising commercial for a tasty product that mixes peanut butter and chocolate. The advertisement in a number of its forms has two people walking around, one eating a chocolate bar, and another eating from a jar of peanut butter. They collide into each other and fall down, and in the ensuing conversation, one person says to the other, "You've got peanut butter on my chocolate". The other responds, "No, you've got your chocolate in my peanut butter". Then both of them taste the resulting mix and come up with smiles on their face.

This is the experience that I envision for all of you. You may be coming from different backgrounds in ASP.NET development, SharePoint development, and administration. You may be the leader of a team of developers looking for some help in navigating unfamiliar waters. You may be a corporate CIO with a technical background looking for the right resource and approach to point your smart and capable team at. From all aspects, my vision for you is to have your peanut butter and chocolate and the same smile on your faces that those individuals in the commercial had. The smile originating from coming up with a unique and wonderful solution that is a mixture of SharePoint and ASP.NET and brings to our world software that brings us more mastery over our world and business environment.

Example Business Scenarios

In discussions with various individuals, there are a number of example cases and types of cases of business problems to solve and scenarios that in my estimation are solution categories. These categories all present markings of solutions that are absolutely going to require a combined SharePoint 2010 and ASP.NET approach to organization, planning, and implementation.

Corporate Internet and Service Portals

This type of scenario is one that is a more generic solution for a corporate presence. SharePoint 2010, with its publishing feature set, offers a great option for a corporate Internet presence. There are many features there such as publishing workflows, great templates and designs, and other aspects of SharePoint 2010 that make it fantastic for corporate Internets.

Yet the reality remains that there are many times it may not represent the best solution to use SharePoint 2010 for the main corporate Internet site. These reasons could be as simple as there is a great deal of effort already invested into the current corporate web site, and replacing it is not the primary goal. The web site has an established brand, sections, and functionality. Other reasons could include some such as the corporate Internet site that exists is not an ASP.NET site, but built with one of the other available web technologies out there, such as Java or PHP.

In this solution, SharePoint 2010 is coming to the table on the services side. With rich content-management features, and excellent document management features, SharePoint is an excellent candidate for a services portal. You can offer users all of the rich access to features of SharePoint 2010 such as we have highlighted in the first chapter of the book as part of the services your company offers. And you can retain the investment in your current Internet presence and web site. Both of these elements need to exist in your current environment, perhaps using the same hardware and IT personnel to maintain and enhance them.

Existing ASP.NET Product

This scenario is one in which either your company or your division has an existing investment in a relatively complex ASP.NET product. The product has a fairly large number of pages, can do complex calculations, ties to many different external systems, and has a complex database involved.

New requirements for the product, or just a general realization, lead you to the fact that document management is a feature that would add a tremendous amount of value to the product. Technical documents, diagrams, pictures, Microsoft Office documents such as contracts, blueprints, contractual reporting, and other similar things are vital parts of the overall business process that your product is involved with. Perhaps your product could offer the generation of and storage of reports in a document library. Perhaps the offering of a lifecycle of documents that involve built-in versioning and workflow approvals routing is vital to your product.

Perhaps your product could benefit from some of the portal capabilities of SharePoint 2010, in that the product could offer the ability to expand using SharePoint 2010 team sites to spin out multiple department-level implementations of your product and solution.

Perhaps your product could benefit from some of the social networking capabilities of SharePoint 2010, incorporating rich internal networking and content capabilities. You might want to incorporate internal blogging as part of your blended solution.

New Blended Solution

This scenario is one where there is no existing investment in either SharePoint 2010 or ASP.NET. However, in evaluating the options for developing the solution, it is seen that SharePoint 2010 offers a rich development platform to build upon that could reduce your time to market for the solution.

Expanding Your Corporate Portal

In this scenario, you have an existing investment in SharePoint, perhaps are just upgrading to SharePoint 2010, and your portal has a large number of departmental users involved. You want to roll out new ASP.NET features and solutions to all of your existing users quickly and in an environment with which they are already familiar. You plan to leverage SharePoint 2010 as your solution delivery platform, and want to deploy your solution in a fashion that will present low impact to your existing environment, but rich features for your solutions.

Talking to SharePoint

In this scenario, you have a new or existing product. The large majority of your customer install base uses SharePoint. You want to develop features on your product or present a solution that allows your existing software to talk to SharePoint and interact with SharePoint data.

■ **Note** These example business scenarios just represent a few of the possible types of use cases or scenarios that could arise. There are many more scenarios that are not represented here—you may find that your scenario is close to one of these, a combination of a couple of these, or a completely different one altogether. The purpose of the examples is to point out a few major categories of scenarios where blended SharePoint 2010 and ASP.NET solutions could make sense or provide business advantages.

Organizational Factors

In addition to constraints in presenting solutions to end users, the reality of developing solutions, staffing projects, and working toward common goals is that you can only develop solutions with what you have, not with what you do not have.

How this comes into play in selecting approaches with blended SharePoint 2010 and ASP.NET solutions is that you need to take into account the makeup of the organization that you currently have to do this with. You can also do this by taking into account the organization that you will see after staffing it with where you want to go.

Where does this matter? In what way, shape, or form does this have anything to do with software development?

Organizational Examples

Take a couple of the business scenarios explained previously as examples. Perhaps your company has an existing ASP.NET product. Your company may not have SharePoint currently, or may currently have a limited SharePoint portal for internal use. What does that organization look like? You probably will have a development team that can range in size from one individual to a few hundred that is involved with the development of your product. You may have another team that manages your SharePoint site. Here, the largest amount of current investment will impact and contribute toward the approach you want to take. The choices you make will most likely be easier to implement if they have a lesser amount of impact on your existing ASP.NET development team, as opposed to ramping up SharePoint expertise in-house or through outside engagements.

In another example, perhaps you have a large investment in a corporate SharePoint portal, including an architect and a team of SharePoint administrators and developers. In this scenario, you have a completely different makeup of organizational interaction, corporate culture, and politics. The choices you make will be easier to implement if you do not do things that will jeopardize your current SharePoint environment and farm. (Of course, the choice to not jeopardize your SharePoint farm is never a bad one.)

SharePoint-Centric Organizations

In evaluating your organization for potential solution approaches, it is important to be cognizant of the current blend of your organization's personnel and culture. If your organization already uses SharePoint to a large extent—if SharePoint team sites are widely used across all organizations, if your corporate Internet presence consists completely of a SharePoint publishing site, or the number of personnel dedicated to the SharePoint side of your IT outnumbers the .NET development side of your company— then your organization can be looked at from a SharePoint-centric viewpoint. It is highly likely in this type of organization that the solutions you will be developing will be SharePoint-centric, and with that comes a particular approach. Some of the questions that you can ask yourself and your leadership to identify a SharePoint-centric organization are as follows:

- What is the ratio of dedicated SharePoint personnel to dedicated .NET development personnel in my company? >1, = 1, <1 ?

- What is the ratio of the dedicated SharePoint hardware to dedicated .NET production hardware? >1, =1, <1?

- Is the scope of the SharePoint farm that we will be dealing with in our solution much greater than the solution itself?

- What is the makeup of the current or envisioned user base of your proposed solution?

Touch Points

In my presentations, discussions, and reflection upon many of the different concepts that we have introduced in the beginning of this chapter, the concept of *touch points* was one that emerged in my thinking. This concept is not a new or unique one in general, but may be when it is applied to the SharePoint 2010 and ASP.NET world. A touch point is simply a way to describe the interaction between two systems. Where two systems touch, there is a "touch point".

In thinking through blending ASP.NET and SharePoint solutions, this term is not meant to be literal or quantitative in that we go and count up the numerous individual points where the solution touches and report them. I am simply using them in more of an adjective format, where the level of interaction and integration is described. *Low* touch point describes a lower level of interaction and integration, *Moderate* Touch point" a higher level, and *high* touch point describes solutions that represent about the highest level of integration possible without going to an exclusive one-way-or-the-other solution.

There is nothing magical about touch points or nothing special about describing them in the fashion that I am doing so. They have simply become of use to me in helping to organize people's thoughts and approaches to SharePoint 2010 and ASP.NET solution development. So in that, they are of use in helping to describe your architectural approach and solution philosophy.

If you are striving toward a *low touch-point solution*, this means that your guiding thoughts and philosophies are going to steer toward your ASP.NET solution and your SharePoint 2010 farm being largely separate entities, running on their own processes (not necessarily hardware), being self-contained, and having a relatively lower amount of areas that they integrate. The rest of Chapter 8, after our introduction to touch points will cover this scenario.

If you choose a *medium touch-point'* approach, this means that there is a medium or moderate amount of integration between your ASP.NET solution and your SharePoint solution. Here, you may have portions of your SharePoint side mixed in with ASP.NET, and portions of your ASP.NET solution mixed in with your SharePoint. Our chapters on the Client Object Model and Business Connectivity Services represented ways that you can accomplish some of that. Chapter 9 will also highlight ways to blend solutions with the medium touch-point approach, as well as introduce some cutting-edge blended approaches with the use of Azure and advanced JavaScript techniques.

■ **Tip** Choosing an approach with respect to touch points does not make an invisible wall come up in your architecture approach or meetings that will force you into doing one specific thing only, or to never include any element of another solution type in your approach. It is simply a guiding principle overall. As a guiding principle, it is designed to help you navigate producing your solution with an organized approach as well as help you navigate your organization and business makeup. It will help in communications across the team and to stakeholders.

Choosing a *high touch-point solution* means that there is a high level of integration that SharePoint 2010 and ASP.NET have, and that the decisions you make ongoing will most likely have to include evaluating the impact on most environments. We will introduce specific examples and considerations in Chapter 10 for this approach.

Over the course of these last three chapters, we will highlight what makes up the particular touch point and examples of what selecting that approach and philosophy entails and how to do it.

Low Touch Point

What is a low touch-point solution approach and philosophy? In explaining this, one key concept to consider is the relative level of complexity of your two different environments. SharePoint 2010 is a very deep and complex product, and it runs in an environment that is tuned for SharePoint. There is performance optimization that comes into play in the interaction between the SharePoint 2010 product, IIS, and the databases. Many ASP.NET applications also have complex elements to them.

So what is the easiest way to integrate the two? Don't.

That, of course, is the simple answer. The more complex answer is contained in all of the content throughout the rest of this chapter. In this philosophy and approach, each of your environments runs on its own. SharePoint 2010 runs self-contained in its own little world and farm, and your ASP.NET application does as well.

■ **Tip** This does not mean necessarily that you need to duplicate or use different hardware to implement a low touch-point solution. There are many options here—SharePoint Web Front-End (WFE) servers can support having other IIS web sites on them. Defining different users that run your IIS Application Pools is a great way to contain impact across systems. SharePoint database servers can have other databases on them; however, it violates a best-practice rule to place other SQL Server databases on the same instance of SQL Server that SharePoint 2010 resides on. So, in this case, if you are using the same SQL Server, define separate instances to house your SharePoint 2010 and other SQL Server databases. Another option that is becoming more and more viable every year is to utilize virtualization for your environments. Microsoft server operating systems such as Windows 2008 Server R2 offer the Hyper-V role for virtualization, and there are other vendors such as VMWare that offer capable virtualization offerings. Virtualization offers many benefits in managing server environments that are worth examining, but a little beyond the scope of this book.

Housing or wrapping ASP.NET solutions within the SharePoint environment can offer increased risk to a SharePoint farm. This is not to say that it is wrong or not recommended, it is just as we move up the scale on integration methods, the higher the touch point, the more it exposes potential risk.

Pros

The pros to implementing a low touch-point solution are as follows:

- Performance maintained in SharePoint farms and ASP.NET applications with no cross-application implications.

- No constraints to ASP.NET application development.

- No additional development training necessary for ASP.NET team.

- Least amount of customization development work.

- SharePoint 2010 farm remains largely intact.

Cons

The cons to implementing a low touch-point solution are as follows:

- Branding is more complex and performed for both the SharePoint 2010 farm as well as the ASP.NET application.

- Authentication and Authorization (AuthN/AuthZ) must be customized to duplicate across platforms.

- Navigation is not seamless—need to plan out user experience navigating through the areas of the two sites.

- Navigation may need customization work.

These are a few of the high-level pros and cons of choosing a low touch-point solution. Now, besides the reasons for choosing to implement low touch-point solutions, we will highlight ways to make them work in your environment.

A blended solution is a solution that presents the front of two applications functioning together. One of the primary ways to accomplish this is through branding. Branding is creating a unified look and user interface for both your SharePoint 2010 and ASP.NET applications. Branding specifically in low touch-point solutions can present to the end user a unified interface that provides common functionality throughout the solutions.

Branding SharePoint Solutions

In this chapter, we will present examples of how to brand a SharePoint 2010 application in a few different ways. We will also cover high-level basics of branding an ASP.NET application. The way in which we will present this is by taking a common HTML template with images, colors, and fonts, such as one that you can purchase commercially on the Internet and utilize in your designs. We will take this design and apply it both to an ASP.NET master page for use in your ASP.NET application, as well as applying it to your SharePoint 2010 environment.

Prior to this example, we'll discuss some of the different options for modifying the user interface in SharePoint 2010, including some of the new functionality built into SharePoint 2010 for branding. Some of what is built in to SharePoint 2010 will depend on which version of the product that you are utilizing. All SharePoint 2010 products, including the free SharePoint Foundation 2010, offer the ability to customize or brand SharePoint. However, there are features within the Standard and Enterprise versions of SharePoint 2010 that offer enhanced abilities in the branding area. The SharePoint Server Publishing Features offers enhanced abilities for branding in SharePoint 2010.

Branding Possibilities, Features, and Tools

There are a number of possibilities when we start to discuss branding a SharePoint site. From an initial perspective, SharePoint has built-in capabilities for changing certain things with respect to the brand, such as colors or font sizes.

Much as we are organizing our overall approach to SharePoint 2010 and ASP.NET blended architecture, we will also present branding options in a similar fashion, using low, medium, and high levels of branding effort.

Low-Effort Branding

The lowest effort to brand your SharePoint 2010 is to utilize some of the built-in themes that come with SharePoint 2010. From any site, you can navigate to Site Settings from the Quick Launch menu, and select Site Themes. You will be presented with the ability to select color themes and palettes from the available installed themes in SharePoint 2010. The window to select these is shown in Figure 8–1.

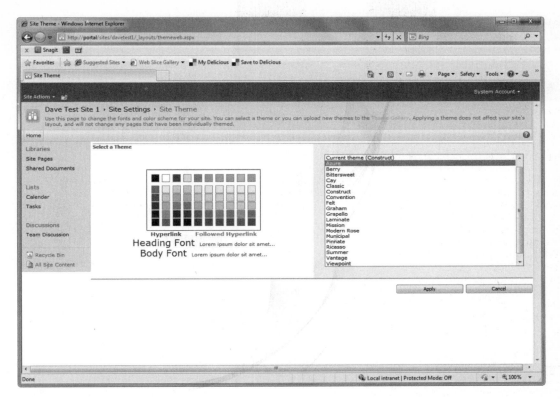

Figure 8–1. *Branding with Site Themes*

Figure 8–1 shows what is available from SharePoint Foundation 2010. If you are using either the Standard or Enterprise products, the built-in themes also allow you to customize colors and fonts in a particular installed theme, as shown in Figure 8–2.

Figure 8–2. Customizable themes—SharePoint Server 2010—Standard and Enterprise

Medium-Effort Branding

Traveling up the scale of effort, the next level of branding control you could take over a SharePoint 2010 site would be to design and import your own theme file. SharePoint supports themes that are created in PowerPoint 2010 for use in SharePoint.

TIP For detailed instructions on how to create a PowerPoint theme and save it, please refer to the Microsoft Office 2010 documentation article here:

---

http://office.microsoft.com/en-us/powerpoint-help/customize-and-save-a-theme-in-powerpoint-2010-HA010338409.aspx

Themes are a new feature in SharePoint 2010 and they are created after the OpenXML format specification. They consist of a packaged zipped file with a .thmx extension. When you create your theme in PowerPoint 2010 and save it, it will be a .thmx file extension. From here, you may import it into

SharePoint 2010 to the Theme Gallery, which should make it available to select along with the default built-in themes that ship with SharePoint 2010. The built-in themes in the Theme Gallery are physically stored on the SharePoint server in the following directory:

```
C:\Program Files\Common Files\Microsoft Shared\Web Server
Extensions\14\TEMPLATE\GLOBAL\Lists\themes
```

To add a new theme to the default ones on your site, navigate to the Site Settings page as shown in Figure 8–1. You will see a link to the Theme Gallery Library. You can scroll down to the bottom of the installed themes and select Add New Item to upload your created theme to your site. After this, you are able to select your customized theme to apply to your SharePoint 2010 site.

Another option for a medium level of effort in branding your SharePoint 2010 solution would be to make changes to the existing CSS in SharePoint. For a publishing site, you are able to specify an alternate CSS file to use in place of the built-in CSS that SharePoint 2010 installs by default. You can select this file along with the Master Pages setting in Site Settings in your SharePoint 2010 site. It is near the bottom of the screen, as shown in Figure 8–3.

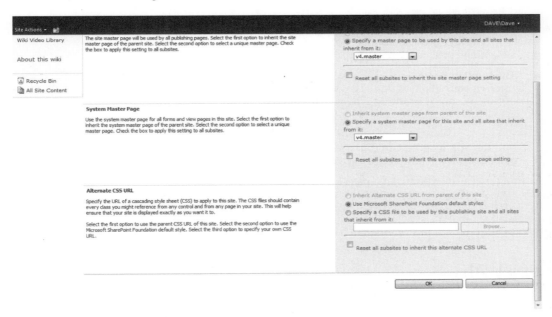

Figure 8–3. Alternate CSS selection in Site Settings ➤ Master Pages

High-Effort Branding

If modifying the look and feel of your standard SharePoint 2010 chrome is not enough, then we will need to get in to a high-effort custom branding solution, with defining the brand for a custom master Page, and possible page layouts and content types.

If your SharePoint solution is of the type that will be published to the Internet, or that is public-facing, you may want to take advantage of SharePoint 2010 Publishing Features. If not, you will still customize a SharePoint 2010 Master Page.

SharePoint Server 2010 Publishing Features

Publishing as a term in SharePoint means the authoring and deployment of branded items such as CSS and images, content, custom assemblies, and configuration files across a Microsoft SharePoint Server 2010 farm. SharePoint Server 2010 Publishing consists of two separate features—the SharePoint Server Publishing Infrastructure feature and the SharePoint Server Publishing feature. The SharePoint Server Publishing Infrastructure feature provides publishing functionality at the site collection level, and the SharePoint Server Publishing feature provides publishing functionality at the site level. The subset of features and functionality of each feature supports the goal of publishing as part of a Web content management solution.

Publishing features come into play in SharePoint 2010 as a design for web content management. Adding or turning on the publishing features in SharePoint 2010 automatically provisions a number of internal components for use in web content management. These components include specific site columns, content types, page layouts, master pages, and lists. Publishing features also changes the way in which the site operates in a number of ways. It applies work flows for publishing content, limits provisioning of subsites to conform to a publishing context, and creates several publishing-specific permissions groups to deal with content management.

One key thing that happens on a site is that a Pages library is created for web content, and this is set up as a document library with versioning and permissions set up. There are two types of publishing sites—the Publishing Portal, and the Enterprise Wiki.

- The Publishing Portal is set up basically ready to be exposed as an external Internet web site. It contains by default a Press Releases site, and a custom brand out-of-the-box. The intent is a head start to help define areas of web content that are specific for exposing to the Internet.

- The Enterprise Wiki, on the other hand, is geared more toward a corporate intranet application with the capability for end users to rapidly modify content in place and create more pages, areas, and links to pages with little restriction.

Publishing sites use customizable page layouts that help to organize the content and how it is displayed in the site. Page layouts can include default layouts such as an image on the left-hand side of the content area and text on the right, or can include columns for content. Page layouts are based upon a content type, which include specific site columns for content. We will discuss publishing layouts later on in the chapter after we define a branded master page to house the layout.

Working With a Brand

We will start out our branding example from what typically would be a real-world example of implementing a template across an ASP.NET application and a SharePoint 2010 site. The first thing that is typically shown to a customer from a web design company is a representative mockup image that represents the interaction between the web designer and the customer. After the customer approves of the direction of the initial mockup, then the designers take the mockup and cut it up into images, CSS, HTML, and possibly JavaScript files. We have an example of this in Chapter 8's downloadable source code. The example consists of an HTML page, CSS scripts, images, and a JavaScript file. The mockup page.html looks like Figure 8–4 in a browser, and the files that make up the web designer deliverable are shown in Figure 8–5.

Figure 8–4. Initial mockup of branding web design

The design has a pencil yellow and blue theme, and a navigation menu at the left as well as the top of the header. There is a main content area in the center. We are mainly concerned with the look and feel of the UI, as opposed to implementing the exact menu items or working in the design.

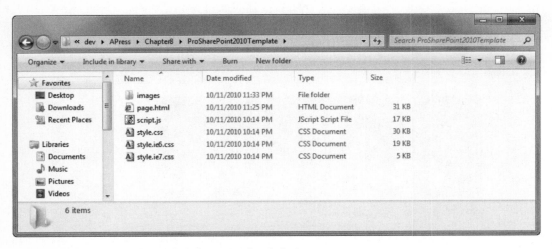

Figure 8–5. *Branding files included in initial web design*

Now that we have received our branding files from our web design company, we are ready to get started. All of the design is contained in one HTML file.

Branding the ASP.NET Application

To apply our brand that is created in one page.html file and controlled by the CSS files style.css and browser-specific versions, we will transfer this brand over to ASP.NET. To do this, we will utilize master pages in ASP.NET, and we will build the sections of the header, the menus, and the sidebar in .ascx controls to place in content placeholders on the Master page. The articles and blocks we will add a little more code to so that they can be reused more than once on the page. The resulting files in our project appear as in Figure 8–6.

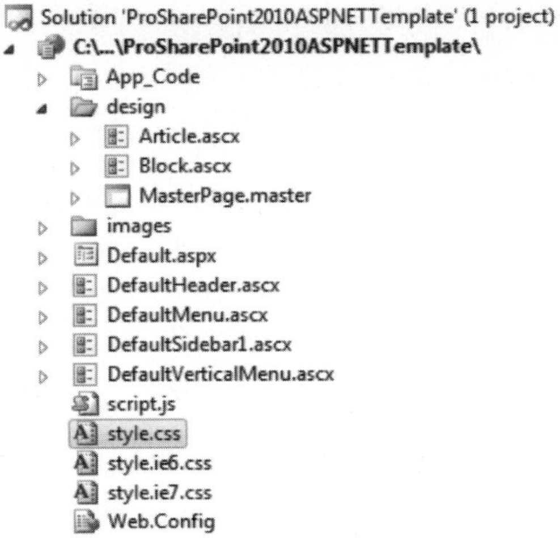

Solution 'ProSharePoint2010ASPNETTemplate' (1 project)
- C:\...\ProSharePoint2010ASPNETTemplate\
  - App_Code
  - design
    - Article.ascx
    - Block.ascx
    - MasterPage.master
  - images
  - Default.aspx
  - DefaultHeader.ascx
  - DefaultMenu.ascx
  - DefaultSidebar1.ascx
  - DefaultVerticalMenu.ascx
  - script.js
  - style.css
  - style.ie6.css
  - style.ie7.css
  - Web.Config

Figure 8–6. ASP.NET branded application

As you can see, we have preserved the images folder just as it was presented to us by the designer, as well as the CSS style sheets. The other components we have broken out so as to best use the built-in feature of master pages in ASP.NET. We are taking the external surrounding elements of our page.html file supplied by the designers and incorporating it into an ASP.NET master page.

The bulk of the approach that I took to brand the ASP.NET application was to take sections that represent certain areas of the layout, and wrap their inner `<div>` tags with a ContentPlaceHolder.

For example, following is the CSS and HTML surrounding the menu content:

```
<div class="art-nav">
                      <div class="l"></div>
                      <div class="r"></div>
                      <ul class="art-menu">
                            <li>
                                    <a href="#" class="active"><span
class="l"></span><span class="r"></span><span class="t">Home</span></a>
                            </li>
                            <li>
                                    <a href="#"><span class="l"></span><span
class="r"></span><span class="t">Menu Item</span></a>
                                    <ul>
                                      <li><a href="#">Menu Subitem 1</a>
                                          <ul>
                                                <li><a href="#">Menu Subitem
1.1</a></li>
                                                <li><a href="#">Menu Subitem
1.2</a></li>
                                                <li><a href="#">Menu Subitem
1.3</a></li>
                                          </ul>
                                      </li>
                                      <li><a href="#">Menu Subitem 2</a></li>
```

```
                                            <li><a href="#">Menu Subitem 3</a></li>
                                 </ul>
                       </li>
                       <li>
                                 <a href="#"><span class="l"></span><span
class="r"></span><span class="t">About</span></a>
                                 </li>
                       </ul>
                 </div>
```

Here in Visual Studio 2010 we add a ContentPlaceHolder that will be populated by the `DefaultMenu` user control.

```
<div class="art-nav">
        <div class="l"></div>
        <div class="r"></div>
        <asp:contentplaceholder id="MenuContentPlaceHolder"
runat="server"></asp:contentplaceholder>
</div>
```

■ **Note** We will not cover in-depth each aspect of how we migrated the brand from the HTML file to the ASP.NET template solution. However, the complete source for both solutions—the HTML page as well as the ASP.NET application are available for download in the code that is associated with this book.

Branding in SharePoint Designer Example

Next, we will highlight the steps to go through to create a brand in SharePoint Designer 2010.

1. Open up Designer, and connect to the Site Collection where we will modify the master page. In this example, we will want to take advantage of the publishing features to get the most use out of our master page. We will also want to define a page layout that will allow us to lay out sections of the page similar to the design delivered to us.

2. Select the Master Pages left-hand link and you will see a window similar to Figure 8–7.

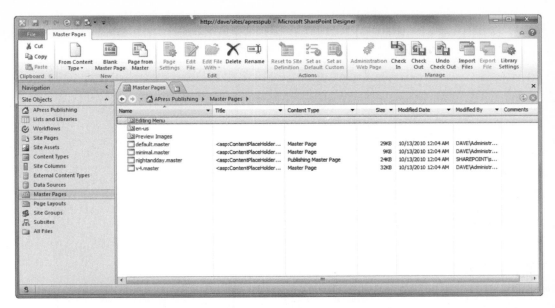

Figure 8–7. SharePoint Designer and Publishing Site Master Pages

3. We will select the nightandday.master Publishing Master Page to modify and apply to the site.

■ **Tip** You can brand a site by using either a publishing master page to affect the publishing content and creating page layouts, or you can brand a site by using the main overall master page, which is v4.master.

---

4. Right -lick nightandday.master, copy it, and paste it in the same library. We will call the corresponding master page pencilblue.master.

5. Once you have renamed the master page, right-click, check it out, and edit it in Advanced mode. You will be in a page editor that looks like Figure 8–8.

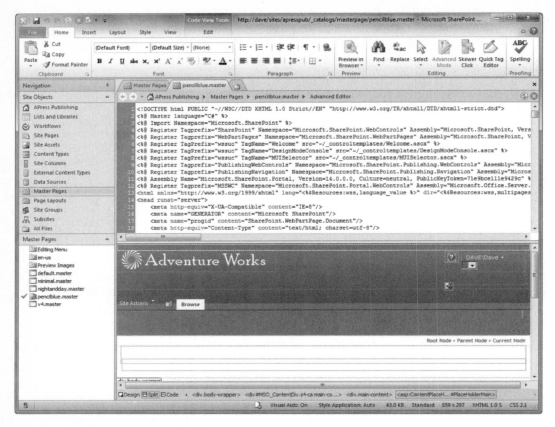

Figure 8–8. Editing a publishing master page

6. To proceed from this point, we will need to choose an approach to our modifications. There are basically two schools of thought as to how to tackle modifying master pages. One school approaches this from the perspective of taking the existing master page provided by Microsoft and modifying it until it meets your needs. The other school of thought is to use a bare-bones type of master page that has the minimal elements in it to allow SharePoint 2010 to remain functional. We will do the latter and use the master pages developed by Randy Drisgill found on Codeplex at http://startermasterpages.codeplex.com. Download them and extract them to somewhere convenient.

■ **Tip** In SharePoint 2007, these pages were called minimal master pages. However, since then, Microsoft has included in the master page lineup in the main SharePoint 2010 product a master page named minimal.master, which has very little chrome on it and is used in scenarios requiring almost no external wrapper functionality.

7. The page we will be using from this project is _starter_publishing.master. If you are modifying a team site, you would instead use the _starter_foundation.master. When you download this file, you can right-click it and edit it directly in SharePoint Designer. To get to the start point, delete all the content in pencilblue.master, and cut and paste the content from _starter_publishing.master into it. You will then get a pop-up window seen in Figure 8–9.

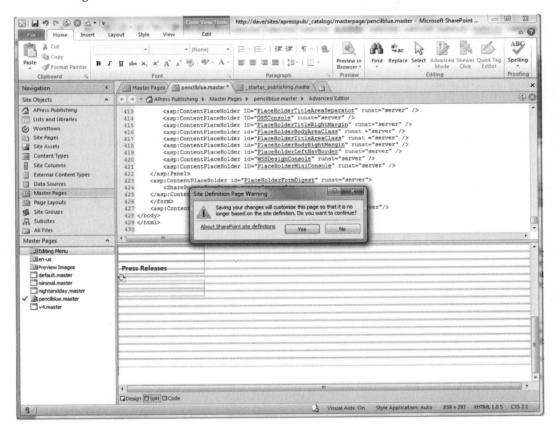

Figure 8–9. SharePoint Designer starter master page and page warning

This warning illustrates the difference between the design work we are doing now with SharePoint Designer, and the finished work that we can deploy to our web site. Customizing the page will make it depart from the page that is stored on the file system, and the page modifications will be stored in the database, as opposed to directly on the file system. It is not recommended to keep your master pages in this state, as it adds overhead to performance on every page. Instead, in a later section of the chapter, we will see how to take the work we have completed here and package a solution up for deployment to your production environment. Packaging a master page up as a solution will ensure that a non-customized page and all the artifacts it references, such as images, CSS files, and JavaScript, are deployed to the file system on your server, as opposed to remaining customized in a database.

■ **Tip** If all the talk about production environments is causing you to ask yourself "*what does he mean by production environment?*", please take a few steps backward, log off of your production environment, and start to see what you need to do to ensure that you are not editing live sites directly in your production environment with SharePoint Designer. At the very least, you can create a new Site Collection for you to hack up with designer change experiments to spare your end users the agony.

At the time of this writing, there are a few corrections to be made to the _starter_publishing.master page to get it to work correctly.

Lines 6 through 8 in the page appear as follows:

```
<%@ Register TagPrefix="wssuc" TagName="Welcome" src="_controltemplates/Welcome.ascx" %>
<%@ Register TagPrefix="wssuc" TagName="DesignModeConsole"
src="_controltemplates/DesignModeConsole.ascx" %>
<%@ Register TagPrefix="wssuc" TagName="MUISelector" src="_controltemplates/MUISelector.ascx"
%>
```

On my publishing site, this was throwing an error when applied. I needed to add a ~/ before the _controltemplates statement in each of these lines to correct this. The corrected lines appear as follows:

```
<%@ Register TagPrefix="wssuc" TagName="Welcome" src="~/_controltemplates/Welcome.ascx" %>
<%@ Register TagPrefix="wssuc" TagName="DesignModeConsole"
src="~/_controltemplates/DesignModeConsole.ascx" %>
<%@ Register TagPrefix="wssuc" TagName="MUISelector"
src="~/_controltemplates/MUISelector.ascx" %>
```

Also, on line 383, the SiteLogo currently does not exist in a freshly installed publishing site:

```
<SharePoint:SiteLogoImage  LogoImageUrl="/Style Library/sitename/logo.png" runat="server"/>
```

You can either correct that by uploading a graphic to the Style Library that does exist, or just change it back to the original Night and Day logo to start by making it the following:

```
<SharePoint:SiteLogoImage  LogoImageUrl="<% $SPUrl:~sitecollection/Style
Library/Images/nd_logo.png %>" runat="server"/>
```

Without the nightandday.css file, this will just show up blank for now, but without an image error.

Next, we will go ahead and check in, publish, approve our changes, and apply the starter master page to our publishing site. This will show the iterative steps necessary to continue to develop your branding solution for low touch-point solutions.

1. Navigate back to your Master Page list view, right-click pencilblue.master, and select Check-in. You will see the pop-up screen shown in Figure 8–10.

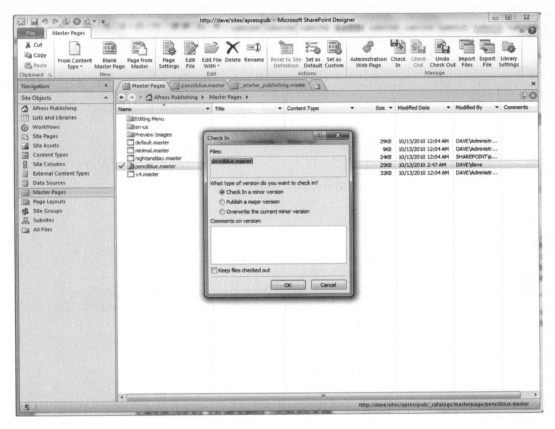

Figure 8–10. Check In master page

2. The options available are either "Check in a minor version," which will save your work in the content database but now allow you to apply it to a site or "Publish a major version." Publishing a major version also brings up the screen in Figure 8–11 to allow you to approve the changes. This will allow you to apply the master page to your site collection.

3. TIP Versioning in document libraries in SharePoint, such as the Pages library, is set by default to use major and minor versions. For an extranet publishing site, you need to select "Publish a major version" to get the approval workflows going and get your page published out so it is visible to the public.

Figure 8–11. Document approval status window

4. Clicking Yes will take you out of SharePoint Designer and directly to your SharePoint 2010 site's master page gallery, where you can select the page approval status and approve it, as in Figure 8–12.

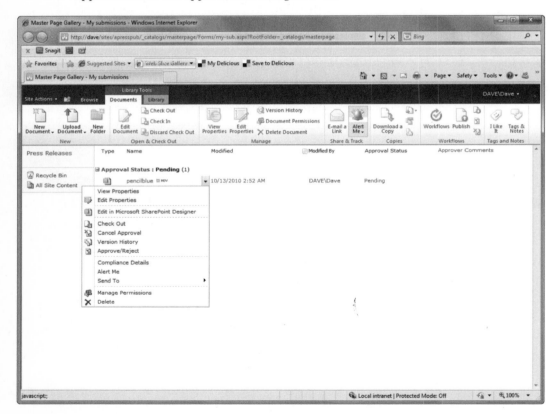

Figure 8–12. Approving a publishing page change

5. There is one more screen after selecting Approve/Reject that will allow you to select the Approve radio button and apply it.

6. After this, you can select Site Settings from the top-left navigation menu, and from there select Master page as shown in Figures 8–13 and 8–14.

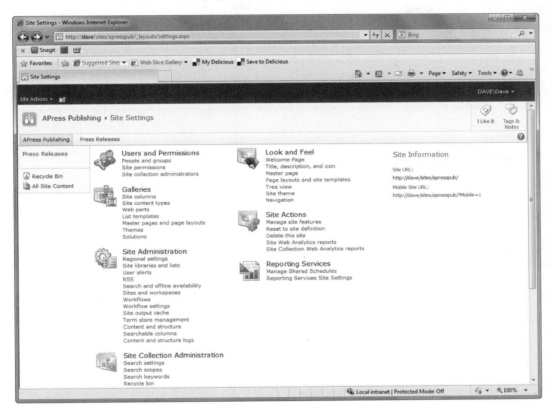

Figure 8–13. *Site Settings*

7. From here, select the Master Page link under the Look and Feel topic.

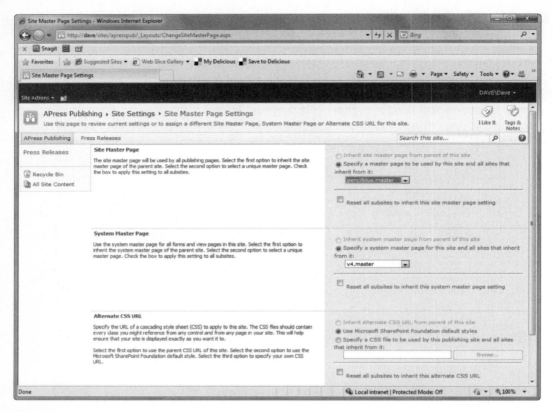

Figure 8–14. Master page selection

Now we have a working starter master page in our publishing site that looks like Figure 8–15.

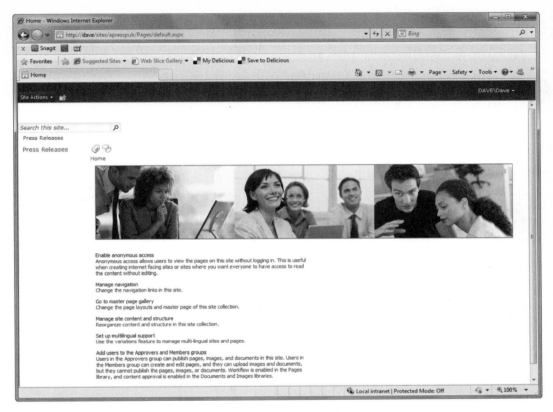

Figure 8–15. Publishing site with starter master page applied

---

■ **Tip** In addition to using Central Administration, you can use PowerShell to set your Master Page. A sample script is included in the downloads for this chapter and is called UpdateMaster.ps1.

From here, we will start to work with the master page in SharePoint Designer to apply the brand. We won't go through every step of branding the page, but just get started to get an idea about some of the process and the tools necessary. The final master page is available as part of the code downloads for the book.

Most of the work of branding will be to take the elements on the HTML page that we obtained from the designer and work them into the SharePoint master page. There are a few tricks to certain elements of SharePoint, but branding and design is an iterative process that changes the page a few small steps at a time, then we will publish the page and look at it on the SharePoint site.

■ **Tip** Because SharePoint master pages can be complex, it really is not recommended to do all your work at once and then deploy it. Doing that will typically result in a page error, which takes time to track down, and you probably will end up taking out at least portions of your changes to ensure that it will display. The best way to approach branding a master page is to start out with the starter master page as we have here, then change the file a little bit at a time, publishing it at every step and examining the results. When we finish this iterative process, we will package it up for deployment in a solution package with Visual Studio 2010. The final solution package is included in the code downloads for the book.

Actually, the first step in branding a master page is we will need to upload the images, scripts, and CSS files provided by our design company to SharePoint.

Cut all of the images from the Images folder, and paste them into the Images folder under the Style Library in SharePoint 2010. You will see the result as in Figure 8–16.

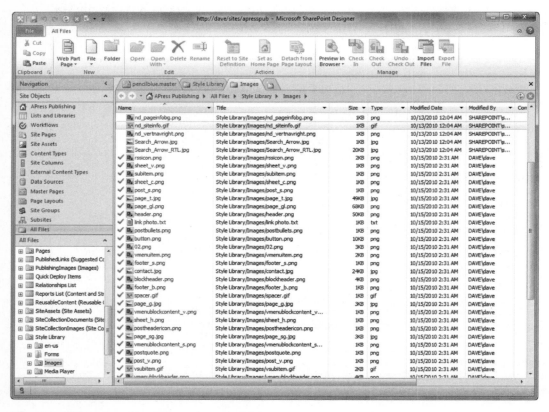

Figure 8–16. Loading images into the Style Library

We will do this similarly with the CSS files and JavaScript. Load the CSS files into the Style Library Core Styles. We are also renaming the files to have pencilblue as the first part, as shown in Figure 8–17.

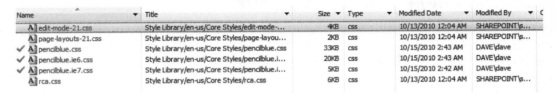

Name	Title	Size	Type	Modified Date	Modified By	
▲		▼	▼	▼	▼	
A] edit-mode-21.css	Style Library/en-us/Core Styles/edit-mode-...	4KB	css	10/13/2010 12:04 AM	SHAREPOINT\s...	
A] page-layouts-21.css	Style Library/en-us/Core Styles/page-layou...	2KB	css	10/13/2010 12:04 AM	SHAREPOINT\s...	
✓ A] pencilblue.css	Style Library/en-us/Core Styles/pencilblue.css	33KB	css	10/15/2010 2:43 AM	DAVE\dave	
✓ A] pencilblue.ie6.css	Style Library/en-us/Core Styles/pencilblue.i...	20KB	css	10/15/2010 2:43 AM	DAVE\dave	
✓ A] pencilblue.ie7.css	Style Library/en-us/Core Styles/pencilblue.i...	5KB	css	10/15/2010 2:42 AM	DAVE\dave	
A] rca.css	Style Library/en-us/Core Styles/rca.css	6KB	css	10/13/2010 12:04 AM	SHAREPOINT\s...	

Figure 8–17. Style Library folder for CSS files

The final version of the PencilBlue.master master page from SharePoint Designer 2010 will be in the downloads section and will be called PenciBlueSPD.master to distinguish it from the one that is included in the Visual Studio Project.

After the brand is applied to SharePoint 2010, the site will look somewhat like Figure 8–18.

Figure 8–18. Branded SharePoint site

■ **Note** With a fixed-width design like this, you will need to adjust your content so that it fits into the space that is available.

Next, we will delve into packaging and deploying your branding solution.

Deploying Branded Solutions

While we are working with SharePoint Designer 2010 in developing our master page, we will not want to be editing master pages directly on our production SharePoint sites. To handle the packaging and deployment of our SharePoint 2010 brand, we will utilize Visual Studio 2010.

1. First, start up Visual Studio 2010 and select the Empty SharePoint Project, as shown in Fig 8–19.

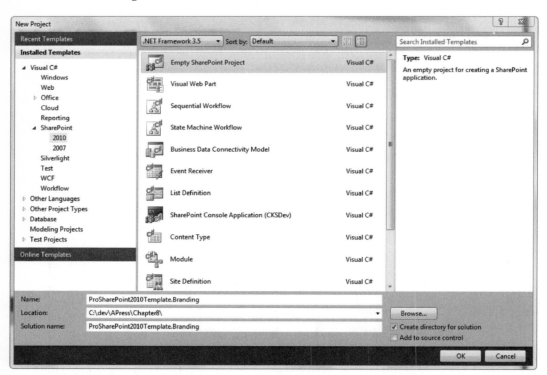

Figure 8–19. SharePoint branding solution—Empty SharePoint Project.

2. Next, we will add a starter master page. I like to use the template that goes along with the CKSDev Toolkit. This is the Community Kit for SharePoint Development, which you can find on CodePlex here:

http://cksdev.codeplex.com/documentation

■ **Tip** The CKSDev Toolkit provides a number of additional project and item templates besides the ones that come out-of-the-box with SharePoint 2010, including a SharePoint 2010 Console application that is great for doing management types of tasks and testing out the SharePoint 2010 objects and libraries. Also included are a number of different helpful item templates, like a Basic Site Page, a Fluent UI Visual Web Part, the Starter Master Page we will be using, a Blank Site Template, a number of items around Custom Actions and Groups, a Delegate Control, a Full Trust Proxy, and a SPMetal Definition that will help you wire up your LINQ to SharePoint 2010 in an automated fashion.

---

3. Add a New Item using the Starter Master Page, as shown in Figure 8–20.

Figure 8–20. Add a Starter Master Page

4. The Project Item template for the Starter Master Page is very helpful in that it not only adds the page, but a Module for deploying it. All of this is automatically added to your Feature setup. Rename your Feature something that you will be able to recognize if you are looking at it in a Site Administration or Central Administration web site, like ProSPBranding. Your entire project will look like Figure 8–21 after you are done with this.

Solution 'ProSharePoint2010Template.Branding' (1 project)
- ProSharePoint2010Template.Branding
  - Properties
  - References
  - Features
    - ProSPBranding
      - ProSPBranding.feature
        - ProSPBranding.Template.xml
  - Package
  - PencilBlue
    - Elements.xml
    - PencilBlue.master
  - key.snk

Figure 8–21. SharePoint 2010 branding project

5. There is one thing that we will have to change in the Elements.xml file so that our master page will be seen by SharePoint 2010 as a master page, show up in the SharePoint 2010 library, and work correctly with the version 4 UI of SharePoint 2010. Add the following line to the File XML node in Elements.xml:

```
<Property Name="UIVersion" Value="4" />
```

6. Next, we will need to change a little where we will deploy our images, CSS files, and JavaScript files. While storing these items in the Style Library for a site is fine for working with developing brands, and is indeed much easier than storing the items on the file system, for our SharePoint farm, we do want our files to be out there on the file system in a non-customized page. We will utilize the Layouts and Images directories on our SharePoint farm to store these artifacts. Right-click your project, select the Add menu, then select Add, as shown in Figure 8–22.

Figure 8–22. Add SharePoint Images and Layouts Mapped Folders

■ **Tip** Since your master page and related artifacts such as images, CSS, and JavaScript files are typically utilized throughout Site Collections, they are accessed very frequently. As such, storing these artifacts in the content database by way of using the Styles Library is not recommended as a best practice. Artifacts in the content database, and a master page stored there especially, are stored as a customization and will affect performance negatively for highly trafficked artifacts such as a master page. Storing these pages on the file system will help all of your pages using the brand be rendered uncustomized, which is the best practice for performance purposes.

7. After you have completed this, your project appears as shown in Figure 8–23. Note that Visual Studio automatically adds a folder under the main layouts and images directories for your project, so that any artifacts that you add there are kept separate from the SharePoint 2010 product artifacts. Note in Figure 8–23 the Images and Layouts directories added to your project. Copy all of the image files you are using to the Images directory under your project folder, and copy the CSS and JavaScript files you are using to the Layouts directory under your project folder.

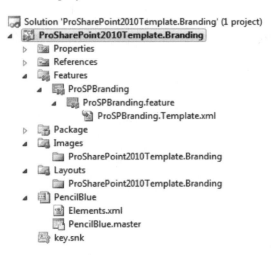

Figure 8–23. SharePoint Branding Project with Mapped Layouts and Images

■ **Tip** Sometimes questions related to internationalization come up when discussing branding. While it is important to utilize resources in our SharePoint 2010 development that support internationalization, when we are discussing branding, for the most part we will either be utilizing one global branding solution for multiple international language sites, including SharePoint 2010 Variations, or we will be developing a custom brand for different languages that may contain images in different languages or to impact different cultures. For this reason, we do not need to be as concerned with aligning our solutions under the language and regional settings in SharePoint 2010 (such as artificially creating en-us folders or 1033 folders underneath the layouts or images folders). It will be sufficient to name our project so that when it is deployed as a .wsp solution, we will know what it is.

8. Now cut and paste your Master Page from your SharePoint Designer 2010 editor directly into the page in your Visual Studio project. You will need to edit your CSS file and do a global Find and Replace to change the references to all of your images from where you have them stored in the Style Library on your development branding site to where they will be located on your production server. This will look something like Figure 8–24.

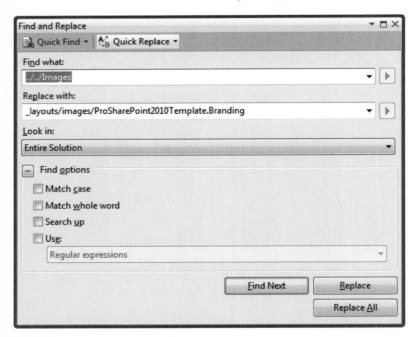

Figure 8–24. Replacing image references in your CSS files

9.   After this, you are ready to deploy your solution to a Site Collection and use your new master page. You can deploy directly to your local environment, but to deploy to your production environment, change the Solution Configuration of your Visual Studio 2010 project to Release, then build your product. Select Package from the Build menu in Visual Studio 2010, as shown in Figure 8–25.

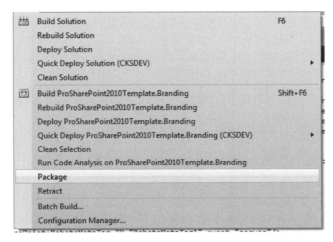

Figure 8–25. Package build in VS2010

10.   When your feature is deployed to your production environment, you will be able to see it in Site Settings ➤ Features. It will look similar to Figure 8–26.

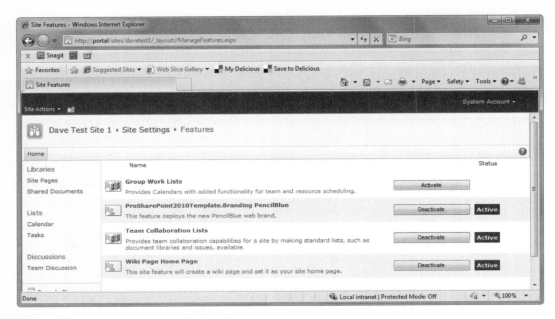

Figure 8–26. Branding feature deployed

Now that we have looked into branding with master pages and packaging a branding solution for deployment to production web sites, the next step is to discuss publishing page layouts, which are utilized in conjunction with SharePoint 2010 Publishing Features.

Publishing Layouts

In beginning to highlight what publishing page layouts are, we will start with the reminder that everything in SharePoint is a list. How does this matter? Well, page layouts sit on master pages. Page layouts are based upon content types. Content types in SharePoint are implemented in lists. So the basic way to define a page layout is by constructing content types from site columns that are either currently in SharePoint or need to be added.

A page layout will have areas that you can place content from a particular content type. Page layouts can contain web-part zones add web parts into, as well as field controls.

All of this information about publishing page layouts contains a few different layers, so it may be helpful to walk through a simple example.

One default page layout is Article Left, which is based upon the Article page layout. Article Left contains an area for an image layout on the left-hand side, and an area for content on the right-hand side. There are many built-in publishing layouts contained in the SharePoint 2010 product that may be fine for you to use directly out-of-the-box. If they are not, you can modify publishing layouts in SharePoint Designer 2010, as shown in Figure 8–27. The built-in publishing layout ArticleLeft.aspx is shown in Figure 8–27.

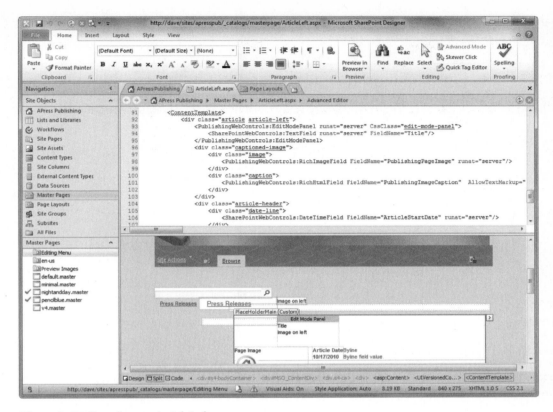

Figure 8–27. Page layout ArticleLeft.aspx

■ **Tip** Don't let all the SharePoint terms confuse you. Publishing page layouts simply will define different areas of display for information. When you edit the page, you are able to modify elements in each particular area. You as a solution provider will provide either the standard publishing layouts to use along with your master pages, or you will also define publishing layouts. End users can edit the published pages on your external facing web site and add content to them.

For example, the main page in our branded publishing page layout, when you edit the page content, appears as shown in Figure 8–28.

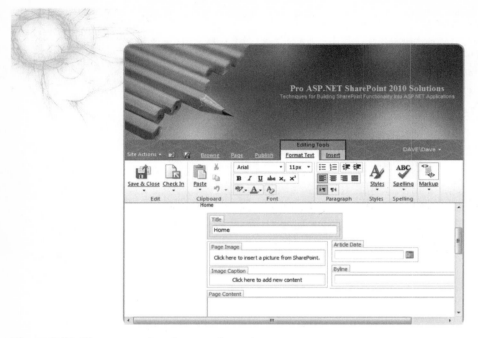

Figure 8–28. Home page showing page layout

As you can see, with all the content types and site columns in back of it, the page layout just presents simple areas to fill content in to the user, such as the title, a selectable image, an image caption, an article date and byline, and page content that is available to edit and includes quite a lot of options.

So when you define your master pages, if you have specific content layout needs on different pages, you may need to define a custom page layout for each page that will use the specifics. If the built-in page layouts will suffice, such as including an image and some content, you can use them.

You can customize page layouts in SharePoint Designer 2010 and packages similar to how we did the master pages in Visual Studio 2010.

Customizing SharePoint 2010 Navigation

SharePoint 2010 offers a number of ways that the user, an administrator, or you as an architect and developer, can customize navigation. SharePoint primarily works with navigation through two main sources:

- Customizing the Quick Launch—this is the left-hand side navigation that is present in most SharePoint sites.

- Customizing the Top Navigation Bar—this is the top navigation menu structure that is shown near the header in most SharePoint sites.

We will highlight how to customize the navigation in SharePoint 2010 so that it will be the most compatible with ASP.NET

Customizing Navigation Through the User Interface

You can update the Quick Launch by adding links and items through the user interface. You can select the Look and Feel section under Site Settings, then select the Quick Launch button. You will see the administrative interface built in to SharePoint 2010 for updating the Quick Launch, as shown in Figure 8–29.

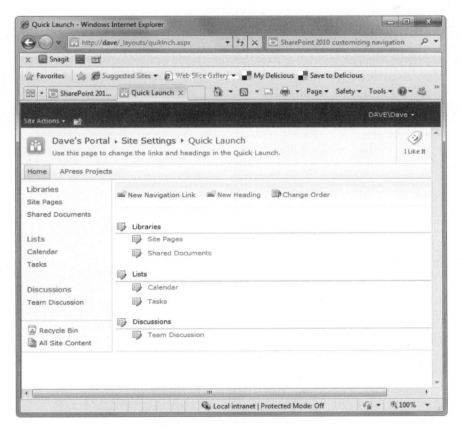

Figure 8–29. Modifying the Quick Launch

You can add new sections and new links to other areas into SharePoint 2010 directly through this interface—Figure 8–30 shows an example of adding a new group heading and two navigation links to a SharePoint Foundation 2010 site. You potentially could duplicate any external links to ASP.NET applications using this method. Figure 8–30 shows the updated links.

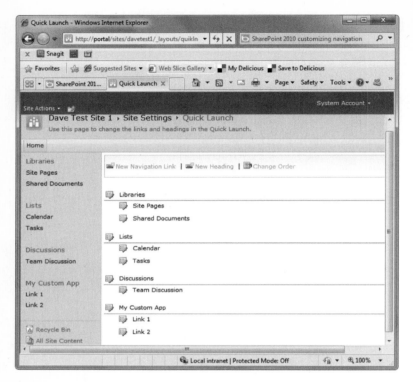

Figure 8–30. *Custom headings and links added*

Similarly, you can update the top navigation area using the user interface. you can add links as top navigation links, as shown in Figure 8–31.

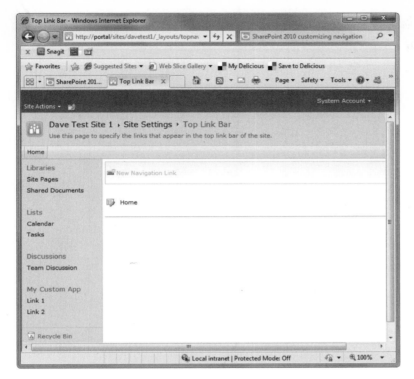

Figure 8–31. *Adding links to the top link bar*

As you can see, simply adding in navigation elements in addition to SharePoint's built-in navigation model can help to blend or integrate ASP.NET applications and SharePoint 2010. This, in addition to branding sites the same, can present a solid front-end experience to the users.

Adding Links Through the Object Model

Navigation in SharePoint 2010 is done through standard ASP.NET controls—the standard Menu control in System.Web.UI.Webcontrols (System.Web.dll) is used for the Quick Launch and the top navigation menus. As such, it is relatively easy to modify the menu selections through the SharePoint Object Model. Following is an example of code that will add a link to the left-hand Quick Nav menu:

```
SPSite siteCollection = SPControl.GetContextSite(Context);
SPWeb site = siteCollection.AllWebs["DavePub"];
SPWeb subSite = site.Webs["DavePubSub"];

SPNavigationNodeCollection nodes = subSite.Navigation.QuickLaunch;
SPNavigationNode navNode = new SPNavigationNode("Dave's Blog", "http://www.davemilner.com",
true);
nodes.AddAsFirst(navNode);
```

Navigation Custom Data Sources

It is also possible to completely override the custom SharePoint 2010 menu system by replacing navigation with a custom data source. The scope of going through this example is a little beyond what we will cover in this chapter, but for more information please see the following MSDN article:

`http://msdn.microsoft.com/en-us/library/ms432695.aspx`

This will step you through what it would take to completely replace the Quick Launch area with a menu provider.

Summary

In this chapter, we have highlighted the approach to implementing professional SharePoint 2010 and ASP.NET applications in a blended environment using the low touch-point method. We have covered specifics by example of branding SharePoint 2010 and ASP.NET environments, have implemented a brand of the type delivered to us from a design company, and have covered many other features related to making the SharePoint UI as compatible to our ASP.NET application as we can. We have also highlighted organizational considerations for low touch-point solutions, and provided several examples of potential candidate solutions that could utilize the low touch-point approach.

CHAPTER 9

■ ■ ■

Medium Touch Point Solutions

A man who straddles the fence gets a sore crotch.

Unknown

In this chapter, I continue exploring the integration between ASP.NET and SharePoint 2010. As you saw in the previous chapter, Low Touch Point solutions center on preserving separate functional areas of performance and delve into modifying the appearance through branding, layouts, and navigation. This perspective is at one end of the spectrum. At the other end of the spectrum are High Touch Point solutions. As you will see in the final chapter of the book, these solutions are designed to package up as one entity and deliver out as a product or a solution integrating SharePoint 2010 and ASP.NET.

Well, if you have one extreme on one hand, and another extreme on the other hand, what exists in the middle?

Medium Touch Points

If you're leaning towards a Medium Touch Point solution, it's likely that your ASP.NET solution and your SharePoint 2010 farm are largely integrated entities in one format or another. This category of solutions has the highest number of possibilities, as it covers all that do not fall under either extreme application. In many ways, the large bulk of the SharePoint customizations that are done by SharePoint developers, architects, and solution providers can be considered as Medium Touch Point solutions. Development from the other end of the spectrum—connecting to SharePoint resources through the Client Object Model (examined in Chapter 6)—can also be a component of this category of solutions.

In many ways, describing the approach that you select as a Medium Touch Point approach is a tool to help categorize your development and solution philosophy. This philosophy can be important, helping to galvanize your different development teams towards collaboration.

■ **Tip** In general, one of the greatest assets of SharePoint is the way it enables collaboration in organizations, cultures, and various groups. This asset is not only a function of the software, but is highly evident in the community that surrounds SharePoint. SharePoint has an amazing amount of support built up around it through its community. Content is developed by Microsoft internally and exposed through blogs, MSDN, TechNet, and conferences such as the bi-annual SharePoint Conference. Microsoft also has an arm specifically designed for interacting with the community in Evangelism roles throughout the world. Microsoft also supports the community by awarding MVP status to top contributors who work with their products. Additionally, many media organizations put on conferences that expose people to what is available and what is currently being done with SharePoint. Likewise, SharePoint Saturdays are put on locally by SharePoint communities in cities across the world, supported by corporate organizations, attended by large numbers, and traveled to by top level speakers. At the lower levels, SharePoint user groups are organizing across the world for monthly meetings that involve ramping up on SharePoint, networking, food, and giveaways. So start getting it into your head that SharePoint = Collaboration, not just as a software product but as a culture as well. Breaking down barriers, increasing communication and collaboration, and sharing your knowledge and expertise is a healthy way to live and build your career. Collaborate!

Medium Touch Point blended solutions offer some of the benefits of housing or wrapping ASP.NET solutions within the SharePoint environment, but they also offer the benefit of being able to maintain separation in layers of the applications. The pros and cons of Medium Touch Point solutions are described below.

Pros

The pros to implementing a Medium Touch Point Solution are as follows:

- Performance is maintained in SharePoint farms and ASP.NET application separately where it makes sense.
- Standardized SharePoint deployment and code management.
- The choice of integration points.
- Utilizing skills from .NET development and SharePoint customizations so that skillsets are not under-utilized or wasted.
- Your SharePoint 2010 farm remains largely intact.

Cons

The cons to implementing a Medium Touch Point solution are as follows:

- Authentication can potentially be combined, but AuthZ with role based access might need to be customized from the .NET side.
- Navigation is not seamless. You need to plan out user experience navigating through the areas of the two sites.
- Navigation may need customization work.

These are a few of the high level pros and cons of choosing a Medium Touch Point Solution. I will highlight ways to make them work in your environment.

Medium Touch Point Examples

In previous chapters, I covered some of the more standard fare of Medium Touch Point examples, such as using the Client Object Model from within SharePoint 2010 and without SharePoint 2010, connecting to external data sources via web parts, and BCS example solutions. So I'll use this chapter to push the envelope a little and provide some examples of utilizing SharePoint 2010 technologies plus some interesting new features from Microsoft such as Azure Cloud Services, which is becoming more and more central to developing on the Microsoft stack.

There are several ways in which Azure can be utilized from within SharePoint 2010, and I'll explore a couple of the more recent offerings. But first let's address what's on the horizon with SharePoint and the cloud.

SharePoint and The Cloud

One of the initial ways that SharePoint and the cloud is starting to make an impact is through Business Productivity Online Services (BPOS). BPOS is an offering that, as of press time, offers Exchange Online, e-mail, and calendaring through integration with Outlook 2010; web conferencing via Microsoft Live Meeting; a My Company Portal through SharePoint Online that features a SharePoint 2007 Team Site; and Instant Messaging with Office Communicator. The goal is to provide smaller companies lacking the resources of an IT department the opportunity to subscribe to those services at a very reasonable rate.

The next versions of BPOS will be a little different, including a new brand for the overall application offering: Office 365. Go to `http://office365.microsoft.com/en-US/online-services.aspx` for a description of the online services that will be provided within the next calendar year. The primary products in this offering are Microsoft Office Professional Plus, Microsoft Exchange Online (2010), Microsoft SharePoint Online (2010), and Microsoft Lync Online, which is the new version of the combination of the previous messaging, live meeting, and phone communications software suite. Details are just starting to emerge, but it promises to be a very compelling solution for SharePoint and the other elements of Office 365 as a subscription service in the cloud.

SharePoint 2010 and Windows Azure MarketPlace

One of the new offerings that is currently in a phase of Community Technology Preview (CTP) is Windows Azure Market DataMarket. The DataMarket is an online offering in a venue where technology partners can expose valuable data via a subscription service in the cloud. This data is provided through RESTful oData feeds that can be consumed by your SharePoint 2010 environment.

■ **Note** You may be wondering what this oData gibberish is all about. oData is an open standard for exposing data over the Internet in a standardized manner utilizing REST, Atom, and JSON. You can read more about it at `http://www.odata.org` . SharePoint 2010 exposes oData through its REST interface, as covered in Chapter 6, with the Client Object Model. oData will be around for a while as a standard, so I recommend getting accustomed to it early.

To get started with this Medium Touch Point blended solution, you will need to set up an account for Windows Azure Marketplace. Navigate to `https://datamarket.azure.com/` and sign up, as shown in Figure 9–1.

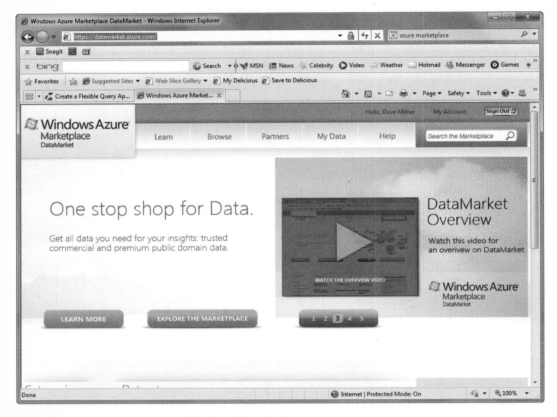

Figure 9–1. Windows Azure Marketplace DataMarket

■ **Tip** DataMarket is the first offering of what looks to become a paid subscription service. At the time of this writing, you can find many free services by browsing through the Market. The price is listed as 0.00. However, to get set up, you need to register with Azure and provide a credit card for charges.

So after your DataMarket account and access is all squared away, you need to download and install the Azure SDK and Visual Studio Azure components to be able to follow along with the rest of the code in this chapter. You may obtain this software at `http://msdn.microsoft.com/en-us/windowsazure/` (see Figure 9–2).

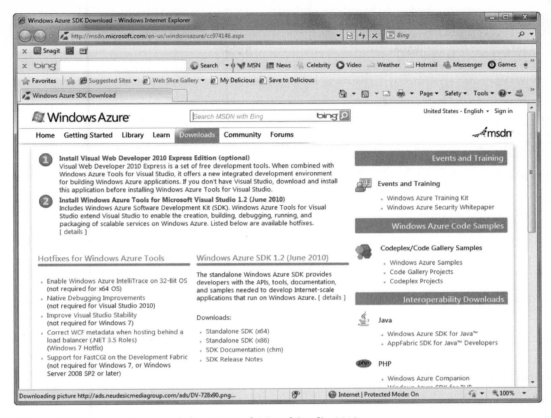

Figure 9–2. Window Azure tools for Microsoft Visual Studio 2010

The next step in working with the DataMarket is to subscribe to a data feed. After you sign up for your account, you can click the "Explore the Marketplace" button shown in Figure 9–1 to see what feeds are currently available and their subscription pricing model. Many are free. I have chosen the United Nations Energy data feed, the alteryx Census demographic data, and the data.gov crime figures in my examples, as shown in Figure 9–3. All three of these are free subscriptions (the Census data has a limit per month on transactions, the others do not).

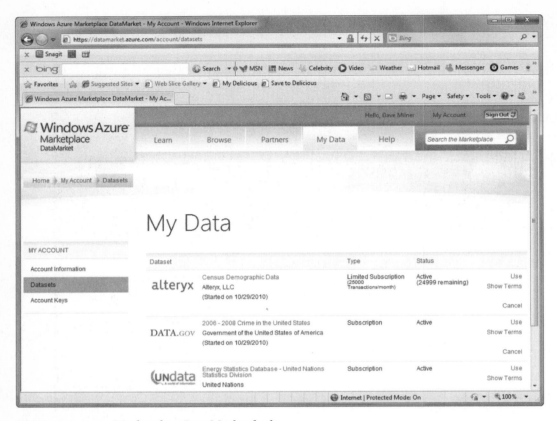

Figure 9–3. Azure Marketplace DataMarket feeds

PowerPivot and Azure

One of the best ways to interact with Azure Marketplace DataMarket feeds is through the tight integration with PowerPivot. PowerPivot is a very powerful data analysis add-in for Microsoft Excel 2010 that offers compelling BI features such as processing millions of rows of data and performing analysis on them as well as creating slices with pivot tables and graphs that help depict your data.

■ **Tip** To see what PowerPivot can do, search for "PowerPivot Demos" on Bing or watch this presentation at
`www.youtube.com/watch?v=MzgMMO-P9F0`.

PowerPivot can also be configured and enabled for SharePoint 2010. I will show you an example of consuming a DataMarket feed directly within Microsoft Excel and then extend the discussion to utilizing PowerPivot on your SharePoint site.

To hook up an Azure feed to PowerPivot, first download and install the PowerPivot add-in from
`www.powerpivot.com`, as shown in Figure 9–4.

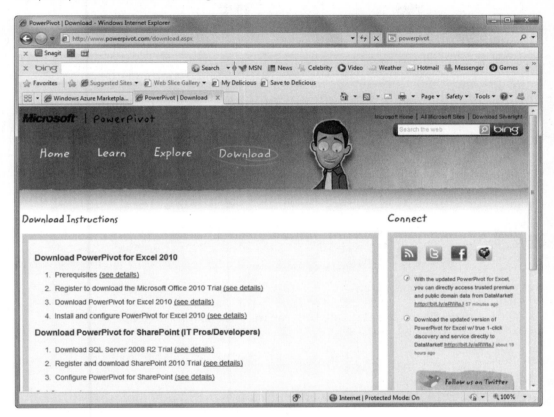

Figure 9–4. *Microsoft PowerPivot*

The PowerPivot site has specific instructions for not only using PowerPivot directly from within
Microsoft Office as an Excel add-in, but also setting up and configuring it for SharePoint 2010.
The steps to do so are as follows:

1. After you have downloaded and installed PowerPivot, go to the PowerPivot tab
   and launch the PowerPivot window. You will see a new PowerPivot window, as
   shown in Figure 9–5.

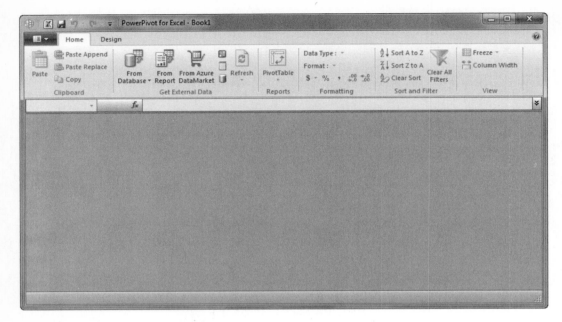

Figure 9–5. PowerPivot Window for Excel

2. Clicking on the "From Azure DataMarket" icon will open up the Table Import Wizard (see Figure 9–6).

Figure 9–6. Table Import wizard

3. Here you can type in the feed of the Azure DataMarket dataset URL, which you can find on the Data Explorer window of your Azure DataMarket page (see Figure 9–7).

4. After you have entered in the URL (you can also go directly to the Azure DataMarket by clicking the "View available Azure DataMarket datasets" link), enter in your personal account key that you generate on your "Account Keys" tab. Then hit the "Test Connection" button.

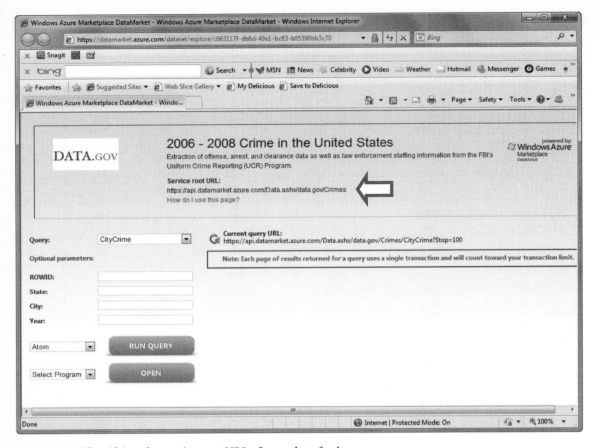

Figure 9–7. Identifying the service root URL of your data feed

5. After testing your connection, you may preview and filter data coming back in the Preview and Filter window in the course of going through your wizard (see Figure 9–8).

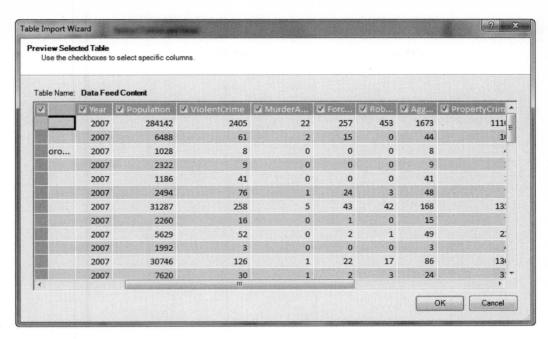

Figure 9–8. PowerPivot preview and filter window

6. After you have filtered out all data that you want, finish the import by continuing through the wizard and selecting Next-Next-Finish. The import can take a few minutes to load, as PowerPivot is designed to be able to work with large datasets. A picture of the import in process can be seen in Figure 9–9.

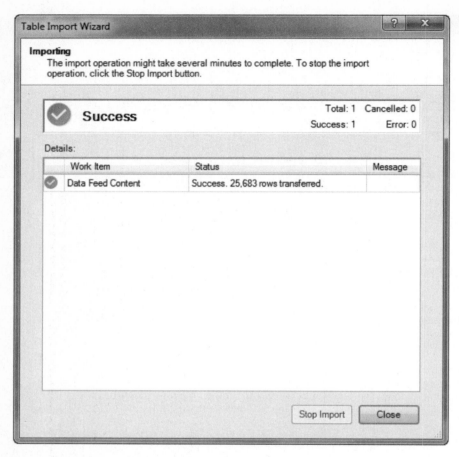

Figure 9–9. Import data feed content in process

The finished feed will appear as in Figure 9–10.

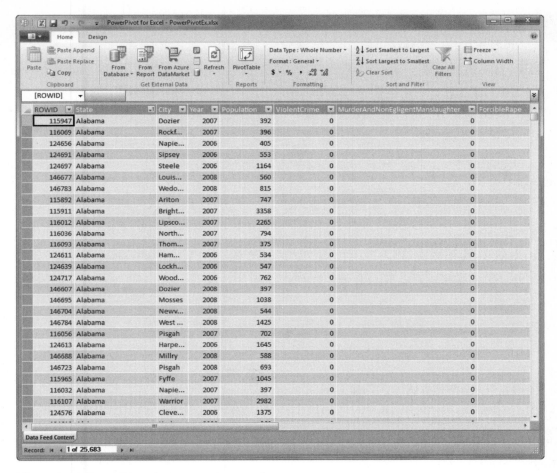

Figure 9–10. PowerPivot data source imported

From this point, you can start to implement other related data feeds, using your own internal data, and slicing and analyzing the data that comes in to build charts like the one shown in Figure 9–11.

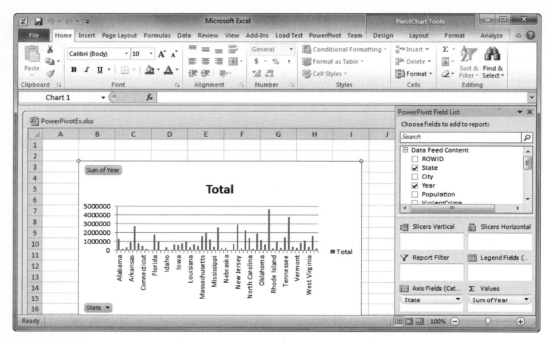

Figure 9–11. *PowerPivot PivotChart*

The advantage that PowerPivot brings to the table is raw processing power. Excel previously had a fast limit of 1 million rows, beyond which it could not run. PowerPivot's engine can handle a much larger data set. In fact, the actual limits will be dependent more upon the hardware resources of your machine than the actual limits that the engine can manage.

PowerPivot also can be set up on a SharePoint 2010 server farm. Instructions on how to set up PowerPivot for SharePoint 2010 can be found at www.powerpivot.com/download.aspx. Follow the links for "Download PowerPivot for SharePoint" for complete instruction on how to set up PowerPivot for SharePoint. Setting PowerPivot up for SharePoint will provide common library so that you can save your PowerPivot workbook .xslx files to a common SharePoint endpoint that can be utilized by other people. Once in SharePoint 2010, other viewers may view and interact with this data through a web browser—not using Excel. A lot of the real-time slice and data manipulation will be available there as well. This is one example of a Medium Touch Point solution, in that a portion of your application is hosted elsewhere—the cloud. The only .NET portion of this is a third party data feed provider in the cloud.

■ **Note** This PowerPivot example shows a no-code solution for connecting to the Azure Marketplace DataMarket. In the following example, I will show a .NET example of connecting to the Azure MarketPlace DataMarket. You should be able to draw from the pattern in the following example if you would like to wire up a .NET WCF Service to do this to expose to SharePoint 2010. I will also show the .NET WCF Service Pattern in the SQL Azure example that follows.

Accessing Azure DataMarket Feeds Through .NET

In another example in the code download, I show how to programmatically wire up access to the Azure DataMarket through a .NET Application. I will walk you through this example.

1. In Visual Studio .NET, Select Project ➤ New ➤ Console Application, as shown in Figure 9–12, and name it `AzureDataMarketConnect`.

Figure 9–12. *AzureDataMarketConnect console application*

2. Next, add service connection endpoints for the DataMarket feeds. Right-click Services in your Solution Explorer and select "Add Service Reference." Enter the URL as in Figure 9–13 and name your service reference `DataGovCrimes`.

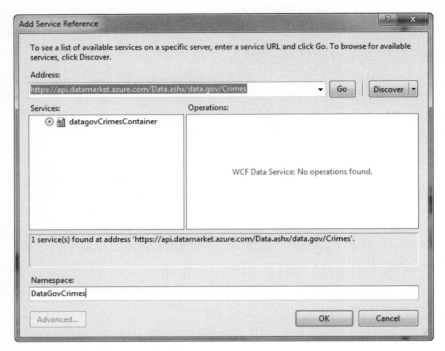

Figure 9–13. Add service reference to data.gov Crimes data feed

3. Add another service reference to the United Nations energy feed at

`https://api.datamarket.azure.com/Data.ashx/UnitedNations/Energy`

4. Name this service reference UNEnergy.

5. Next, add classes that interact with the service feeds and obtain consumable data from them. Define a new class in your project named DataGovCrimesData.cs. Then, add the code in Listing 9–1 to the class.

Listing 9–1. DataGovCrimesData.cs

```
using System;
using System.Collections.Generic;
using System.Linq;
using System.Text;
using AzureDataMarketConnect.DataGovCrimes;
using System.Net;
namespace AzureDataMarketConnect
{
    public class DataGovCrimesData
    {

        private Uri serviceUri;
        private datagovCrimesContainer contextCrimes;
```

```
        private const string SERVICE_URI =
"https://api.datamarket.azure.com/Data.ashx/data.gov/Crimes";
        private const string USER_ID = "unDataReader";
        //NOTE - you need to get your own key here - this is what it looks like, but some
values have been changed to protect my account
        private const string SECURE_ACCOUNT_KEY =
"XNUJ6mU1O3p1r57lgCdabcFQAE+fFgAsio3tSLKX1/Q=";

        public DataGovCrimesData()
        {
            serviceUri = new Uri(SERVICE_URI);
            contextCrimes = new datagovCrimesContainer(serviceUri);
            contextCrimes.Credentials = new NetworkCredential(USER_ID, SECURE_ACCOUNT_KEY);
        }

        public IList<CityCrime> GetCrimeData()
        {
            IEnumerable<CityCrime> query;
            query = from crimes in contextCrimes.CityCrime
                    select crimes;

            try
            {
                return query.ToList();
            }
            catch (Exception ex)
            {
                Console.WriteLine("Error: {0}", ex.Message);
                return null;
            }
        }


    }
}
```

In the class in Listing 9–1, note that you are doing the following:

- Defining private variables and constants that hold your credentials, URIs, and internal objects related to connecting to Azure DataMarket

- In the constructor, you are providing a dataContext to the Azure DataMarket services.

- You expose a method GetCrimesData() that uses LINQ to obtain the CityCrime data from the DataMarket feed and expose it in an IList for consumption by a client calling this class.

You will also do the same thing for the Energy data from the United Nations feed.

Finally, as an example of a client feed that obtains data from the classes you wrote, add the code in Listing 9–2 to Program.cs.

Listing 9–2. *Code to Add to Program.cs*

```csharp
using System;
using System.Collections.Generic;
using System.Linq;
using System.Text;
using System.Net;
using AzureDataMarketConnect.DataGovCrimes;
using AzureDataMarketConnect.UNEnergy;
using System.Collections.Specialized;
using System.Collections;


namespace AzureDataMarketConnect
{
    public class Program
    {
        static void Main(string[] args)
        {

            IList<UNEnergy.Values> energyList;  //UNEnerby.Values is the entity type returned
by the service
            UnitedNationsEnergyData energyData = new UnitedNationsEnergyData();
            energyList = energyData.GetEnergyData();

            if (energyList != null)
            {
                foreach (Values value in energyList)
                {
                    Console.WriteLine("{0,20} {1,-15} {2,-5}", value.CountryName,
value.CommodityTransactionName, value.Quantity);
                }
            }

            IList<CityCrime> crimeList;  // CityCrime is the entity type returned by the
service
            DataGovCrimesData crimeData = new DataGovCrimesData();
            crimeList = crimeData.GetCrimeData();

            if (crimeList != null)
            {
                Console.WriteLine("{0,4} {1,-12} {2,-15} {3,10} {4,13}", "Year", "City",
"State", "Population", "Violent Crime");

                foreach (CityCrime crime in crimeList)
                    Console.WriteLine("{0,4} {1,-15} {2,-15} {3,13} {4,10}", crime.Year,
                                                                    crime.City,
                                                                    crime.State,
                                                                    crime.Population,

crime.ViolentCrime);
            }
            Console.Write("Tap any key to exit. ");
            Console.ReadKey();
```

```
        }
    }
}
```

Listing 9–2 is an example of self-contained classes that encapsulate connecting to the Azure Marketplace DataMarket and obtain feeds for use with consumption by other clients. Other objects that can consume these classes include .NET middle tier objects, .NET WCF Services, and other application objects such as Silverlight middle tier objects.

Integrating External Feeds Through .NET WCF Services and jQuery

The next example of a Medium Touch Point solution builds on solutions in ASP.NET and SharePoint 2010 that allow for connecting to external data feeds from SharePoint through jQuery and WCF Services. I will continue to build upon this solution by migrating the data feed from a local SQL Server data store to the cloud with SQL Azure. This represents a Medium Touch Point solution that integrates some of the latest Microsoft technologies available; it should serve to point the way towards innovative solutions for you and your teams.

For this blended solution, you will have the following components:

- ASP.NET Web + WCF .NET Application named SalesStores that talks to a SQL Azure endpoint and exposes JSON.

- SharePoint 2010 jQuery and JavaScript code implemented simply with a Content Editor Web Part.

- A SQL Server database named AzureTest that you create and populate locally, and then migrate to SQL Azure in the cloud.

You will build this blended solution by performing the following steps:

1. Take a local SQL Server database and migrate it to SQL Azure.

2. Build your ADO.NET Entity Data Models against the Azure database.

3. Set up a .NET WCF Data Service that consumes the oData REST feed from your Entity Data Models.

■ **Tip** For working with AJAX and great tools that build up that front such as jQuery and the related libraries, it is not necessary to write server side code in .NET as a SharePoint 2010 solution and incur the overhead of solution packages and deployment. JavaScript code can be embedded in a SharePoint page through the use of a Content Editor Webpart. This can provide the rapid deployment of solutions and will also work in controlled environments such as hosted solutions.

■ **Note** Since you are setting up data access through SQL Azure, I'll take this moment to explain how to set up data in a SQL Azure Database. A SQL Azure database is simply a cloud option for database services. Microsoft is investing a lot of resources into making this service a workable business model, so it presents a pay-for-service model of data storage as opposed to a server licensing option for SQL Server. For some companies, this option may prove to be a cost-saving one, depending upon business factors. More information about SQL Azure can be found at http://msdn.microsoft.com/en-us/windowsazure/sqlazure/default.aspx.

Setting Up and Migrating Data to a SQL Azure Database

The first step to using SQL Azure databases is to sign up for an account. This can be done at www.microsoft.com/windowsazure. Once your account is set up, you will be able to name a SQL Azure project (see Figure 9–14).

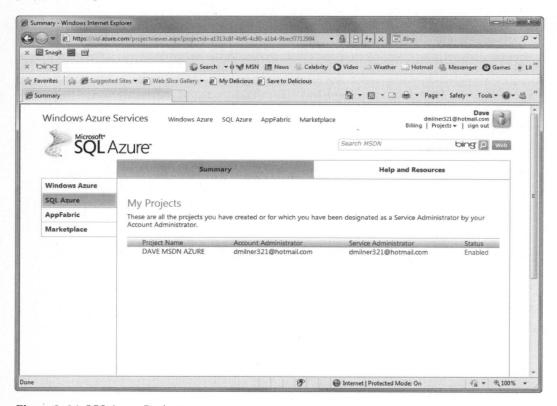

Figure 9–14. SQL Azure Project

Next, you will create a database, as shown in Figure 9–15.

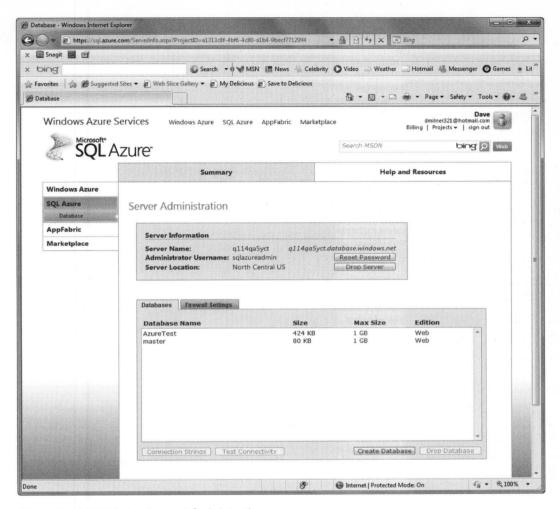

Figure 9–15. SQL Azure Server Administration

As you can see, the server name in your created instance of SQL Azure is shown. You have the option to specify the location of the server as well as assign an Administrator username and password for managing your data. You can use your SQL Server Management Studio to connect to the server directly.

■ **Tip** For security purposes, connecting up to your database through SQL Server Management Studio is only specifically allowed by setting Firewall Settings, such those shown in the tab in Figure 9–19. Determine which IP address or ranges of IP addresses you want to enable to connect up to your Azure databases, and enter the rules in on the Firewall Settings Page.

To upload or migrate data to SQL Azure, first you create the data in a local SQL Server database. An overview of the data that I created in the database AzureTest for this example can be seen in Figure 9–16.

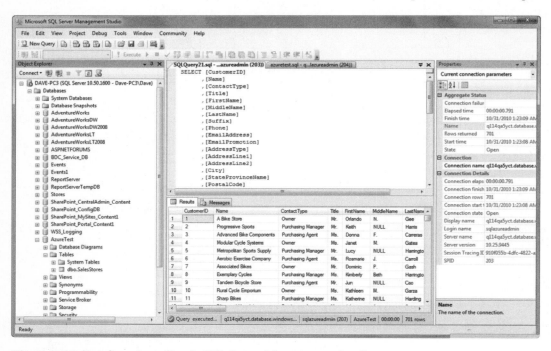

Figure 9–16. Database AzureTest in SQL Server Management Studio

Once you have the data mocked up in a local database, you will generate a script to migrate it to SQL Azure. You can do this by following these steps:

1. Select your database, right click, and select Tasks ➤ Generate Scripts

2. In the next window, select "Script entire database and all objects."

3. In "Set Scripting Options," save your script to a single file. Click the "Advanced" Button.

4. In the "Advanced Scripting Options" window, make the following selections:

- Set "Script for the database engine type" to "SQL Azure Database."
- Set "Convert UDDT's to Base Types" to "True."
- Set "Types of data to script" to "Schema and data."
- Finish out the wizard and save to your local script file.

■ **Tip** All Azure databases need to have a unique clustered index, so be sure to set one in your table either through designating a primary key or by creating the index directly.

---

5. Next, in SQL Server Manager, click the "Connect" button on the left, and connect to your SQL Azure database instance, as shown in Figure 9–17.

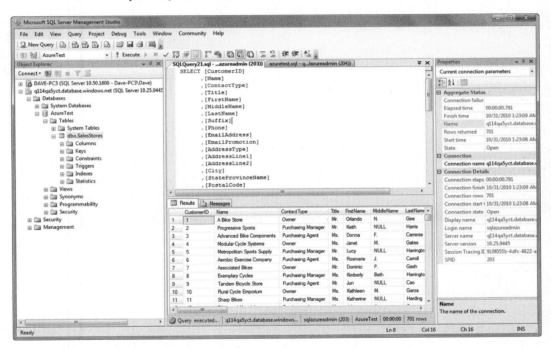

Figure 9–17. Connecting to SQL Azure through SQL Server Management Studio

6. From there, open the new script window on your SQL Azure database, open the script file that you saved locally, and run your script against the Azure database. You now have data in the cloud.

Developing an ASP.NET Application with SQL Azure, WCF, and jQuery

The steps for developing an ASP.NET application with SQL Azure, WCF, and jQuery are as follows:

1. First, fire up Visual Studio and create a new web application project, as shown in Figure 9–18.

Figure 9–18. *ASP.NET web application*

2. Next, add an ADO.NET Entity Data Model to talk to your SQL Server database SalesStores by selecting "Add New Item" and "ADO.NET Entity Data Model" (see Figure 9–19).

Figure 9–19. ADO.NET Entity Data Model

3. In the Entity Data Model Wizard that comes up next, select "Generate from database" as shown in Figure 9–20.

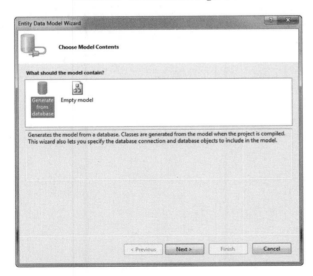

Figure 9–20. Choose model contents

4. Next, you have the ability to choose your database connection. In this case, instead of choosing a local SQL Server database, you are going to use the SQL Azure database that you have set up. The connection credentials appear as in Figure 9–21.

Figure 9–21. SQL Azure database connection

Now you can generate your ADO.NET Entity Data Model entities directly from the cloud connecting to your SQL Azure data store by following these steps:

1. Select your connection information as shown in Fig 9–22.

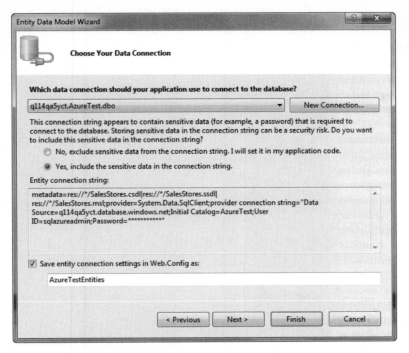

Figure 9–22. Choose Entity Data Model Connection

2. Finalize your test model as shown in Figure 9–23, and select Finish to complete adding the generation of the Entity Data Model to your project.

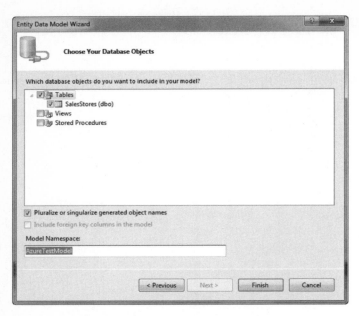

Figure 9–23. Choose Your Database Objects

■ **Tip** If you would like to work with the exact data that I am using in this example, the script is included in the code downloads for the chapter. It has both the schema and data, and you can run the script both locally and in a SQL Azure instance to take advantage of the data. The data itself is an extract from the AdventureWorks sample database, but has additional fields of Lat and Long for geocoding.

3. You will end up with the following entity in your Entity Designer window, as shown in Figure 9–24.

Figure 9–24. SalesStore Entity Model

4. Next, to create a REST oData endpoint that you can connect to from SharePoint 2010, go to Add ➤ New Item ➤ WCF Data Service, as shown in Figure 9–25.

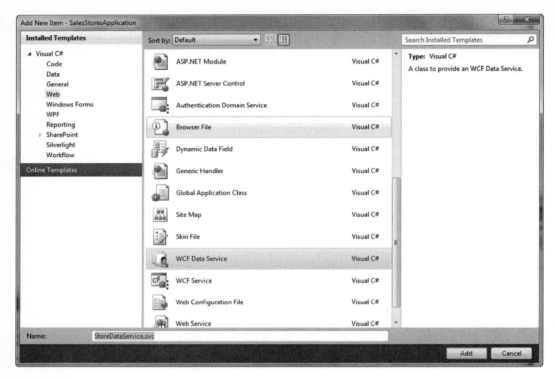

Figure 9–25. *Add WCF Data Service*

　5.　Change the StoreServiceData.cs to contain the code in Listing 9–3.

Listing 9–3. *Changes to StoreServiceData.cs*

```
namespace SalesStoresApplication
{
    public class StoreDataService : DataService<AzureTestEntities>
    {
        // This method is called only once to initialize service-wide policies.
        public static void InitializeService(IDataServiceConfiguration config)
        {
            config.SetEntitySetAccessRule("SalesStore", EntitySetRights.AllRead);

        }
    }
}
```

　6.　Next, add a client application by right clicking the solution file and selecting
　　　Add ➤ New Project. Select Cloud and Azure Cloud Services, and name the
　　　application SalesStores (see Figure 9–26).

Figure 9–26. *Add Cloud Service*

7. In the next window, select the ASP.NET Web Role as shown in Figure 9–27.

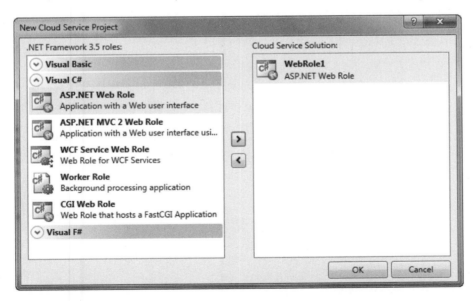

Figure 9–27. *Cloud Service role window*

8. Next, in the WebRole1 project that is created for the cloud service, add a Service Reference and click the "Discover" button to reference your SalesStoreServiceReference (see Figure 9–28).

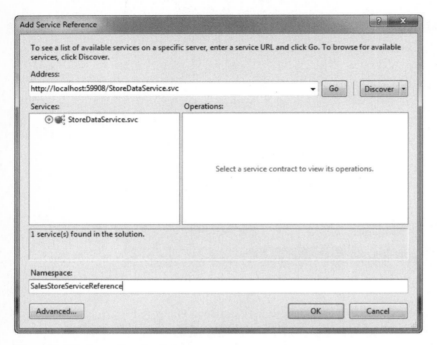

Figure 9–28. Azure Service Reference

■ **Note** Because you have cached data from your Azure DataMarket work previously, notice that before you click the "Discover" button, you have access to add ServiceReferences to your DataMarket feeds as well.

---

9. Next, add the code in Listing 9–4 to your default.aspx page.

Listing 9–4. Code to Add to default.aspx

```
<div>
   <asp:DropDownList ID="StoreList" runat="server"
onselectedindexchanged="StoreList_SelectedIndexChanged"
      AutoPostBack="True">
   </asp:DropDownList>
   <br />
   <br />
   <asp:Label ID="infoLabel" runat="server"></asp:Label>
   <br />
```

```
</div>
```

10. Add the code in Listing 9–5 to the codebehind of your default page in your default.aspx.cs file.

Listing 9–5. Codebehind Code

```
public partial class _Default : System.Web.UI.Page
{
    private AzureTestEntities storeContext;
    private Uri svcUri = new Uri("http://localhost:59908/StoreDataService.svc");

    protected void Page_Load(object sender, EventArgs e)
    {

        //Instantiate the DataServiceContext
        storeContext = new AzureTestEntities(svcUri);

        //Get all person entities from the data service
        DataServiceQuery<SalesStores> stores = storeContext.SalesStores;

        //Add each person to the drop down list
        foreach (SalesStores s in stores)
        {
            StoreList.Items.Add(new ListItem(s.Name.ToString(), s.CustomerID.ToString()));
}
    }


    protected void StoreList_SelectedIndexChanged(object sender, EventArgs e)
    {
        //Define a LINQ query that returns information
        // about the selected store.
        var storeInfo = (from s in storeContext.SalesStores
                            where s.CustomerID ==
Convert.ToInt32(StoreList.SelectedItem.Value)
                            select s).FirstOrDefault();

        //Display information about the store
        infoLabel.Text = String.Concat("ID: ", storeInfo.CustomerID.ToString(), "<br /> ",
                                        "Business Type: ",
storeInfo.BusinessType.ToString(), "<br /> ",
                                        "City: ", storeInfo.City.ToString(), "<br /> ",
                                        "State: ", storeInfo.StateProvinceName.ToString(),
"<br /> ",
                                        "Annual Revenue: ",
storeInfo.AnnualRevenue.ToString());

    }
}
```

11. At this point, you have your REST oData feed service wired up as well as your application to test it out, and you can set the WebRole1 project as the startup project and hit F5. The results should appear as in Figure 9–29.

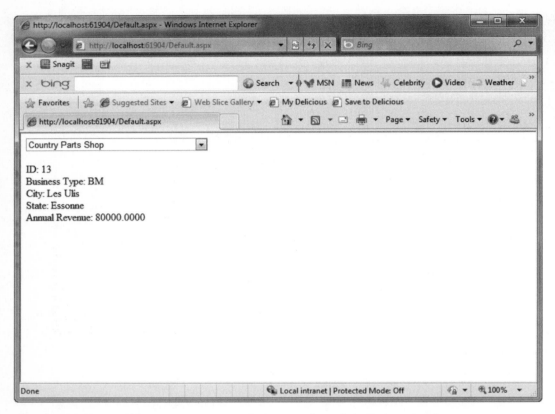

Figure 9–29. Test application connecting to SQL Azure through WCF Data Service.

12. Notice also that you can connect directly up to a browser to tap into your WCF
    Data Service oData feed. Locate the URL of your service (here on my local
    machine it is `http://localhost:59908/StoreDataService.svc/SalesStores` as
    I entered the base Uri into my codebehind page). You get the standard page in
    IE showing the Atom feed as shown in Figure 9–30.

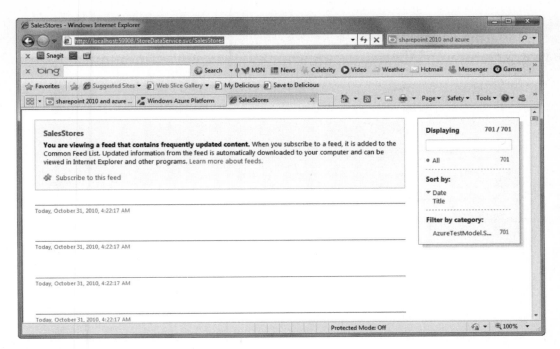

Figure 9–30. *SalesStores oData feed*

13. Selecting Page ➤ View Source will show you your feed data (see Figure 9–31).

Figure 9–31. *Atom Feed oData for SalesService WCF Data Service*

Note that this works in the debugger view, but you can certainly publish this WCF Data Service to an ASP.NET application server in an IIS 7 instance for consumption just as easily.

At this point, I've introduced and provided examples of how to utilize WCF Data Services to produce oData feeds through Atom connecting up to SQL Azure services. This represents a number of the latest and greatest pieces of the current Microsoft stack in ASP.NET development, and this looks to be the wave of the future as far as interacting with data. The advantage to using SQL Azure is that you can connect to data feeds that extend far beyond the reach of your local systems. Also, if you have budget constraints concerning SQL Server hardware, software, and personnel, SQL Azure is a viable alternative. If you have a scenario of this sort now, you know how to work with it. If not, then you know how to work with it in the future when it happens.

Consuming an oData Feed with jQuery in SharePoint 2010

For the last piece of the integrated SharePoint 2010/ASP.NET Medium Touch Point solution, I will show you how to integrate your REST oData feeds in SharePoint 2010 through client side JavaScript using the jQuery library.

For your development approach to this, instead of working directly in SharePoint you will go ahead and add in an HTML page that includes your jQuery references and JavaScript directly in your project.

Once you have all the kinks worked out of your client side code, you can port it into a Content Editor Web Part on your SharePoint 2010 server and integrate it.

Add a new HTML page to your project named ClientTest.htm. Then add the code in Listing 9–6 to the page.

Listing 9–6. Code for ClientTest.htm

```
<head>
    <title>SalesStores</title>
    <link href="http://ajax.microsoft.com/ajax/jquery.ui/1.8.5/themes/ui-lightness/jquery-
ui.css" rel="stylesheet"
        type="text/css" />
    <script src="http://ajax.microsoft.com/ajax/jquery/jquery-1.4.2.min.js"
type="text/javascript"></script>
    <script src="http://ajax.microsoft.com/ajax/jquery.ui/1.8.5/jquery-ui.min.js"
type="text/javascript"></script>
    <script type="text/javascript">
        (function ($) {
            $.widget("ui.salesstore", {
                options: {
                    address: "http://localhost:59908/StoreDataService.svc/SalesStores"
            },
                _create: function () {
                    var el = this.element;
                    var o = this.options;

$.getScript("http://ajax.microsoft.com/ajax/jquery.templates/beta1/jquery.tmpl.js",
                function () {
                    $.template("table",
'<table><thead><tr><th>Customer</th><th>Address</th><th>City</th><th>State</th><th>Annual
Revenue</th></tr></thead>' +
                        '<tbody>{{each
d}}<tr><td>${Name}</td><td>${AddressLine1}</td><td>${City}</td><td>${StateProvinceName}</td><t
d>${AnnualRevenue}</td></tr>{{/each}}</tbody></table>');
                    $.ajax({
                        url: o.address,
                        dataType: "json",
                        success: function (result) {
                            this.valueTable = $.tmpl("table", result).addClass("ui-widget")
                                    .find("thead").addClass("ui-widget-header").end()
                                    .find("tbody tr").addClass("ui-widget-content").end()
                                    .appendTo(el);
                        }
                    });

                });
            },
            destroy: function () {
                this.valueTable.remove();
                $.widget.prototype.destroy.apply(this, arguments); // default
            }
        });

    })(jQuery);
```

```
        $(function () {
            $("#store").salesstore();
        });
    </script>

</head>
<body>
    <div id="store" />
</body>
```

Note that in the jQuery code, you are making use of several jQuery plugins, the jQuery UI, jQuery widgets, and jQuery templates. All of this makes for very compact client side code to interact with your local WCF Data Service that connects to SQL Azure data.

The result of the code in Listing 9–6 looks like Figure 9–32.

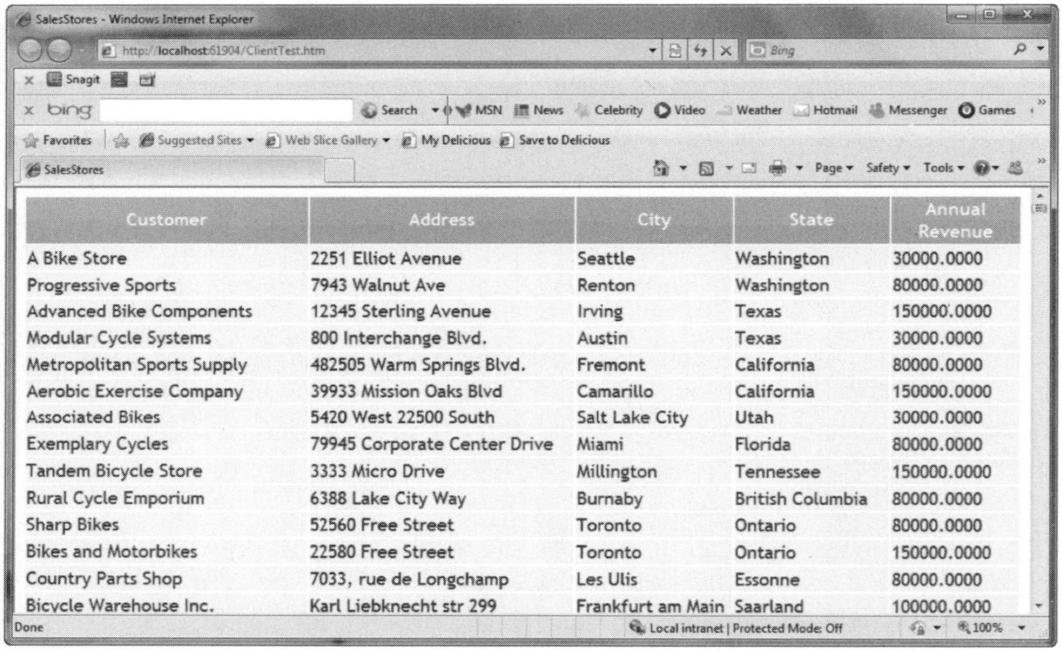

Customer	Address	City	State	Annual Revenue
A Bike Store	2251 Elliot Avenue	Seattle	Washington	30000.0000
Progressive Sports	7943 Walnut Ave	Renton	Washington	80000.0000
Advanced Bike Components	12345 Sterling Avenue	Irving	Texas	150000.0000
Modular Cycle Systems	800 Interchange Blvd.	Austin	Texas	30000.0000
Metropolitan Sports Supply	482505 Warm Springs Blvd.	Fremont	California	80000.0000
Aerobic Exercise Company	39933 Mission Oaks Blvd	Camarillo	California	150000.0000
Associated Bikes	5420 West 22500 South	Salt Lake City	Utah	30000.0000
Exemplary Cycles	79945 Corporate Center Drive	Miami	Florida	80000.0000
Tandem Bicycle Store	3333 Micro Drive	Millington	Tennessee	150000.0000
Rural Cycle Emporium	6388 Lake City Way	Burnaby	British Columbia	80000.0000
Sharp Bikes	52560 Free Street	Toronto	Ontario	80000.0000
Bikes and Motorbikes	22580 Free Street	Toronto	Ontario	150000.0000
Country Parts Shop	7033, rue de Longchamp	Les Ulis	Essonne	80000.0000
Bicycle Warehouse Inc.	Karl Liebknecht str 299	Frankfurt am Main	Saarland	100000.0000

Figure 9–32. *HTML page using jQuery to connect to WCF Data Service and SQL Azure*

The last step to complete your cycle is implementing this in SharePoint. Copy all of the text in the head portion of the file and also the div tag in the body, and paste them into a text document in Notepad. Name it `SalesStores.txt` to help keep track of it.

■ **Note** You can remove the `<head>` and `<body>` tags in the Notepad document. The text file is included in the example folder and named `SalesStores.txt`.

Next, upload the SalesStores.txt document to your Shared Documents library in your site. Finally, on the page where you want to include the results, add a Content Editor Web Part, and then configure it to point to the text file in your Shared Documents library. The URL I am pointing to is /Shared Documents/SalesStores.txt. When you save the Web part, you will see your content as in Figure 9–33.

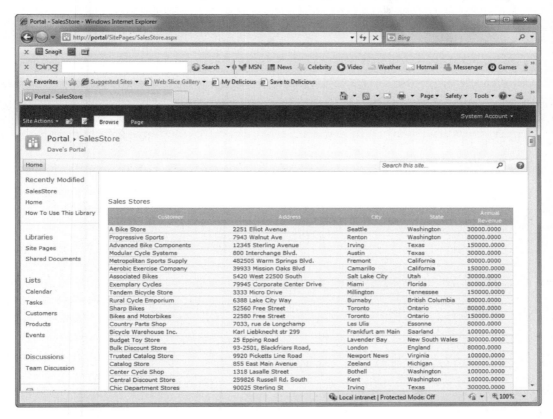

Figure 9–33. Finished Web Part for a Medium Touch Point solution

Summary

In this chapter, I introduced the concept of Medium Touch Point solutions, which are the most flexible of approaches to blending SharePoint 2010 with ASP.NET. I also introduced several cutting edge techniques for development in SharePoint 2010 including Azure cloud services utilizing both the Azure Marketplace DataMarket as well as SQL Azure storage, WCF Data Services with REST and oData, and jQuery client-side development with jQuery advancements including jQuery UI widgets and jQuery templates. Next, I will demonstrate the final technique for blending SharePoint 2010 and ASP.NET solutions: High Touch Point solutions.

CHAPTER 10

■ ■ ■

High Touch Point Solutions

If I'd had some set idea of a finish line, don't you think I would have crossed it years ago?

Bill Gates

In building blended SharePoint 2010 and ASP.NET solutions, the final area to investigate the High Touch Point solutions. High Touch Point solutions are the ultimate in integration between ASP.NET and SharePoint 2010. There does not exist a tighter integration or more blended solution in terms of wrapping the functionality of an ASP.NET application completely within the SharePoint 2010 engine, product, and feature set.

This will be the most complicated integration that you will do with SharePoint 2010, although maybe not the most elegant. The advantages are that you can be in complete control of your ASP.NET solution, which presents a tremendous vertical business advantage, and you can wrap much of the core functionality of SharePoint 2010 within it, including rich document management with versioning capabilities, routing capabilities, alerts, RSS feeds, workflows, and all of the other features that SharePoint 2010 documents support such as offline capabilities with both SharePoint 2010 Workspace and Windows Phone 7 Office Hub. The collaboration factor means that you can present your unique application solution along with a model for being able to build out portal collaboration through multiple layers of organizational user support. While the last chapter expanded your horizons by showing what's available in blending Medium Touch Point solutions, this chapter should expand your options in a different direction.

The core concept of a High Touch Point solution is going to involve a Layouts directory implementation of your ASP.NET solution. This will involve the endpoint where your ASP.NET solution, whether it is an existing one or a new one you are developing, will be deployed to the same directory structure as the bulk of the application pages in the standard SharePoint 2010 solution.

In this chapter, I will cover the pros and cons for High Touch Point solutions and highlight some dos and don'ts with respect to best practices and other considerations. Then I will build out an example High Touch Point solution, modify it, and deploy it to SharePoint 2010. I will also discuss considerations for migrating existing ASP.NET solutions into SharePoint. Finally, since there is a lot of talk about load testing in these environments, I will dig into Visual Studio 2010 and set up a load test for the High Touch Point solution that will set a threshold for page load times and performance profile the application.

Pros

The pros to implementing a High Touch Point solution are as follows:

- Your ASP.NET application is self contained

- Changes involve master page changes only

- Advanced DB interaction

- - Transactional support
  - Many-to-many database relationships
- Performance tuning is easier for .NET applications
- Cons

The cons to implementing a High Touch Point solution are as follows:

- Performance constraints carry over to SharePoint environment. You need to load test!
- Deployment will not be standardized with SharePoint Solution Packages (.wsp files)
- You need to keep farm in sync
- Performance tuning is more difficult for SharePoint 2010 farm

Now, besides the reasons for choosing to implement High Touch Point solutions, I will highlight ways to make them work in your environment.

Tenets and Constraints for High Touch Point Solutions

Since High Touch Point solutions will involve the deployment to the Layouts directory in a SharePoint installation, there are some rules and constraints surrounding what to do for this type of solution as well as setting expectations for what can realistically work with a High Touch Point solution using SharePoint 2010.

High Touch Point solutions represent the extreme end of a blended ASP.NET and SharePoint 2010 environment. You would not typically use it for an existing SharePoint 2010 farm that already has a fair amount of user traffic and documents stored in it. These solutions work best if they are considered a "one-off" type of solution or package for a particular purpose that makes sense from a business perspective strategically.

The appeal to this type of solution is that it can offer a great deal of built-in feature support from SharePoint 2010 at a very low cost. SharePoint Foundation 2010 is a free product download, and is a proven document management portal. You can wrap an ASP.NET application into a SharePoint 2010 Foundation Team Site and have built-in features that encapsulate meeting feature requirements for solutions that need to wrap document management into their base offering.

■ **Note** One example of a High Touch Point solution that I designed and developed was for a client that had government requirements surrounding documentation. Certain work flows needed to be documented consistently, changes in documentation needed to be maintained and updated frequently, and reports needed to be maintained within the system. I implemented a WSS 3.0 solution that involved a web farm with two Web Front-End (WFE) servers as a front-end. The solution contained one site collection only, used NTLM authentication, and had the complicated SharePoint end of things very neatly encapsulated.

High Touch Point Blended Solution Example

As part of delving into blended solutions, let's start off by doing a High Touch Point solution example from start to finish. This example will be a new ASP.NET web site that will be integrated in with SharePoint 2010.

New ASP.NET Web Site Example

To start your example of High Touch Point solutions, you will begin by coding a simple example of an ASP.NET Website that integrates with the SQL Server AdventureWorks database. This database represents an external SQL database with line of business (LOB) data in it. You will show an ASP.NET application hooking up to the SQL Server database, and then migrate it to SharePoint 2010.

■ **Note** SQL Server and SharePoint best practices indicate that it is best to not include production SQL Server databases on the same instance as your SharePoint farm. Basically, there's the potential for slowing down your SharePoint environment doing this. SharePoint Health Analyzer will come up with an error if you set SQL databases up in the same instance as your SharePoint farm. The resolution to this is simple: install your SharePoint farm on the default instance of your SQL Server installation. Then install your transactional SQL databases on a second named instance of SQL Server. It doesn't have to be physically on a different server; it's enough to use a second named instance. The reason to recommend setting up the named instance for your other databases is that it's a little easier administratively to deal with SharePoint installed on a default instance of SQL Server. This, however, is not really important, as the workaround to any instance is to simply set up a SQL Server Alias to an instance that is a single name; for example, DAVE-PC3\AdventureWorks is my server \ instance connection, so I set up DaveAdventureWorks as my SQL Alias to that transactional database instance and DaveSharePoint as my SQL Alias to my SharePoint database instance.

Fire up Visual Studio 2010, and start a new web site, as shown in Figure 10–1.

Figure 10–1. New ASP.NET web site

Your web site must use the .NET Framework 3.5. This will ensure that all of the technologies and libraries that you are using will be compatible with SharePoint 2010, which uses .NET 3.5. In this example, you are choosing the ASP.NET Web Site template as opposed to an ASP.NET Application template simply to make porting the solution as easy as possible. ASP.NET web sites all actively compile the code on the fly with the built-in IIS support of the .NET Framework. This means that you can migrate smaller subsets of the components of your solution easily as opposed to depending upon a large compile-and-package approach.

■ **Note** Depending upon the complexity of your application, defining a High Touch Point solution is the one approach where you may not depend upon the existing packaging solutions for SharePoint development in finalizing your builds. The tradeoff here is that your site is accessible from a universal place with respect to the site collection, yet it can implement a large portion of the ASP.NET application. This means that instead of doing .wsp package deployments, you may choose to do a Layouts directory direct deployment on each of your WFE servers. This would be about the ONLY time that doing this would be recommended. Note that you'll need to manage the code on each WFE server. Also, load testing and monitoring are recommended for usage. And last, this solution is primarily at the site collection level, as all sites will have access to your pages.

Add Web Forms Customers and Orders

Next, you add two web forms to your web site solution. Name them Customer and Orders, as shown in Figure 10–2.

Figure 10–2. Customers and Orders pages

On the default.aspx page, add in links to the two new pages, as in the markup in Listing 10–1.

Listing 10–1. Add Links to the Two New Pages

```
<html xmlns="http://www.w3.org/1999/xhtml">
<head runat="server">
    <title></title>
</head>
<body>
    <form id="form1" runat="server">
    <h1>AdventureWorks Pages</h1>
    <div>
        <ul>
            <li><asp:HyperLink ID="hypCustomers" runat="server"
                NavigateUrl="~/Customers.aspx">Customers</asp:HyperLink></li>
            <li><asp:HyperLink ID="hypOrders" runat="server"
                NavigateUrl="~/Orders.aspx">Orders</asp:HyperLink></li>
        </ul>
    </div>
    </form>
</body>
</html>
```

In Listing 10–1, you use the landing page to the application or the default.aspx page as the one containing navigation elements to the other pages in your application; you may also use other means for navigation. When you migrate the solution to SharePoint 2010, all of the SharePoint built-in navigation elements become available as well.

Next, you need to set up access to your AdventureWorks database. Ensure that your web.config file has the connection listed for your environment similar to the following:

```
<connectionStrings>
<add name="AdventureWorks" connectionString="data source=DAVE-PC3;Integrated
Security=SSPI;Initial Catalog=AdventureWorksLT2008"/>
</connectionStrings>
```

■ **Note** When you migrate this application to SharePoint 2010, you'll use the built-in capabilities of IIS 7 and the .NET Framework to recursively read directories for configuration information.

Next, you add the markup in Listing 10–2 to your Customer page.

Listing 10–2. Adding Code to Customer Page

```
<body>
    <form id="form1" runat="server">
    <h1>AdventureWorks Customers</h1>
     <div>
     Customer:  <asp:DropDownList ID="ddCustomer"
OnSelectedIndexChanged="ddCustomer_SelectedIndexChanged" AutoPostBack="True" runat="server">
        </asp:DropDownList>
          <asp:DetailsView ID="dvCustomerDetail" runat="server" Height="50px" Width="125px">
          </asp:DetailsView>
        <asp:Label ID="lblErrorMessage" runat="server"></asp:Label>
    </div>
     <div><asp:HyperLink ID="hypDefault" runat="server"
NavigateUrl="~/Default.aspx">Home</asp:HyperLink></div>
    </form>
</body>
```

Add ASP.NET Code

Next, add code in the codebehind page `customer.aspx.cs` to load the data into these controls. Modify the Page Load function as shown in Listing 10–3.

Listing 10–3. Modifying the Page Load Function

```
protected void Page_Load(object sender, EventArgs e)
    {
            if (!Page.IsPostBack)
            {
                string queryString = "SELECT CustomerID, CompanyName FROM
[AdventureWorksLT2008].[SalesLT].[Customer]";

                using (SqlConnection connection = new
    SqlConnection(ConfigurationManager.ConnectionStrings["AdventureWorks"].ConnectionString))
                {
                    using (SqlDataAdapter sdaSO = new SqlDataAdapter(queryString, connection))
                    {
                        try
                        {
                            DataTable dtSO = new DataTable();
                            sdaSO.Fill(dtSO);
                            ddCustomer.DataSource = dtSO;
                            ddCustomer.DataTextField = "CompanyName";
                            ddCustomer.DataValueField = "CustomerID";
                            ddCustomer.DataBind();
                            ddCustomer.Items.Insert(0, "Select Customer");
```

```
            }
            catch (Exception ex)
            {
                lblErrorMessage.Text = "Error retrieving data " + ex.Message;
            }
        }
    }
}
}
```

Now, add the function in Listing 10–4 to handle the drop-down list change.

Listing 10–4. A Function to Handle the Drop-down List Change

```
public void ddCustomer_SelectedIndexChanged(object sender, EventArgs e)
    {
        string queryString = "SELECT CompanyName, EmailAddress, Phone, FirstName, LastName
FROM [AdventureWorksLT2008].[SalesLT].[Customer] WHERE CustomerID = " +
            ddCustomer.SelectedValue.ToString();

        using (SqlConnection connection = new
SqlConnection(ConfigurationManager.ConnectionStrings["AdventureWorks"].ConnectionString))
        {
            using (SqlDataAdapter sdaSO = new SqlDataAdapter(queryString, connection))
            {
                try
                {
                    DataTable dtSO = new DataTable();
                    sdaSO.Fill(dtSO);
                    dvCustomerDetail.DataSource = dtSO;
                    dvCustomerDetail.DataBind();
                }
                catch (Exception ex)
                {
                    lblErrorMessage.Text = "Error retrieving data " + ex.Message;
                }
            }

        }
    }
```

In the Page_Load function, you are using standard ASP.NET / ADO.NET SQL connection objects to connect to the AdventureWorks database to load the Customer drop-down control. This control is marked to post back the page, so when the index changes, you use the function to fill your DataView with data from the selected Customer.

In a similar fashion, add the markup in Listing 10–5 to your Orders.aspx page.

Listing 10–5. Code for the Orders.aspx Page

```
<body>
    <form id="form1" runat="server">
    <h1>Orders</h1>
    <div>
```

```
        Sales Order:  <asp:DropDownList ID="ddSalesOrder"
OnSelectedIndexChanged="ddSalesOrder_SelectedIndexChanged" AutoPostBack="True" runat="server">
        </asp:DropDownList>
        <asp:GridView ID="gvSalesOrderDetail" runat="server">
        </asp:GridView>
        <asp:Label ID="lblErrorMessage" runat="server"></asp:Label>
    </div>
    <div><asp:HyperLink ID="hypDefault" runat="server"
NavigateUrl="~/Default.aspx">Home</asp:HyperLink></div>
    </form>
</body>
```

And add the following to your page load function in the orders.aspx.cs file:

```
protected void Page_Load(object sender, EventArgs e)
        {
            if (!Page.IsPostBack)
            {
                string queryString = "SELECT SalesOrderId, SalesOrderNumber FROM
[AdventureWorksLT2008].[SalesLT].[SalesOrderHeader]";

                using (SqlConnection connection = new
SqlConnection(ConfigurationManager.ConnectionStrings["AdventureWorks"].ConnectionString))
                {
                    using (SqlDataAdapter sdaSO = new SqlDataAdapter(queryString, connection))
                    {
                        try
                        {
                            DataTable dtSO = new DataTable();
                            sdaSO.Fill(dtSO);
                            ddSalesOrder.DataSource = dtSO;
                            ddSalesOrder.DataTextField = "SalesOrderNumber";
                            ddSalesOrder.DataValueField = "SalesOrderId";
                            ddSalesOrder.DataBind();
                            ddSalesOrder.Items.Insert(0, "Select Sales Order");

                        }
                        catch (Exception ex)
                        {
                            lblErrorMessage.Text = "Error retrieving data " + ex.Message;
                        }
                    }
                }
            }
        }
```

Then add the function in Listing 10–6 to handle your drop-down selection change.

Listing 10–6. Drop-down Selection Function

```
public void ddSalesOrder_SelectedIndexChanged(object sender, EventArgs e)
    {
        string queryString = "SELECT OrderQty, ProductID, UnitPrice, UnitPriceDiscount,
LineTotal FROM [AdventureWorksLT2008].[SalesLT].[SalesOrderDetail] WHERE SalesOrderId = " +
            ddSalesOrder.SelectedValue.ToString();
```

```
    using (SqlConnection connection = new
SqlConnection(ConfigurationManager.ConnectionStrings["AdventureWorks"].ConnectionString))
    {
        using (SqlDataAdapter sdaSO = new SqlDataAdapter(queryString, connection))
        {
            try
            {
                DataTable dtSO = new DataTable();
                sdaSO.Fill(dtSO);
                gvSalesOrderDetail.DataSource = dtSO;
                gvSalesOrderDetail.DataBind();
            }
            catch (Exception ex)
            {
                lblErrorMessage.Text = "Error retrieving data " + ex.Message;
            }
        }

    }
}
```

Here, similar to the Customers page, you are using standard ASP.NET / ADO.NET SQL connection objects to connect to the AdventureWorks database to load the Orders drop-down control. This control is marked to post back the page, so when the index changes, you use the above function to fill your DataGrid with data from the selected Order.

Run this simple application with the F5 button and you will see something similar to that in Figures 10–3 thru 10–5.

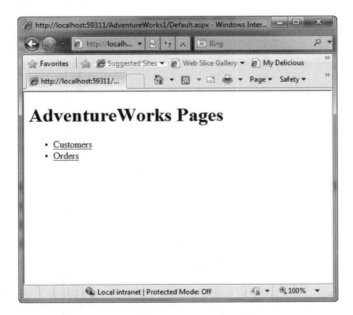

Figure 10–3. *AdventureWorks application home page*

■ **Tip** This application is using standard .NET Forms in its coding approach. You can also use a jQuery with templates, such as is shown in Chapter 9's examples, and Silverlight, as shown in Chapter 6. One approach that will not mix well with the current feature set in SharePoint 2010 is the MVC templates such as a MVC 2 or 3 application. This is because the URL rewrite features in MVC are not currently compatible with SharePoint 2010's handling of navigation and web pages. While it may be possible to integrate it, a solution of this nature has too many points of potential failure. I do not recommend this approach.

Figure 10–4. AdventureWorks Customers page

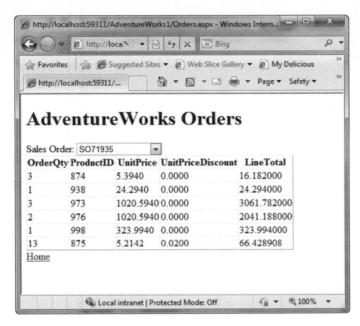

Figure 10–5. AdventureWorks Orders page

From this point, you have a working ASP.NET application that connects to an external SQL Server database. This particular application does not really require a High Touch Point solution in that it doesn't contain many-to-many database table relationships or support transaction modeling. It is just a simple solution to illustrate the concepts, and one that is short enough to cover in the context of a book chapter. The finished code will be included as part of the book code downloads.

Next, you will work on the changes that need to happen to migrate your ASP.NET Web Site to SharePoint 2010.

Modifying Our ASP.NET Web Site for SharePoint 2010 Integration

One of the first changes that you will make to your ASP.NET application to get it to work with SharePoint 2010 is to modify the pages to work with master pages. In the same step, you will mock up a master page in your web site that contains some of the same elements as the SharePoint 2010 master page you will use when you migrate the solution.

To begin, copy your AdventureWorks1 Web Site into another directory: AdventureWorks2 (this is the same as it appears in the code downloads). You will work with AdventureWorks2 to modify it for the High Touch Point solution approach. Next, in the root of your web site, create a folder named _layouts. This will imitate the application page duplicating the route to the WSS _layouts folder in IIS. Next, create a master page, and name it applicationv4.master. This is the same name as the SharePoint 2010 application master page that you will use in SharePoint 2010. After you have completed this, you will see something in your solution explorer window similar to that in Figure 10–6.

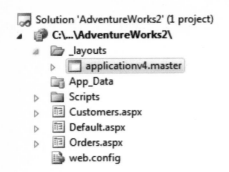

Figure 10–6. Modified ASP.NET web site

Create Master Page

To begin with, you will add only one ContentPlaceHolder control to AdventureWorks2, as follows:

```
<body>
    <form id="form1" runat="server">
    <div>
        <asp:ContentPlaceHolder id="PlaceHolderMain"
runat="server"></asp:ContentPlaceHolder>
    </div>
    </form>
</body>
```

This is the same place holder name that appears on the applicationv4.master page in SharePoint 2010.

■ **Tip** If you would like to add more content placeholders from applicationv4.master, you can find this file at C:\Program Files\Common Files\Microsoft Shared\Web Server Extensions\14\TEMPLATE\LAYOUTS. There are many other content placeholders of interest, such as PlaceHolderPageTitle, PlaceHolderAdditionalPageHead, and many others. I tend to use only the main placeholder at first to get all of the functionality incorporated from my ASP.NET application with little distraction, then I deal with titles, page heads, naming conventions, and other things later.

Reference Master Page on Application Pages

Next, you will a reference the applicationv4.master page from all of your application pages. Add the following MasterPageFile reference to the Page markup on every page on your site:

```
<%@ Page Language="C#" AutoEventWireup="true" CodeFile="Customers.aspx.cs"
MasterPageFile="~/_layouts/applicationv4.master" Inherits="Customers" %>
```

Also, replace the markup surrounding your custom code. Basically, you replace all of the HTML containers on your page down to the div tag that surrounds your drop-down control or hyperlink control with a contentplaceholder control as follows:

```
<asp:Content ID="contentMain" ContentPlaceHolderID="PlaceHolderMain" runat="server">
</asp:Content>
```

As an example, what would be left on the default.aspx page would look like the code in Listing 10–7.

Listing 10–7. An Example of the default.aspx Page

```
<<%@ Page Language="C#" AutoEventWireup="true" CodeFile="Default.aspx.cs"
MasterPageFile="~/_layouts/applicationv4.master" Inherits="_Default" %>
<asp:Content ID="contentMain" ContentPlaceHolderID="PlaceHolderMain" runat="server">
<h1>AdventureWorks Pages</h1>
<div>
    <ul>
        <li><asp:HyperLink ID="hypCustomers" runat="server"
NavigateUrl="~/Customers.aspx">Customers</asp:HyperLink></li>
        <li><asp:HyperLink ID="hypOrders" runat="server"
NavigateUrl="~/Orders.aspx">Orders</asp:HyperLink></li>
    </ul>
</div>
</asp:Content>
```

After you complete this, you should be able to run your application through F5 and obtain the same results as shown in Figures 10–3 through 10–5.

Modify web.config

The next step in modifying your ASP.NET web site to run within SharePoint 2010 is to clean up and remove the majority of content from your web.config file. The idea here is that the SharePoint environment can provide the bulk of the host information that is necessary to use your application, and the only things that are necessary to include are application-specific information such as connection strings and application settings. Your web.config file should appear similar to that in Listing 10–8 when you are finished.

Listing 10–8. Modified web.config File

```
<?xml version="1.0"?>
<configuration>
        <appSettings/>
        <connectionStrings>
                <add name="AdventureWorks" connectionString="data source=DAVE-PC3;Integrated
Security=SSPI;Initial Catalog=AdventureWorksLT2008"/>
        </connectionStrings>
        <system.web>
                <compilation debug="true"/></system.web>
</configuration>
```

Run your application one more time to ensure that no remaining reference errors remain, and correct them as necessary. You are now ready to deploy your application to a SharePoint 2010 environment.

Deploy to SharePoint 2010 Layouts Directory

The next and nearly-final step in integrating your ASP.NET application to work with SharePoint 2010 is to work directly with the SharePoint root and deploy your application as a Layouts directory deployment. The reason you do this is that the amount of maintenance and re-work that it would take to wrap the features, pages, controls, and other code in any medium to large sized ASP.NET Application within feature sets would be significant. The changes that you have incorporated already within each of the application pages have required you to touch every page in the solution already, if only to update the master page reference (most ASP.NET applications are usually built with existing master pages).

Go to the Layouts directory and create a new folder with the same name as your ASP.NET Web Site: AdventureWorks2.

The Layouts directory is at `C:\Program Files\Common Files\Microsoft Shared\Web Server Extensions\14\TEMPLATE\LAYOUTS` for most deployments. SharePoint can be installed on other drives as well.

Next, copy all of the files within AdventureWorks2 to the new folder you have created: `C:\Program Files\Common Files\Microsoft Shared\Web Server Extensions\14\TEMPLATE\LAYOUTS\AdventureWorks2`.

This is all that it takes to make your application available from within a SharePoint 2010 environment. A page reference to `http://portal/_layouts/AdventureWorks2/default.aspx` (where "portal" is your site collection) will bring up your ASP.NET application pages. Your application will appear as in Figure 10–7.

You will notice that your ASP.NET Web Site and content will pick up the styling of the surrounding SharePoint 2010 site.

So this is the basic development and deployment story for High Touch Point solutions. There are a few things to note about this solution.

First, as a deployment to the Layouts directory, these pages will be accessible by all web applications that are defined in SharePoint 2010 on the server you deployed to. The _layouts reference is a universal one within all web applications. So, any access control will have to be done as customized code for yourself or handled within the `web.config` of your local folder. Also, the entry point for your blended solution is not necessarily known. For instance, I may be coming to AdventureWorks from my parent site collection of `http://portal/`. I could also be coming from a subsite such as `http://portal/sites/mysite1/subsite/`. If there is different desired behavior depending upon entry point, a custom coded solution will need to be provided to accommodate it.

Second, you will need to handle navigation elements within your solution. You can certainly include the ContentPlaceHolder tag and specific navigation elements that appear on normal SharePoint pages. You can also specify the _layouts/AdventureWorks2/page.aspx links in links libraries or on other navigation elements.

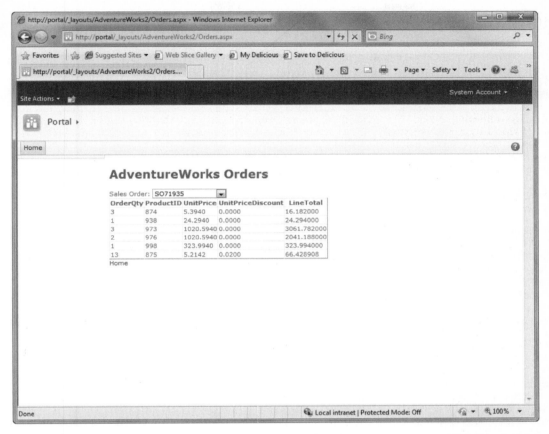

Figure 10–7. AdventureWorks ASP.NET web site deployed to SharePoint 2010 as a High Touch Point solution.

Third, as I will show you in the last part of this chapter, these application pages have not been load tested for performance, unlike the standard SharePoint 2010 pages. Also, since they are running in the same application pool in IIS as your SharePoint site collection, any adverse performance in your application will also affect your SharePoint environment. It is recommended to do solid load testing on any High Touch Point solution to be able to deliver concrete numbers as to the requests per second (RPS) and number of concurrent users that you can support with your solution.

This wraps up the coverage and detail for your example of a High Touch Point solution. Next, you will learn the aspects that apply to migrating an existing ASP.NET application over.

Migrating An Existing ASP.NET Application

In many ways, the simple example that you created for coding a new ASP.NET Web Site and deploying it to SharePoint 2010 should give you the pattern that you need for planning a High Touch Point solution for integration with SharePoint 2010. As stated previously, several candidates are appropriate for selection in this type of blended solution, including standard ASP.NET web forms development in many different flavors. Unfortunately, just saying ASP.NET web forms doesn't really cover enough detail to help out in planning, as there are so many different possibilities in consideration with third party control libraries, open source inclusions, and other factors. I will point out what I have seen work or what should work with certain approaches.

Client Side Libraries

You may be wondering if your "x" JavaScript library work with High Touch Point Solutions. For "x", you can plug in any number of the most popular client side JavaScript libraries. Obviously, as I made liberal use of jQuery in the Chapter 9 examples, that works very well. I have found that MOST of the client side JavaScript libraries I have tested work seamlessly. This would include ext-js, Yahoo-UI (yui), and even some older school predecessors to jQuery like scriptaculous. Client-side code, and JavaScript especially, really plays well in a SharePoint 2010 environment. Even some of the .NET wrappers around the client-side code seems to work pretty well (e.g. Coolite wrapper for ext-js).

Third-Party Libraries

Most of these libraries seem to work pretty well for these considerations as well. One thing that you may have to deal with is the Code Access Security (CAS) aspect and permissions. From my experience, to use .NET control libraries, you will have to register the assemblies in the appropriate `web.config` files and add them to SafeControls.

■ **Tip** Including third party libraries in a SharePoint 2010 install is a whole other topic. Basically, you are going to need to modify the `web.config` file either directly. A better practice would be to add a solution package .wsp that includes the .dlls you need referenced and added to safe controls. You can update your `web.config` file through a feature event receiver that fires on a feature activation and uses SPWebConfigModification as the classes involved in adding the necessary elements to your configuration.

That said, outside of getting the .dlls and controls registered and available, most third party controls, especially those from some of the larger vendor names in the business seem to work well with SharePoint 2010 and High Touch Point solutions. This would also include the Ajax Control Toolkit, a blend between .NET assemblies and client-side code. You can register it in your `web.config` file and use it in SharePoint.

■ **Tip** The key to using these elements is to make your SharePoint `web.config` file look similar in sections to the ASP.NET `web.config` file, especially when it concerns assemblies, controls, and other elements. You may have to do some work to figure out which elements SharePoint removes and handles.

Silverlight

In general, Silverlight works well with SharePoint 2010. As you saw in the chapter on the Client Object model, there are specific libraries provided directly to Silverlight for communication with the SharePoint object model. For High Touch Point solutions, the only real consideration is anything to do with cross domain access to services, which need a web shim setup. I recommend an excellent video by Microsoft Silverlight Team member Tim Heuer at `www.silverlight.net/learn/videos/silverlight-videos/how-to-use-cross-domain-policy-files-with-silverlight`.

Otherwise, most of the underlying knowledge presented in earlier chapters should be of great benefit to you in planning High Touch Point solutions. You have seen specific tools for working with SharePoint 2010 and have investigated from a File System perspective as well as an IIS .NET application perspective. These approaches will be beneficial if you run into hurdles when blending your ASP.NET and SharePoint 2010 solutions in a High Touch Point way.

Finally, along with the recommendation for load testing your solution, I will cover a simple example of setting up a Load Test with Visual Studio 2010.

Load Testing Your Blended Solution

Load testing your High Touch Point solution is a best practice. While there are a number of tools out there that can perform Load Testing, the one I will cover is a Microsoft tool that you may already have in your toolbox: Visual Studio 2010.

■ **Note** The load testing features that I will cover here in Visual Studio 2010 are only found in the Ultimate Edition SKU of VS2010. You can see which version you have by selecting Help ➤ About in your Visual Studio 2010 IDE. If you do not have Visual Studio 2010 Ultimate and have no way to obtain it, don't panic. There are a number of other tools that can help you accomplish your goal, and many of them work in somewhat the same fashion as this example for VS 2010. A good gateway site for testing tools is `http://www.softwareqatest.com`

First, check your local SQL Server database to see if you have a database that is named "LoadTest2010". If you do not, you will have to create one. Open up SQL Server Management Studio (SSMS), and from there select File ➤ Open. Navigate to `C:\Program Files (x86)\Microsoft Visual Studio 10.0\Common7\IDE`, or to the install directory of your Visual Studio instance, and select the `loadtestresultsrepository.sql` file, as shown in Figure 10–8.

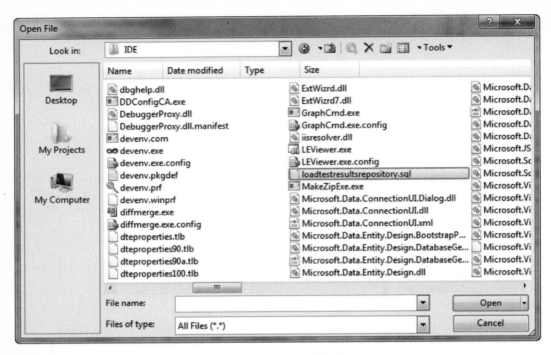

Figure 10–8. Creating a Load Test Results Repository in SSMS

Run the script that you loaded, which will perform all the actions necessary to create the LoadTest2010 database. The results of this can be seen in Figure 10–9.

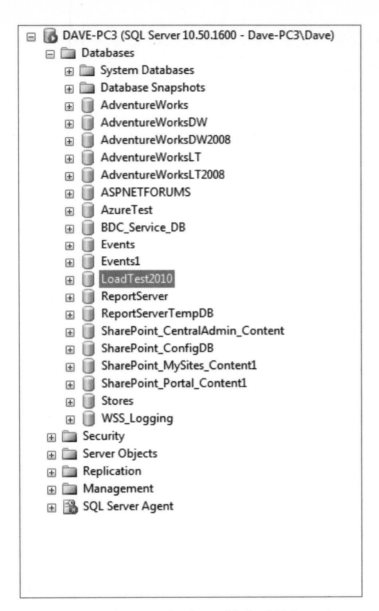

Figure 10–9. LoadTest2010 database added to SQL Server instance

From there, in your Visual Studio 2010 IDE, select Test ➤ Manage Test Controllers. You will see a dialog window as shown in Figure 10–10.

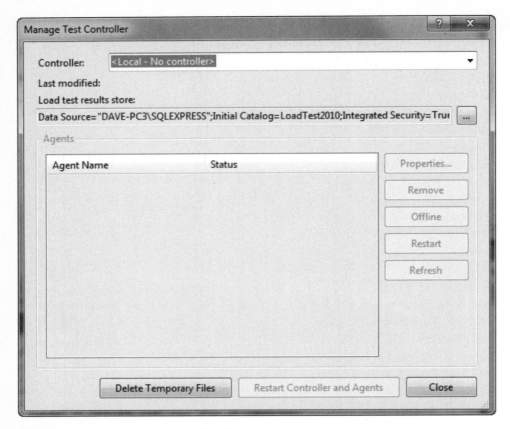

Figure 10–10. Manage Test Controller dialog window

From there select the ellipses … and configure the connection window to point to the SQL Server where you just created your LoadTest2010 database, as in Figure 10–11. Note that in this case there is no controller other than locally; however, you can set up a multi-server farm to handle controllers and agents to truly test load in a balanced web farm environment. For more information on that and other more advanced testing questions, see the *Visual Studio Performance Testing Quick Reference Guide* on Codeplex at `http://vsptqrg.codeplex.com`.

Figure 10–11. Connection Properties window

This sets up your SQL Server instance to hold results of tests. Next, go to your AdventureWorks2 solution and add a test project as shown in Figure 10–12.

Figure 10–12. *Add Test Project*

Next, add a Web Performance Test to your Test Project. Select the Test menu drop-down, and pick New Test from it. You will see a window similar to Figure 10–13.

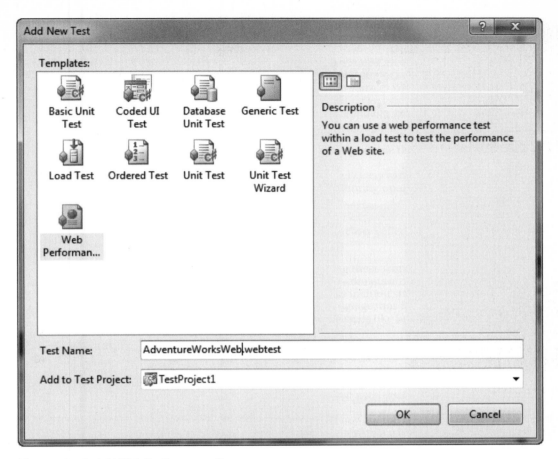

Figure 10–13. *Add Web Performance Test*

Once you add and name the Web Performance Test to your project, it will bring up an instance of Internet Explorer, with a Web Test Recorder window in the left hand side, as shown in Figure 10–14.

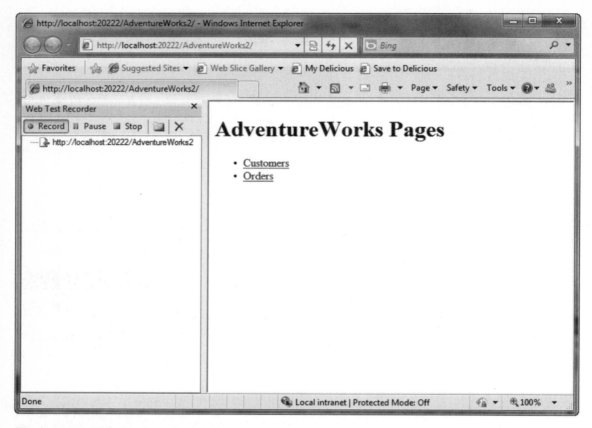

Figure 10–14. Web Test Recorder window

From this browser window, browse to the web site you want to do load testing on and select "Record."

■ **Note** In Figure 10–14, you can see that I am performing a load test on the local development web server, or Cassini server. This is fine if it is on; however, to better simulate load on IIS, you can install your app on IIS and browse to it to start. You can also browse to the _layouts/AdventureWorks2/default.aspx start page to test your load in your SharePoint 2010 High Touch Point solution. Here, you'll simulate testing the ASP.NET application alone to get a baseline picture for load.

This will record your browsing session, and you can manually navigate through your website as a normal user would. After you have completed browsing, select "Stop." You will see the completed webtest file in your Solution Explorer window. You can change parameters or settings on your Web Test to target a certain threshold load time for your pages for example. A picture of this and some other things available are in Figure 10–15.

Figure 10–15. AdventureWorksWeb.webtest test items

This example can be set up just as a baseline test for how long pages load. For actual performance testing in your environment, select the very far right icon in the above window, "Create Performance Session for this test." The following wizard items will show up, shown in Figures 10–16 through 10–19.

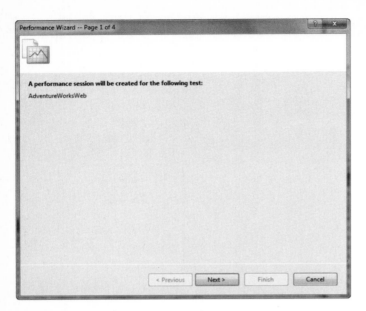

Figure 10–16. Performance Wizard step 1 test setup

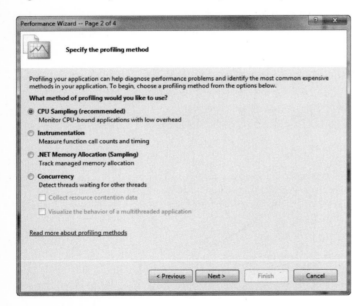

Figure 10–17. Profiling method

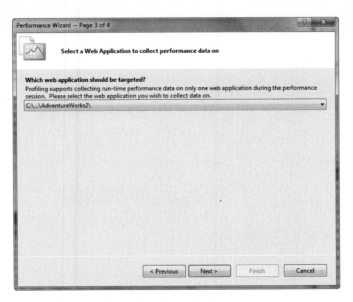

Figure 10–18. *Web application selection*

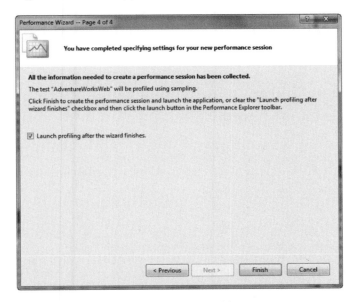

Figure 10–19. Finalize and launch profiling

The results of the Profiling report can be seen in Figure 10–20.

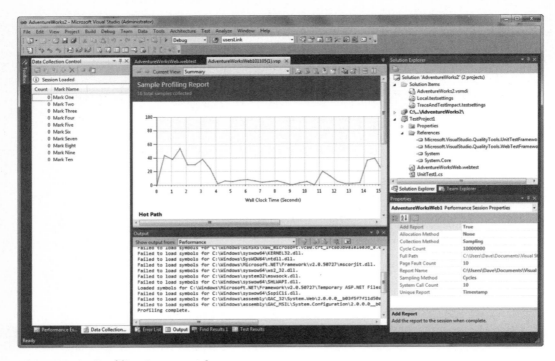

Figure 10–20. *Profiling Report results*

The Profiling Report indicates the CPU load under the profile test. Graphical results as well as specific performance session results can be seen in the output. The whole field of Load Testing is a very large one. To set up load tests that are more specific to your environment or on multiple machines, consult the *Visual Studio Performance Testing Quick Reference Guide* on Codeplex at http://vsptqrg.codeplex.com as well as the MSDN forums at http://social.msdn.microsoft.com/Forums/en/vstswebtest/threads.

This concludes the Load Testing section and wraps up the considerations for High Touch Point solutions in general.

Summary and Conclusion

In this chapter, I have highlighted High Touch Point blended solutions, provided guidance for selecting this model for implementation, highlighted the pros and cons of this approach, and then delved into specific examples of code. You produced an ASP.NET application from scratch, modified it to fit within a Layouts directory deployment, and deployed it to SharePoint 2010. I also discussed migrating existing ASP.NET Applications into SharePoint 2010. To wrap up that section, you produced a specific example on Load Testing and learned how to set up a Load test for the ASP.NET application and perform Performance Profiling. Both of these sections will help in providing measurements and numbers for High Touch Point solution deployments.

In conclusion, I want to thank you, the reader, for sticking with me through this journey of Pro SharePoint 2010 Solutions. It has been a pleasure digging deep to teach you all. Throughout the book, I have endeavored to not only provide the mundane examples including standard SharePoint 2010 coding techniques, but also to place them within a strategic context. The approaches I have highlighted have been experientially calculated to address the architectural considerations of solutions of this nature including organizational components.

My goal was to provide the tools so that you can expand the horizons of those you serve in your organizations in terms of what is available with collaboration. Keep your tools sharp and your eyes on the horizon because the best in software is yet to come! I hope to see you down the road on your SharePoint journey. If there is anything I can do to help you, please don't hesitate to get in touch!

Dave Milner

Index

■■■